Religion,
Altered States of Consciousness,
and Social Change

Religion,
Altered States of Consciousness,
and Social Change

Edited by Erika Bourguignon

Ohio State University Press
Columbus   1973

Library of Congress Cataloging in Publication Data
Bourguignon, Erika.
  Religion, altered states of consciousness, and social change.
  1. Psychology, Religious. 2. Trance. 3. Sects. 4. Religion and sociology.
I. Title
BL53.B643 200'.19 72–8448
ISBN 0–8142–0167–9

Contents

Preface   vii

Introduction: A Framework for the
Comparative Study of Altered States
of Consciousness   3
Erika Bourguignon

Part I: Cross-Cultural and Comparative Studies

           1. Societal Correlates of Possession
              Trance in Sub-Saharan Africa   39
              Lenora Greenbaum

           2. Possession Trance in Sub-Saharan
              Africa: A Descriptive Analysis of
              Fourteen Societies   58
              Lenora Greenbaum

           3. Social Change, Ecology, and
              Spirit Possession among the
              South African Nguni   88
              Judith Gussler

Part II: Field Studies

           4. Spirit Mediums in Palau: Transfor-
              mations in a Traditional System   129
              Anne P. Leonard

5. Apostolics of Yucatán: A Case
Study of a Religious Movement   178
Felicitas D. Goodman

6. The Shakers of St. Vincent:
A Stable Religion   219
Jeannette H. Henney

✮ 7. Umbanda in São Paulo: Religious
Innovation in a Developing
Society   264
Esther Pressel

Part III: Some Conclusions

8. An Assessment of Some
Comparisons and Implications   321
Erika Bourguignon

Epilogue: Some Notes on
Contemporary Americans and
the Irrational   340
Erika Bourguignon

Appendix   359
Notes on the Contributors   377
Index   379

Preface

Altered states of consciousness have moved, in the course of the past ten years, from being a subject of quiet and even esoteric research to one proclaimed loudly in newspaper headlines. Where once questions concerning such states were studied by psychiatrists dealing with sick people or by anthropologists writing about exotic societies, the drug culture of the 1960s has promoted altered states to being subject matter for public debate.

During the same period, there have also been a great revival and expansion among the hundreds of marginal religious groups in this country. Simultaneously, anthropologists have discovered a renewed interest in the study of religion, particularly in the study of rituals and symbols. Our work must be seen in the context of these developments.

Yet this book does not deal primarily with the drug culture or with the renewed vigor and appeal of minority religions in this country, where the search for altered states is part of the ritual, part of the higher good sought by converts. Nonetheless, we hope that some of what my coauthors and I report of our findings concerning the place of altered states among the religions of other societies may be seen to have some relevance to the current situation in the United States. I have attempted to indicate some of this relevance in the Epilogue.

This volume is the outcome of a research project conducted under my direction at the Ohio State University between 1963 and 1968, as well as some work carried on subsequent to its formal termination. Titled "A Cross-Cultural Study of Dissociational States," it was supported in whole by Public Health Service Grant MH 07463 from the National Institute of Mental Health. The project was initiated by me in collaboration with a physical anthropologist, Dr. Louanna Pettay, now of Sacramento State University, and a psychiatrist, Dr. Adolf Haas, of the Ohio State University. Our aim was a multifaceted analysis of what appeared to be a widespread psychocultural phenomenon, about which, however, curiously little of a systematic nature was known. The phenomenon with which we were concerned was the religious evaluation, often as possession by spirits, of a psychological state variously termed "dissociation," "trance," or, more recently and more generally, "altered states of consciousness." Having myself carried out anthropological field work in Haiti, I had had the opportunity to study such behavior at first hand and to investigate it and its institutional context in some depth. I was also aware of the debate concerning the "pathology" or "normalcy" of such states.

To develop perspective on this and other issues, two approaches to the subject of altered states appeared necessary. On the one hand, we wished to gather a body of comparative materials, appropriate for statistical analysis, of the relationship between various aspects of society and the presence or absence of institutionalized forms of altered states of consciousness with their associated belief systems. On the other hand, we proposed to carry out a series of highly focused field studies in societies where such patterns of behavior were known to exist in a religious context.

The present volume contains some of the results of both of these types of research. As our title indicates, the behaviors under investigation are institutionalized within a religious framework. We have chosen not to concern ourselves with other types of altered states. We have focused our presentation on the complex interrelationships between religious beliefs and institutions in which altered states of consciousness are utilized and on the problems of cultural change that confront human societies and offer such a crucial challenge to all of us.

Since the initiation of our research, interest in this area of investigation has grown, and more systematic studies in our area of interest are now available. Several symposia to which I have contributed dealing with related matters have been held in recent years. Among these are: A Symposium on Trance and Possession States, of the R. M. Bucke Memorial Society, in Montreal (1966); Le Colloque International sur les Cultes de Possession, in Paris (1968); and most recently the Conference on Marginal Religious Groups in America Today, at Princeton (1971).

A number of ethnographic studies dealing with altered states have also appeared recently, such as those included in Beattie and Middleton's volume *Spirit Mediumship and Society in Africa* (1969). I. M. Lewis's recent volume *Ecstatic Religion* (1971) provides an interesting summary of much descriptive material as well as a particular theoretical approach to the subject. What claim to distinctiveness our enterprise may have lies in several features: we have utilized both large-scale statistical studies and highly focused field studies; we have attempted to deal with the psychobiological aspects as well as the societal and cultural ones; and finally, the contributors to this volume are a team of collaborators, informed by a common orientation as well as by individual specializations and interests.

We have received assistance from many persons, from colleagues and from out students, with whom we have discussed various aspects of our work, and whose criticism we have benefited from, but not always accepted.

I wish to thank all of them. Also, I was fortunate to receive assistance in the preparation of this volume from the Ohio State University Development Fund, for which I wish to express my appreciation. I also wish to thank Miss Marilyn Walker, for her valuable help in typing most of the manuscript. Dr. Goodman took on the task of preparing the index, for which I wish to express my appreciation. We are especially indebted to Mrs. Sarah T. Millett, our editor, who has struggled bravely with our problems; only she knows how much we owe to her efforts. The final responsibility for the contents of this volume, however, is our own.

Erika Bourguignon

Columbus, Ohio
February 18, 1972

Religion,
Altered States of Consciousness,
and Social Change

Introduction: A Framework for the Comparative Study of Altered States of Consciousness

Erika Bourguignon

Altered states of consciousness, which in American society are thought of mostly in relation to psychopathology and to the drug culture (which some would consider the expression of a type of pathology) appear in a variety of forms among the peoples of the world. Often, they are institutionalized and culturally patterned and utilized in specific ways. The word *utilized* is chosen intentionally here, because I wish to suggest that these states do indeed have utility for the societies that employ them. The cultural meaning supplied for these states and the institutional framework within which they operate vary from society to society, and thus the specific functions they fulfill vary also. Yet, there are some common trends. In traditional societies—and to a considerable extent in modern societies as well—the context in which such patterned states are viewed most often by the people concerned is one that we may broadly call "religious." I mean here that altered states tend to be spoken of in connection with supernatural entities such as "spirits" or "souls." Thus, a person in an altered state may be thought of as "possessed" by certain spirits or, on the other hand, his soul, or one of his souls, may be thought to be temporarily absent. Such beliefs account for the individual's altered behavior as well as for his altered subjective experience of himself and of the world. If he behaves strangely, the behavior may be attributed not to him but to a possessing spirit. If he sees or hears unusual things, these may be spirits he is seeing or hearing, or messages from spirits he is receiving. To assist him, if assistance is needed, specialists in dealing with spirits or with sacred matters are called upon. Spirits and souls, individuals with special power or expertise in matters of spirits and souls these define a supernatural realm, which we may consider to be the realm of religion. Religion, however, deals with those areas of life beyond the empirical skills of a society's specialists: the intractable illness, the uncontrollable weather conditions, the fertility or availability of game, the social conflicts unamenable to a rule of law, the mysterious and unanswered questions concerning the whys of the universe and the beings and forces within it. Among such problems beyond the control of individuals are the frequently cataclysmic consequences of change—social, cultural, economic, and political. And when we consider the relationship of religion to change, its double role as a bulwark against change on the one hand and as a mediator or even initiator of change on the other, we often find that key individuals in this process experience altered states of consciousness. It is on this point of juncture—between religious institutions (beliefs, practices, and personnel) and the processes of sociocultural change, where altered states of consciousness may play a critical role—that we wish to focus in this volume. This introduction intends to provide a framework for such an undertaking.

To do so, we must start with definitions of terms and with an indication of the quantitative importance of the phenomena under discussion. In the ethnographic literature, altered states of consciousness are often referred to by words such as "trance" or "spirit possession." These words are used widely, inconsistently, and often interchangeably. We may also read of dissociation, fugue states, hysteria, hallucinations, catalepsy, epilepsy, hypnosis, somnambulism, and so on. For our purposes all of these psychiatric terms may be subsumed under the broad heading of "altered states of consciousness." We may do so without committing ourselves here to any particular explanatory theory, to the exactness of what is often amateur diagnosis in any particular case or, indeed, to the appropriateness of a language of psychopathology in general to a discussion of the behaviors in question. Let us merely note that the words "altered states of consciousness," as well as "trance" and "dissociation"—broad terms that we have also found it convenient to use—refer to a category of psychobiological states and types of behavior amenable to objective observation and study.

A number of different classifications and models of states of consciousness have been developed. One such model is presented by Fischer (1969, 1970), who constructs a "biocybernetic model of conscious experience" (1970:323), for which he finds a neurophysiological basis. Fischer orders states of consciousness along a continuum varying in terms of central nervous system arousal (or "ergotropic excitation"). The "normophrenic" state, ranging from daily routine to relaxation and characterized by perception, is at the center of this model. It is flanked, on the one hand, by a continuum of reduced arousal, ranging from tranquil states to hypoaroused states whose extreme point is found in the Yoga state of samādhi. This is the continuum of meditation, in contrast to perception. On the other hand, we find the states of increased arousal, ranging from sensitivity, creativity, and anxiety to the hyperarousal of acute schizophrenia and reaching an extreme in the ecstatic state of mystical rapture. This is the continuum of hallucination. The states themselves are conceptualized as the individual's symbolic interpretations of the state of arousal of his own central nervous system. Ecstatic mystical rapture is thus interpreted as a subjective symbolization of maximal arousal, samādhi

meditation of minimal arousal (or maximal tranquilization).

In this view, altered states of consciousness are characterized by deviation in quantity of central nervous system
arousal from a central, normal state, since the deviation
may be one of greater than normal arousal or less than
normal arousal, i.e., greater tranquilization.

This classification of states of consciousness is important because it is based on a neurophysiological factor—the arousal of the central nervous system. In effect,
a neurophysiological and biocybernetic model is set up
here, into which the altered states described in the ethnographic literature could be placed. Like the drug states
that Fischer discusses, as well as REM (Rapid Eye Movement) sleep associated with dreaming, these are, for the
most part, states of above-normal arousal. However, an
assignment of our states to positions within this continuum model would require better and more precise
neurophysiological data than are now available on persons in such states. It would also require an expansion
of the model to accommodate these data. As we shall
see, for example, one category of altered states that concerns us principally is characterized neither by hallucination nor by meditation. It will be necessary to say more
about this later on.

A rather different classification, limited to altered states
of consciousness, is offered by Ludwig (1968). He dif-
ferentiates states according to the variables involved in
their induction, grouping them into five categories: (A)
reduction of exteroceptive stimulation and/or motor
activity; (B) increase of exteroceptive stimulation and/or
motor activity and/or emotion; (C) increased alertness
or mental involvement; (D) decreased alertness and relaxation of critical faculties; and (E) presence of somato-
psychological factors. In Fischer's terms, A and D represent decreased arousal below the threshhold of normal

6

activity; B and C represent increased arousal. E is a mixed category: thus, "drowsiness secondary to hyperglycemia" appears to be a state of tranquilization and reduced arousal, whereas certain drug states, such as those produced by LSD, are hyperarousal states (p. 75).

In spite of the great variety of states included in his classification, Ludwig finds that they share a series of ten general characteristics: alterations in thinking, disturbed time sense, loss of control, change in emotional expression, change in body image, perceptual distortion, change in meaning or significance (that is, the attributing of heightened significance to subjective experiences, ideas, or perceptions in this state), sense of the ineffable, feelings of rejuvenation, and hypersuggestibility. It will be helpful to keep these characteristics in mind in our discussion of altered states of consciousness and to note in the following chapters how they are utilized in various cultural contexts. In any given instance, the importance of each of these characteristics may be of greater or lesser significance.

Whereas Fischer presents us with a model involving the neurophysiological underpinnings of states of consciousness, Ludwig offers a classification based on modes of induction that relate to modifications in central nervous system excitation. He also provides us with another level of analysis—the subjective, psychological, largely perceptual, modifications undergone by individuals whose level of arousal varies from the normal range of daily waking activity. A further analysis of the classification provided by Ludwig, however, is possible. Thus, it must be emphasized that his categories order the states according to the psychobiological manner in which they come into being, not according to the sociocultural contexts in which they occur or the meanings assigned to them by those experiencing or witnessing them. Thus, with respect to such contexts and meanings his categories are, in fact, heterogeneous. We may differentiate between the private, individual, unpatterned states and those that occur in culturally patterned, institutionalized forms. In Ludwig's category A, for example, are included such diverse types as "highway or road hypnosis," "experimental sensory deprivation states," and "healing or revelatory states during 'incubation' or 'temple sleep' as practiced by the early Egyptians, Greeks and Romans" (Ludwig 1968:71–72). In category B, we find, among other examples, "panic states, rage reactions," "brainwashing states," "religious conversion and healing trance experiences during religious revival meetings," and "spirit possession states, either by the Holy Ghost or tribal spirits" and so forth (Ludwig 1968:72–73). Similar citations may be made for the other categories. In terms of sociocultural contexts, "highway or road hypnosis" and "panic states, rage reactions" may be considered individual phenomena, into which cultural patterning enters only marginally. On the other hand, "experimental sensory deprivation states" and "brainwashing states" are culturally patterned and occur in highly structured, institutionalized settings as often as the "healing or revelatory states" that are also mentioned, or the "religious conversion and healing trance" and the " 'spirit possession' states." However, the former two are types of states patterned within secular institutions and given secular or "profane" meanings, whereas the latter three are patterned within religious institutions and are given religious or "sacred" meanings. Each of Ludwig's five categories of altered states, grouped by method of induction, may then be subdivided along two further dimensions: (1) states that are personal and not culturally patterned or minimally patterned in contrast to those that are given an institutional context and culturally patterned form and meaning; (2) this institutional patterning may be of two types, either profane or sacred.

This sort of analysis will quickly reveal that a given type of state, considered only in terms of the method or process of induction involved, may be individual and secular in one society and institutionalized and sacred in another. To cite just one example: under the heading of "increased alertness or mental involvement," Ludwig cites "trance states reported among radar screen operators." I interpret this as an individual, secular type of state. Yet the same process of increased alertness and involvement occurs in the method of divination known as scrying, in which the "operator" uncovers hidden facts through intent concentration on gazing at a crystal ball, a surface of water, or other reflecting substance. This is an example of a culturally patterned sacred trance.

This discussion indicates the great variety of states referred to under the broad heading of "altered states of consciousness." We shall limit ourselves in our analysis to only a segment of this broad field—specifically, to institutionalized, culturally patterned altered states. In traditional societies, these are almost without exception sacred states.[1] We shall discuss the matter of particular cultural interpretations and societal institutionalizations presently. For the moment, however, we must ask a basic and important question: In studying institutionalized altered states of consciousness, for the most part in traditional societies and in a sacred context, are we dealing with a rare and exotic phenomenon of interest only to specialists, a bit of anthropological esoterica? Or are we dealing with a major aspect of human behavior that has significant impact on the functioning of human societies? A quantitative answer to this question is in order.

Table 1 provides such an answer. It shows that of a sample of 488 societies, in all parts of the world, for which we have analyzed the relevant ethnographic litera-

TABLE 1

Institutionalized Forms of Altered States of Consciousness (T and/or PT): Distribution by Major Ethnographic Regions

	Total		Sub-Saharan Africa		Circum-Mediterranean		East Eurasia		Insular Pacific		North America		South America	
	N	%	N	%	N	%	N	%	N	%	N	%	N	%
Total Societies Coded.............	488	100	114	100	44	100	65	100	86	100	120	100	59	100
Altered States Present............	437	90	94	82	35	80	61	94	81	94	116	97	50	85
Altered States Absent.............	51	10	20	18	9	20	4	6	5	6	4	3	9	15

ture, 437, or 90% are reported to have one or more institutionalized, culturally patterned forms of altered states of consciousness. This sample of 488 societies, which we have utilized in our research for a variety of comparative statistical analyses, was drawn from a worldwide universe of adequately described cultures. This universe is the total number of societies included in the *Ethnographic Atlas* (Murdock 1967), and our sample, in fact, represents 57% of the societies of that universe.[2]

The presence of institutionalized forms of altered states of consciousness in 90% of our sample societies represents a striking finding and suggests that we are, indeed, dealing with a matter of major importance, not merely a bit of anthropological esoterica. It is clear that we are dealing with a psychobiological capacity available to all societies, and that, indeed, the vast majority of societies have used it in their own particular ways, and have done so primarily in a sacred context. Yet some societies have not done so, or had abandoned the practice before the time period for which the report, on which our coding is based, is valid.

Table 1 presents another striking finding in the observation that there exists a remarkable interregional difference with regard to the probability that a society will have institutionalized forms of altered states of consciousness. The *Ethnographic Atlas* divides the world into six major ethnographic regions, as shown in table 1. The incidence of altered states is seen to range from a high of 97% of the societies of aboriginal North America to a low of 80% in the Circum-Mediterranean region. The latter region includes North Africa, the Near East, and southern and western Europe as well as overseas Europeans. Thus, we note that the probability of a society's utilizing this universal psychobiological capacity varies from region to region. We shall consider this matter more closely in a moment, but for now we may note that such regional variation is coherent with what we know of the distribution of other cultural features (Bourguignon and Greenbaum 1968; Driver and Schuessler 1967; Barry 1968). It must be stressed that although the *capacity* to experience altered states of consciousness is a psychobiological capacity of the species, and thus universal, its utilization, institutionalization, and patterning are, indeed, features of culture, and thus variable.

We may now take a close look at the cultural classifications of these states. We have found it useful to group these into two broad types: (1) states interpreted by the societies in which they occur as due to possession by spirits (termed "possession trance" [PT]), and (2) states not so interpreted (termed "trance" [T]). In effect, this is a residual and diversified category. Nonetheless, most typically it involves the experience of hallucinations or visions, interpreted in the particular societies as experiences of the (or, a) soul of the person, its temporary absence, its journeys and adventures, and so on. Trance (T) may involve the repetition of messages of spirits to an audience, the imitation of the actions of spirits, or the narration of the subject's spirit journey; or it may involve a private, isolated experience of the individual, as in the vision quest of North American Indians. The experience is remembered by the trancer, for the memory of the experience and often its report to others is of particular importance in many cultures. With its pattern of hallucinations (or visions), T thus fits clearly into Fischer's scheme, which we have discussed. PT, on the other hand, generally involves the impersonation of spirits—the acting out of their speech or behavior. It does not involve hallucinations, and it is typically followed by amnesia. The absence of hallucinations presents difficulties in fitting this type of state into Fischer's model. Here the distortion of perception refers to the self, not to other sense objects. One might ask whether it is not this radical discontinuity of personal identity, which is so characteristic of PT, that accounts for the observation that it is typically followed by amnesia, an amnesia that is absent in the case of T (see Bourguignon 1965).

Although it is true that these two interpretations—possession trance and trance—each cover a broad range of theories and tend to shade into each other in an area of partial overlap, they are for the most part clearly distinguishable. Treating them as separate categories rather than as a continuum has proven useful not only as a device of classification but also, as we shall see, as a tool of further analysis.

Whereas the term "altered state of consciousness" refers, as already stressed, to a psychobiological level of observation, terms such as "possession trance" and "trance," as used here, refer to categories of cultural interpretation. To discover these, to find out whether a dissociated person is undergoing "possession trance" or "trance," ethnographic rather than psychobiological methods of investigation are required. We must not merely observe the subject or note how the state was induced; we must ask his fellows—and afterward, the individual himself—how they explain the individual's transformation. We must note the cultural context in which the observed event occurs. Only in this way can we discover whether we are, in fact, dealing with an individual, private, perhaps deviant event or a patterned and institutionalized one; whether we are dealing with a profane or secular phenomenon, one that is positively evaluated and desired or one that is negatively evaluated and feared. Only by inquiry can we discover its meaning to the participants. Yet, the distinction between PT and T does not relate only to the meaning the behavior has to the participants. This very meaning affects the behavior itself, so that we may expect a person experiencing PT

13

to know what is expected of him and to behave according to the rules, rules that are quite different from those for T should both of these types of states exist in the same society, which is not infrequently the case. Thus, the cultural theory actually structures the behavior and experience of altered states of consciousness. This cultural variation, in spite of a series of psychobiological constants in PT behavior, is strikingly documented in the several papers that follow. All of the field studies in this volume, as well as the comparative ones, report on PT behavior, yet there is a broad range of variation to be discovered in these behaviors that is clearly and explicitly linked to their cultural contexts and to the expectations with which they are associated. The spirits believed to possess the Nguni of South Africa (Gussler) have different characteristics from those of the Palauans (Leonard) or those of the modern Brazilians (Pressel); and all of these diversified spirits are impersonated in behaviors quite different from those that are linked to possession by the Holy Ghost, whether in St. Vincent (Henney) or in Yucatán (Goodman). Even in the latter two cases, there is sufficient cultural diversity between these two enthusiastic Christian churches so as to yield significant differences in behavior during PT.

The implications of these observations are quite clear: behavior during PT (as well as during T) is not a simple biological or biochemical "given," but is subject to a greater or lesser, but always significant, amount of learning. How some of this behavior is learned is reported in several of our chapters.[3]

I have suggested elsewhere (Bourguignon 1972) that altered states of consciousness may be viewed as representing a continuum, in which dreams during REM (Rapid Eye Movement) sleep would represent one extreme, possession trance linked to impersonation behavior the other, with visionary trance roughly at midpoint between them.

They may be compared along a variety of dimensions, such as with reference to methods of induction (see above) or with respect to subjective experience. Thus, as already noted, trance visions, and dreams with which they are often confused when the latter are given particular religious or ritual significance, are remembered, whereas possession trance behavior is forgotten by the subject. Similarly, dreams, and most often visionary trance, are covert, relatively passive experiences, whereas possession trance is an overt, often highly active performance. Thus, dreams are entirely private until shared verbally with others; trance is often private, though it may be carried out for others and mimed; and possession trance is generally a public procedure.

Thus, although our concerns here are primarily with trance and possession trance, it is worth noting the related phenomenon of REM sleep dreaming, which is also a state of altered consciousness and also frequently ritualized. When we enlarge the scope of our investigation in this way, we find that we are dealing not simply with an opposition between T and PT but, indeed, with two high points on a continuum.

Before turning to a consideration of the distribution of our trance types (T and PT) among the societies of the world, another word concerning the concept of "possession" is in order. So far we have spoken of possession belief as an explanatory category for altered states of consciousness and also, pari passu, as a factor structuring behavior in states so interpreted. However, possession belief may be found in a variety of contexts, altered states being only one such context. A belief in "possession" may also be linked to the modification of a person's behavior, capacities, or state of health, in the absence of an altered state of consciousness. We might speak of such nontrance possession as referring to an "alteration of capacity" rather than of consciousness. We refer to

TABLE 2

BELIEF IN POSSESSION BY SPIRITS (P AND/OR PT): DISTRIBUTION BY MAJOR ETHNOGRAPHIC REGIONS

	TOTAL		SUB-SAHARAN AFRICA		CIRCUM-MEDITERRANEAN		EAST EURASIA		INSULAR PACIFIC		NORTH AMERICA		SOUTH AMERICA	
	N	%	N	%	N	%	N	%	N	%	N	%	N	%
Total Societies Coded...........	488	100	114	100	44	100	65	100	86	100	120	100	59	100
Possession Belief Present..........	360	74	92	81	35	77	57	87	76	88	62	52	38	64
Possession Belief Absent	128	26	22	19	9	23	8	13	10	12	58	48	21	36

it simply as "possession" (P) in contrast to PT. Both types of belief may coexist in a given society, or only one or the other may be present. It might also be noted that there are societies in which both T and P are found, but PT is not.[4]

We may then briefly look at the distribution of possession beliefs, including both P and PT. Table 2 furnishes this information. It will be noted that such beliefs occur in 74% of our sample societies, with a maximum of 88% in the Insular Pacific and a minimum of 52% in North America. The beliefs are thus characteristic of the great majority of our societies, but are far from universal, being less widely distributed than institutionalized altered states. Again, however, we find a very great amount of interregional variation.

As institutional altered states and possession beliefs vary by regions, so do *types* of altered states. This is seen in table 3. As noted, we distinguished between Possession Trance (PT) and Trance (T) and found that a given society may be characterized by having one or the other, both, or neither. We thus obtain a typology of societies (not of states). The types are: Type I (T), Type II (T/PT, that is, having both forms), Type III (PT), and Type O (O/O, i.e., having neither T nor PT). As we have already come to expect, the distribution of these types among the six major ethnographic regions of the world is highly diverse. Although Type O is rare, it ranges from 3% in North America to 18% in Sub-Saharan Africa; and though Type I (T) has the highest incidence in our worldwide total, this is largely due to its great predominance (72%) in North America. Indeed, two points stand out about this distribution:

1. The Americas are radically different from the Old World areas and are also different from each other.

2. Each region is seen to have its particular ranking of

TABLE 3

Types of Altered States (Trance Types):
Distribution by Major Ethnographic Regions

Codes*	Trance Types	Total		Sub-Saharan Africa		Circum-Mediterranean		East Eurasia		Insular Pacific		North America		South America	
		N	%	N	%	N	%	N	%	N	%	N	%	N	%
1,5	Type I (T).......	186	38	19	16	10	23	14	22	25	29	86	72	32	54
4,7	Type II (T/PT)..	116	24	23	20	6	14	22	34	27	31	25	21	13	22
3,6	Type III (PT)....	135	28	52	46	19	43	25	38	29	34	5	4	5	8
2,8	Type 0 (0/0).....	51	10	20	18	9	20	4	6	5	6	4	3	9	15
	Total	488	100	114	100	44	100	65	100	86	100	120	100	59	100

*See Appendix for listing of societies and for coding.

types: Sub-Saharan Africa and the Circum-Mediterranean are characterized by Type III [PT]; yet they are distinguished by the fact that the second place is taken by Type II in Africa and Type I in the Circum-Mediterranean area. East Eurasia shows an almost equal preference for Type III and Type II, and the Insular Pacific is almost equally divided between Types III, II, and I, in that order. In all four of these regions, Type III predominates, however slightly. As noted, in North and South America, however, Type I is much more prevalent, with Type II second.

In an earlier publication (Bourguignon 1968 *b*), I cited examples to show that all types are represented in all regions. This assertion is accurate and must stand. However, the advantage for a comparative study of a sampling procedure and the use of large numbers of societies is clear: we can now go beyond such an assertion to point to the incidence—and thus to variations in frequency from area to area—of the types of altered states that we have identified. This leads us to the further question, then, of how we may account for this difference in incidence. And here we discover that the distinction we have made between T and PT is important in yet another respect: these types of institutionalized states vary significantly in their societal concomitants.

As reported in greater detail elsewhere (Bourguignon 1968 *a*), we compared societies of Type I (T), Type II (T/PT), and Type III (PT) with respect to sixteen societal variables. We did so for our entire worldwide sample and also separately for each of the major ethnographic regions. For our worldwide sample, the differences between the three types yielded chi squares significant at or below the .05 level of probability for twelve of the sixteen characteristics.[5] Six of the twelve characteristics were clearly related to societal complexity: estimated size of population, size of local group, presence of stratification, presence (or recent presence) of slavery, settlement patterns, and jurisdictional hierarchy above the local level. In each instance, the PT group of societies (Type III) are the most complex, that is, have the largest population and the largest local group, stratification, slavery, sedentary settlement pattern, and a complex hierarchy of jurisdictional levels. The T societies (Type I) are the simplest, and the T/PT societies (Type II) are intermediary. Several of the remaining characteristics appear also to belong to this pattern. Thus, Type III societies are more likely to have marriage by bride price or other consideration rather than marriage without compensation, and to have extended rather than independent nuclear families. Textor (1967) finds both of these characteristics to be present with a statistically significantly greater probability among societies having stratification.[6] In addition, Type III societies are more likely to have polygynous marriage, and this Textor (1967) finds to be true also of societies having slavery. Other features are less clearly linked to complexity as indicated by stratification or slavery: thus, with respect to kin groups, Type III societies are more likely than the others to have either patrilineal or matrilineal kin groups, but least likely to have other types of kin groups; they also are more likely to have duolateral cousin marriage as well as to practice the segregation of adolescent boys.

Yet although a case may be made for the argument that complexity is also revealed in this second group of societal characteristics, which differentiate our three types of societies, another hypothesis may be suggested. Thus, each of the three types appears to represent a particular profile of societal characteristics. It is of some interest to note, therefore, that each type also predominates in one, and to a lesser extent in a second, of the six major ethnographic regions, and that, to an important extent, the characteristics of the type profile and those of the regional profile tend to coincide. Thus, Type I, as we have seen, predominates in North America and, to a lesser extent, in South America. Although 48% of Type I societies are migratory or seminomadic with respect to settlement patterns, this is also true of 74% of aboriginal North American societies and 31% of those of South America.[7] Another example may be found in the case of slavery, which is present (or was recently present) in 61% of Type III societies. It is (or recently was) also present in 78% of the societies of Sub-Saharan Africa and 61%of those of the Circum-Mediterranean region, in both of which Type III societies predominate.

This discussion suggests that the linkage of trance type and major ethnographic region is the product of two groups of factors. On the one hand, there is statistical evidence, in the form of chi squares and levels of probability, that each of the types is associated with a different degree of societal complexity. On the other hand, the similarity between the societal profiles of trance types and of certain ethnographic regions suggests historical and ecological factors as well.

When we divide the world into six major regions and study the association between societal factors and trance types separately for each, we obtain somewhat different results for each region. For example, stratification is found to differentiate trance types to a degree that is statistically significant below the .05 level of probability in three areas only: Sub-Saharan Africa, East Eurasia, and North America. Greenbaum (this volume) analyzes in detail both the methodological and substantive issues in the study of a single area, namely, Sub-Saharan Africa. Here the issue is the presence or absence of possession trance in a society, and for that purpose PT societies are grouped with T/PT societies and contrasted with societies in which PT is absent, that is, T societies and societies having no type of altered states.

Comparison between trance types shows, as we have seen, an association between the presence of possession trance and certain indicators of societal complexity, such as social stratification and slavery. This is true whether we study a worldwide sample or a regional one, such as that investigated by Greenbaum. That is, there is greater probability that stratified societies and/or those with slavery will have PT than that nonstratified, nonslave societies will have this pattern. We might ask why this should be so. Possession trance, for the most part, involves the impersonation of spirits by human actors. These spirits may be ancestors, foreigners, or other humans, animals, or spirits that never had been embodied in human or animal form. An inspection of spirits represented in possession trance rituals reveals for the most part, it appears, a symbolic rendition of human society. Thus, Gussler shows us the importance for the Zulu of ancestor spirits, representing the well-defined kin groups into which the society is divided. In more recent times, however, with severe acculturative pressures on the Zulu, possession, we are told, may be by spirits of foreigners—Swazi, Thonga, or even East Indians. Leonard tells us that in Palau, the traditional mediums served the gods of the clans and villages, that is, societal divisions are reproduced and reenacted on the spirit level. In the Umbanda cult of present-day Brazil, Pressel shows us, possession is by a variety of highly individualized spirits representing different segments of the population. A great many other examples can be cited from the broad literature on possession trance that tend to confirm the view that complex societies offer a great repertoire of roles. It is from this repertoire of actual and potential roles that some are selected for enactment in possession trance.

On one level, this may be viewed as a symbolic expression of a society's model of its social structure. On another level, it may be viewed as a means by which an individual can play roles otherwise not available to him, that is, a woman may play a male role or vice versa; an adult may play the role of a child; a Zulu may play the role of an East Indian; a young person the role of an older, more powerful one; a lower class person the role of a powerful individual; and so on. This playing of alien roles may not only be a way of providing temporarily various options to the individual, it may also be a symbolic and ritualized way of coming to terms with the foreign or the dangerous. However, these suggestions can at present only be explored by example; we cannot confirm them in any systematic manner.

Although there is, as we have noted, a link between societal complexity and possession trance institutions, there are exceptions to be found. We note the presence of possession trance in some simple, unstratified, non-slave societies; and, also, we find some complex societies that do not show the expected behavior. Greenbaum, in chapter 2, addresses herself to this problem. She notes that complexity alone is not sufficient to explain the presence of possession trance, and offers an additional hypothesis: she suggests that societal rigidity in complex societies enhances the likelihood of the presence of possession trance. She reasons that possession trance practices provide the individual in rigid societies some greater degree of elbow room, and that they provide the society with a channel for innovation that would not be otherwise available.

In the concluding chapter, we shall attempt to determine whether this hypothesis is also supported by the descriptions of societies offered elsewhere in this volume.

It should be noted that this hypothesis of the relationship between social rigidity and PT is tested by the frequency with which PT is present in societies of a given type. It tells us nothing about attitudes toward the PT phenomenon. Societies where it is welcomed or induced voluntarily are not differentiated from societies in which it is feared and/or occurs spontaneously. Nor is there any argument that PT represents an attempt—conscious or unconscious—at psychological compensation or control. Greenbaum's primary concern is with the functioning of the society, the assumption that rigid societies without a "safety valve" to allow for some play of individual variations and social decision-making could not survive. Thus, it is similar to the underlying hypothesis of Nadel's (1952) comparative study of witchcraft beliefs in two pairs of African societies.

Oesterreich in his classic study of possession (1922) differentiated between "voluntary" (or induced) and "involuntary" (or spontaneous) states. He did not, however, relate these differences to the types of societies in which they occurred. Recently, Douglas (1970) has formulated a hypothesis about the relation between social control and attitudes toward dissociation. Thus, she hypothesizes that "the inarticulateness of the social organisation in itself gains symbolic expression in bodily dissociation" and "as trance is a form of dissociation, it will be more approved and welcomed the weaker the structuring of society" (Douglas 1970:74). The hypothesis says nothing about *incidence*, but about *attitudes*. Douglas tests her hypothesis by comparing three Nilotic groups (Dinka, Nuer, and Mandari) and shows how the least structured of these groups, the Dinka, welcomes trance as the expression of a benign power, whereas the Nuer, more highly structured, view it as dangerous, as do the Mandari. The Nuer cosmos is rational and regulative; they believe sickness to be caused by sin. Sacrifices are offered to expiate transgressions, the principal ones of which are those that contravene the principal social relations:

24

adultery and homicide. The Mandari, too, consider possession dangerous and are highly concerned with sin. The Dinka, by contrast, live in a largely irrational universe that they cannot control, and they are much less concerned with sin and pollution. Also, the Dinka live in an economically expanding society; the Nuer, in a constricted one. Douglas distinguishes between the constraints of "group" ("the experience of a bounded social unit," [p. viii]) and "grid" ("rules that relate one person to others on an ego-centered basis," [p. viii]). She compares the Mandari, the Dinka, and the Nuer with respect to these two variables and finds that for the Mandari, group is strongest; for the Nuer, it is weaker but grid is stronger; and for the Dinka, both grid and group are the weakest of the three societies.

There appears to be some overlap here with Greenbaum's concepts with respect to the fixity or fluidity of groups, but not with respect to the concept of "grid." On the other hand, the concept of cultural complexity, which we have discussed with respect to the contrasting incidence of PT and T societies, is not relevant to Douglas, as the contrast between PT and T is not. Douglas is concerned with all types of "bodily dissociation," and the examples of societies she selects cut across levels of complexity, from the Bushmen to the West Indians of London.

The fact that a given society may have more than one type of dissociation, favoring one and fearing another, is recognized by Douglas but does not appear to her as a problem in making a general assessment of the prevalent attitude. Such a single statement of attitude appears necessary in this scheme. Douglas links this contrast in attitudes toward dissociation to a contrast between "ritualism" and "effervescence," stating (p. 81), "A social structure, which requires a high degree of conscious control will find its style in ritualism, and in the shunning of experiences in which control of consciousness is lost.'" Douglas (1970:81) states another hypothesis, however, that is not, it seems to me, merely a restatement in somewhat different terms of the original hypothesis: "The fullest possibilities of abandoning conscious control are only available to the extent that the social system relaxes its control over the individual." Perhaps, then, it is more meaningful to consider dissociation as a way to escape from the controls—indeed, a way to get the system to relax its controls on the individual, by making spirits—good, bad, or ethically neutral—in some way responsible for the breach in the patterning of social controls, and thus to modify the individual's position in the network of groups and grids.

Another approach to altered states must also be mentioned: I. M. Lewis (1966) has suggested that spirit possession cults (read possession trance cults) are linked to deprivation. He speaks of "a widespread use of spirit possession by means of which women and other depressed categories exert mystical pressures upon their superiors in circumstances of deprivation and frustration, when few other sanctions are available to them" (Lewis 1966:318). Several of the papers in this volume (Henney, Gussler) consider this hypothesis. Douglas rejects it as a broad generalization, pointing out, for example, how some deprived groups, such as the "Bog Irish," do not engage in such practices; and she substitutes her own hypothesis to account for the data on the Somali that Lewis presents.

Lewis elsewhere (n.d.) suggests a grouping of societies with possession cults into three types: those having "amoral peripheral possession cults," those having "main morality cults," and those having both types of possession cults. Deprivation theory applies to the first of these, the primary subjects of his concern. In his discussion, he suggests that Haitian "voodoo" is such an amoral peripheral cult, since the main morality cult in Haitian society is represented by Christianity. This I would question on two grounds. Most Haitian *voduists* are not, I believe, conscious of a conflict of world views between Catholicism and their folk religion. They speak of *Bon Dieu*, indentify their spirits with the Catholic saints, and go to church to have their children baptized and, where possible, their marriages blessed. Nor can it fairly be said to be the religion of the downtrodden. Quite aside from the much discussed role that *vodû* may, or may not, have played in the régime of the late François Duvalier, it appears to be the religion of the majority; and its function of supernatural coercion of the powerful, to the extent to which it exists, is, at best, a limited and partial function. Pentecostalism and related revivalistic religions also represent a case in point. This religion, whether in the United States, in Haiti, in St. Vincent, in Yucatán, or elsewhere, may well appeal selectively to some of the poor. But as Henney shows, for St. Vincent, the aim of the cult is not supernatural coercion of the powerful. Furthermore, since the possessing spirit in the case of this type of Christian church is the Holy Ghost, we are, in fact, dealing with a main morality cult, it would seem, rather than with a cult of amoral peripheral spirits. More precisely, Pentecostalism appears to partake of the characteristics of both of Lewis's types of cults.

It might be noted in this context that Douglas is concerned with "bodily dissociation," regardless of what kind of interpretation it is given in the particular culture—whether it is, in our terminology, T or PT. But, in fact, the emphasis of her discussion is on PT. Lewis, on the other hand, is concerned with possession as a cultural interpretation of the "condition, behaviour, or conduct" of individuals, "whether this involves trance or not and whether it is induced 'voluntarily' or 'involuntarily' " (Lewis n.d.:1). Thus, in our terminology, he does not make a distinction between P and PT; but in fact, he, too, deals primarily with PT. Whereas Douglas is concerned with the physiological alteration and cultural *attitudes* toward it, Lewis is concerned with *interpretations*, with cultural concepts, of altered conditions or behaviors; thus, he is primarily interested in the kinds of spirits thought to operate these transformations. Where Douglas sees in possession trance a symbolic representation of a type of social order, Lewis sees it as a means of social action.

The views formulated by Douglas are, as she herself points out, based on the sociological approach of Durkheim. The views of Lewis are based on the sociology of religion of Max Weber.

Our own scheme in some ways cuts across the approaches of Douglas and of Lewis. Like Douglas, we are interested in altered states of consciousness ("trance," "dissociation"); but unlike her, and like Lewis, we find it necessary to distinguish between types of altered states as related to different sorts of cultural interpretations. Thus, we have adopted the categories "trance" and "possession trance." In dealing with a large sample for statistical purposes, our approach is ethnographically less differentiated than that of Douglas in that we do not distinguish between different types of attitudes toward altered states, that is, welcomed states versus feared states. This is due, in part, to the fact that we have found ourselves unable to arrive at a single judgment for each society; some societies display more than one attitude, either because of different contexts in which altered states occur or because different groups within a population exhibit different attitudes. We do, however, consider such distinctions in some detail in our descriptive studies.

Unlike Lewis, we distinguish between different types

of possession beliefs—those linked to altered states (PT) and those not so linked (P). Again, in our statistical studies, we do not, at this stage of our work, distinguish between the types of spirits who are thought to possess persons and their varying relations to the moral system of the society.

We are, however, concerned with the relationship between the presence of institutionalized altered states (T and/or PT) and a series of societal variables, applied consistently to a large number of societies. We are concerned with formulating generalizations on the relationship between trance types, as we have defined them, and societal variables, which can be tested statistically. Seeking to test the applicability of a number of hypotheses to our data, we attempt in our descriptive studies to explore in depth the complex interrelationships between possession trance (PT) and possession belief (P) where it exists, as well as trance (T) where it exists as a separate form of altered state, and a variety of aspects of social and psychological functioning.

As noted earlier, however, the present volume centers its attention on one specific area of concern: the relationship between institutionalized, sacred altered states of consciousness and social change. So far, we have attempted to develop a perspective toward the subject of altered states. We may now briefly address ourselves to the matter of social change. Here it may be helpful to distinguish two kinds of processes that, for the sake of simplicity, we may term "microchange" and "macrochange." Microchange, in this usage, refers to modifications in the social situation of an individual without implying a modification in the social structure. This may take the form of making choices between alternative courses of action in any given situation, that is, there is no stereotypy in regard to solutions of individual problems. If I understand him correctly, this is what Firth

(1951:83–84) discusses under the term "organizational change" in contrast to "the massive form" of organizational change, which he refers to as structural change and which I speak of as macrochange. We may illustrate the contrast with respect to the operation of possession trance, dealing first with microchange in the life of the individual and second with macrochange in the life of the society. I have discussed elsewhere (Bourguignon 1965) the uses of possession trance for an individual in providing a greater range of actions. In this example, in the context of Haitian *vodû*, a woman who wished her former common-law husband to marry her was possessed by a female spirit during a curative ritual. The spirit agreed to perform the cure but required the man to do two things: to enter into a ritual marriage with the spirit and to enter into a legal marriage with the spirit's human impersonator. If we interpret the spirit identity as an alternate set of roles for the person, under appropriate ritual conditions, it is clear that such a set of roles makes it possible for the individual to modify the situation in which he or she must live, to introduce changes in the social framework of his own life. Yet, these changes do not affect the structure of the society. Individuals can utilize this option on the condition that the responsibility for the behavior is assigned to the spirit and not to the person. Again, such microchanges are characteristic of many of the East and South African societies, in which women in particular are afflicted by illnesses that require them to join cult groups and to meet the demands of their possessing spirits. The Nguni, discussed by Gussler, offer an example of such a situation. Possession trance and possession illness lead to a modification in the social position of the afflicted individual; they do not lead to a restructuring of the society. As Gluckman (1954) has shown with respect to the types of behavior that he calls "rituals of rebellion," these patterns, though expressing dissatisfaction with the social structure as it exists, in fact help to preserve it by offering a "safety valve" for accumulated pressures. As noted, Nadel (1952), in part, offers a similar explanation for witchcraft beliefs, pointing out that the stresses under which the society labors are not removed, but are allowed temporary expression, permitting the unsatisfactory system to continue its existence. Microchanges, rather than leading to macrochanges, may, in fact, in a situation of relative equilibrium, serve to maintain the social structure. The Shakers of St. Vincent, described by Henney, appear to present a case in point.

The possibility that possession trance may make possible microchange for individuals for whom such change is not available elsewhere suggests, as noted, the greater probability that such a mechanism will exist in more rigid societies. However, it also suggests that greater use of the mechanism will be made by those who suffer the greatest inability to modify their lives under the existing circumstances. The types of problems individuals cannot cope with will also be identified in this manner, as is illustrated by Pressel's discussion of the Umbanda religion of contemporary Brazil and the problems treated there not only by mediums in consultation but also by the actions of individuals during possession trance on their own behalf.

With respect to change on the level of social structure, the possession trance institution may play several roles. To begin with, we find a situation that corresponds to what Lewis has called the "major morality cult" (n.d.) or "central possession cult" (1971). We find an example of this in traditional Palauan society, as described by Leonard. Mediums, chosen from appropriate clans, were subject to the approval of the chiefs. As such, they were tied closely to the centers of power. And though becoming a medium might have provided opportunities for microchange for the individual and, indeed, altered the person's position in the society, there is no evidence that mediums were innovators, although they could influence a chief's decisions. On the other hand, the founder of the new religious movement, Modekngei, that arose in response to foreign contact, was able to gain followers by his apparent supernatural connections. The African separatist churches, discussed by Gussler with respect to the Zulu, take their authority for their innovative practices from possession by the Holy Ghost, as did the leaders in the abortive movement for social change among the Yucatán Maya, described by Goodman. Here, the message of the immediacy of the Second Coming was translated into a great missionary effort, to save as many as possible before it was too late. In order to undertake this effort, the church community was to be reorganized, developing a novel and alien type of social structure. It should be noted here that innovators, launching, in Wallace's (1956) terms, revitalization movements, aim toward the restructuring of the entire society. They begin in a personal crisis with a restructuring of their own personal world and their operation within it. (Wallace has termed this process "mazeway resynthesis.") They gain followers: as these followers and their leader develop the movement toward the reorganization of society, they have, in part, already removed themselves from that society and have created a small, new society for themselves. Thus, change is brought about and legitimized by supernatural sanction, possession trance, or visionary trance. But, in addition to the benefits that altered states bestow on members of such a group, membership itself is a transforming experience, on the level of personal behavior and personal identity and on the level of social action, as well. In Yucatán, individuals experienced baptism in the Holy Spirit and felt themselves saved. They also altered their style of life by giving up the "things of this world," and they developed new ties to the quasi family represented by the congregation. Life in such a congregation has its major compensation, even if the larger society is not changed. Henney's discussion of the Shakers of St. Vincent also shows this clearly: these people do not constitute a revitalization movement; they do not aim at the transformation of the society but at personal salvation. Yet membership in the group, besides the satisfaction of the possession trance and visionary experiences, also offers more mundane satisfactions, such as positions of authority for individuals, particularly for the men.

We may conclude, then, that altered states in general, and possession trance in particular, are related in a complex and multistranded manner to the subject of social change. To the extent that such states offer opportunities for a larger number of personal options to the individual within the existing social framework, they help to maintain that framework and thus act as a conservative force. Also, to the extent that such altered states are linked to "central possession cults" in Lewis's phrase (1971), they are tied to the centers of power and thus act in a conservative manner. On the other hand, by providing a sanctioned and prestigious form of decision-making, they may, in situations of social crisis, provide an avenue for the expression of dissatisfaction with existing patterns and for the introduction of massive innovations. The precise place of the trancer as a vehicle for such introductions or institutionalizations of change in connection with movements of change deserves further study. However, our framework for the study of altered states, involving a series of levels of analysis, offers, I believe, an avenue of approach to this complex subject.

1. One such often-cited exception are the Samburu, whom I have mentioned elsewhere (Bourguignon 1968 *b*). Several others are given by Lewis (1971:40–44); however, some of his examples deal with insufficiently documented situations. Also, it should be noted that, although the native interpretation may be secular, as in tarantism, the cure, or part of it, may nonetheless be sacred.

2. Detailed information on sampling is provided in Bourguignon (1968 *a*) and Greenbaum (1970). Discussion of research procedures and a list of bibliographic sources for data of our sample societies is to be found in Bourguignon (1968 *a*). Greenbaum's chapter in the present volume, entitled "Societal Correlates of Possession Trance in Sub-Saharan Africa," presents a detailed analysis of a portion of our data. Of the 422 "cultural clusters" identified by Murdock (1967), 72% are represented in our sample (Bourguignon 1968 *a*:34, table 4). To test the representativeness of our sample with respect to its universe, we compared the sample for each of the six regions with the *Atlas* total for that region by means of the z test, which tests the standard error of a proportion (Bryant 1966:112). We calculated z values for 18 dimensions for each of the six regions. Of the total 108 values obtained, only three were significant at the .05 level or below. Thus, although we do not have a random sample of the *Ethnographic Atlas* universe, it is, indeed, a representative one.

3. It happens that none of the societies under investigation here use drugs for purposes of inducing altered states. However, the generalization made here is applicable to drug-induced states as well, since cultural factors have been found to affect them profoundly. See Wallace (1959) and Dobkin de Rios (n.d.).

4. The Appendix lists the societies in our sample together with their coding for T, P, and PT.

5. For a full discussion of the codes used in this study, see Bourguignon (1968 *a*) and Bourguignon and Greenbaum (1968).

6. I have shown (Bourguignon 1972) that societies that use dreams to seek and control supernatural powers are more likely to be of Type I and II than of Type III, that is, trance and dreams are used similarly. Textor (1967) shows that such use of dreams is significantly less likely in stratified societies than those that are not stratified. This is consistent with our finding that societies of Type III, which typically are stratified societies, do not use dreams in this way.

7. For regional profiles, see Bourguignon and Greenbaum (1968), where settlement patterns are presented in table 17.

REFERENCES

Barry, Herbert III. 1968. Regional and worldwide variation in culture. *Ethnology* 7:207–17.

Bourguignon, Erika. 1965. "The self, the behavioral environment and the theory of spirit possession," in *Context and meaning in cultural anthropology* (editor M. E. Spiro). New York: The Free Press of Glencoe.

——. 1968a. *A cross-cultural study of dissociational states: Final report.* Columbus: the Ohio State University Research Foundation.

———. 1968*b*. "World distribution and patterns of possession states," in *Trance and possession states* (editor Raymond Prince). Montreal: R. M. Bucke Memorial Society.

———. 1972. "Dreams and altered states of consciousness in anthropological research," in *Psychological anthropology* (editor F. L. K. Hsu). New ed. Cambridge, Mass.: Schenkman Publishing Co.

———and Lenora Greenbaum. 1968. *Diversity and homogeneity: A comparative analysis of societal characteristics, based on data from the Ethnographic Atlas.* Occasional Papers in Anthropology, no. 1. Columbus: Department of Anthropology, the Ohio State University.

Bryant, E. C. 1966. *Statistical analysis.* 2d ed. New York: McGraw-Hill.

Dobkin de Rios, Marlene. n.d. Healing hallucinogens: Cultural variables affecting drug-induced altered states of consciousness. *Proceedings, 39th International Congress of Americanists* [Lima, Peru], forthcoming.

Douglas, Mary. 1970. *Natural symbols: Explorations in cosmology.* New York: Pantheon Books.

Driver, H. E., and K. F. Schuessler. 1967. Correlation analysis of Murdock's 1957 ethnographic sample. *American Anthropologist* 69:332–52.

Firth, Raymond. 1951. *Elements of social organization.* London: Watts and Co.

Fischer, Roland. 1970. Über das Rhythmisch-Ornamentale im Halluzinatorisch-Schöpferischen. *Confinia Psychiatrica* 13:1–25.

———. 1970. "Prediction and measurment of perceptual-behavioral change in drug-induced hallucination," in *Origin and mechanisms of hallucinations* (editor W. Keup). New York: Plenum Press.

Gluckman, Max. 1954. *Rituals of rebellion in South-East Africa.* The Frazier Lecture, 1952. Manchester: Manchester University Press.

Greenbaum, Lenora. 1970. Evaluation of a stratified versus an unstratified universe of cultures in comparative research. *Behavior Science Notes* 5:251–90.

Lewis, I. M. 1966. Spirit possession and deprivation cults. *Man* 1:307–29.

———. 1971. *Ecstatic religion: An anthropological study of spirit possession and shamanism.* Harmondworth, Middlesex, England: Penguin Books.

———. n.d. Possession cults and public morality. *Proceedings of the Colloque:* Cultes de Possession [Paris], forthcoming.

Ludwig, Arnold. 1968. "Altered states of consciousness," in *Trance and possessions states* (editor Raymond Prince). Montreal: R. M. Bucke Society.

Murdock, George Peter. 1967. *Ethnographic atlas: A summary.* Pittsburgh: University of Pittsburgh Press.

Nadel, S. F. 1952. Witchcraft in four African societies: An essay in comparison. *American Anthropologist* 54:18–29.

Oesterreich, T. K. 1922. *Die Bessessenheit.* Halle: Wendt und Klauwell.

Textor, R. B. 1967. *A cross-cultural summary.* New Haven: HRAF Press.

Wallace, A. F. C. 1956. Revitalization movements. *American Anthropologist* 58:264–81.

———. 1959. Cultural determinants of response to hallucinatory experience. *A.M.A. Archives of General Psychiatry* 1:58–69.

I

Cross–Cultural and Comparative Studies

1 : Societal Correlates of Possession Trance in Sub-Saharan Africa

Lenora Greenbaum

INTRODUCTION

Among the Nyoro of East Africa, it is believed that a spirit can inflict an illness upon a person. The illness is interpreted as evidence of possession by the spirit and can be cured when the spirit speaks through the ill person and makes requests. Granting the spirit's wishes is thought to effect a cure. A person so cured can, through a lengthy process, become a medium and participate in curing others so afflicted (Beattie 1963). The Swazi of South Africa believe that diviners (people who assist others in the solution of personal problems) become possessed by ancestral spirits. The diviners reach a high pitch of excitement and then stop and speak. Often the spirit will identify itself at this time (Kuper 1947). In West Africa, the Ashanti hold the belief that the god Bonsam reveals himself in the form of a man every ninth day. On this day, his priest dresses in a special way. Drums beat. The god comes closer. The priest trembles. "The person of the entranced priest fades into the person of the god." The priest then speaks in the language of the gods and helps solve problems brought by other people (Lystad 1958). Among the Jukun of the Sudan, there exist cult groups composed of women believed to be possessed by spirits. The high priestess is considered the mouthpiece of the ancestors and the gods. She pronounces oracles and foretells the future. Membership in the cult is hereditary; the spirit is passed on from mother to daughter (Meek 1950).

These are but a few examples of the phenomenon of possession trance found in various parts of Africa. Possession trance is a widespread phenomenon throughout the world and appears in many different forms. Despite the variety of manifestations, however, in each case the belief exists that a change of identity occurs to an individual. During a trance period this individual behaves in a manner different from that of his normal identity and often like the inhabiting or possessing spirit.

Of interest in this chapter is whether possession trance occurs at random among societies or whether societies with possession trance are in some way similar to each other. In other words, is there something in the nature of the larger society that makes for such unusual changes of identity? If these societies have no similarities, then possession trance may be a random phenomenon, needing a unique explanation wherever it occurs.

Purpose

The purpose of this study is to seek correlations between characteristics of societies and the presence of possession trance. This is a first step in understanding possession trance as a sociological as well as psychological phenomenon. A comparison is made between societies with and without possession trance in terms of their economy, social stratification, political organization, settlement pattern, marriage and kinship arrangements, and population size. These variables, which will be detailed later on, relate mainly to status and role relationships, that is, ways in which the society is organized or structured. Hence, they are referred to here as structural variables.

Background

With the development and availability of computers since World War II, interest in cross-cultural statistical studies has been high. White (1967) in a partial listing of work prior to 1967, indicates more than 60 studies done between 1945 and 1967. The topics of these studies cover a wide range, for example, residence and kinship patterns (Murdock 1949), food taboos (Ayres 1967), cultural evolution (Carneiro and Tobias 1963), art styles (Fischer 1961), and many more. Since 1967, the volume of work has continued, namely, McNett and Kirk (1968), Murdock (1968 *a*), Bourguignon and Greenbaum (1968), Chaney and Revilla (1969), Wolfe (1969), Abrahamson (1969), among others.

In the area of belief systems and religion, both Swanson (1960) and Whiting (1959) attempted to establish societal correlates of particular institutionalized beliefs. Each used a sample of 50 societies chosen from all over the world. Swanson found that societies in which a belief in a high god exists are likely to have three or more levels of administrative sovereignty. Whiting tried to show that societies in which sorcery is present tend to rely on a system of "coordinate" justice and punishment rather than "superordinate." Her findings were inconclusive because of the sparsity of data available to her at the time.

The present study continues the tradition of cross-cultural statistical work, with particular reference to correlates of an institutionalized religious belief and practice, that is, possession trance. It differs from previous works in some respects. First, only one geographic area of the world is studied, Sub-Saharan Africa. Several independent teams (Driver and Schuessler 1967; Bourguignon and Greenbaum 1968;

Murdock and White 1969; among others) have found that regional differences are great and warrant regional rather than worldwide analysis. Further, the present study uses every society listed in the *Ethnographic Atlas* of April 1967 (Murdock 1967) in Sub-Saharan Africa for which sufficient data were available to make a determination as to the presence or absence of possession trance. Although the 114 societies used cannot be considered a true statistical sample of Sub-Saharan African societies, they do represent all the available societies that can be used for the subject at hand. The degree to which this group is representative of all African societies in the *Ethnographic Atlas* is indicated later on.

Definitions

Possession trance, the dependent variable used in this study, refers to a condition in which a person is believed to be inhabited by the spirit of another person or a supernatural being. During this "possession" by a spirit other than his own, the person is in an altered state of consciousness, evidenced by one or more of the following: talking and acting like the inhabiting spirit, lapsing into a coma-like state, speaking unintelligibly, exhibiting physical symptoms such as twitching, wild dancing, frothing at the mouth, and so on. Upon regaining his original identity, the person generally retains no conscious memory of the activity of the spirit.

Possession trance may be an individual or a group phenomenon. It may be induced by drugs, music, or other methods external to the individual, or it may be a spontaneous manifestation by the person possessed. It may be a phenomenon restricted to a particular status or role (for example, a diviner, medium, priest) or it may occur at random in the society. In all cases however, the phenomenon is accepted within the society as a trance induced by a spirit entering the person possessed, and not as an individual psychological aberration.⌉

All the coding for the presence or absence of possession trance in the African societies analyzed here was done by the Cross-Cultural Study of Dissociational States, and appears in the final report of this research project (Bourguignon, 1968). The *structural societal characteristics* used as independent variables were selected from the coded data of the *Ethnographic Atlas* as revised and consolidated by Bourguignon and Greenbaum (1968). Fifteen variables are used in all. The basis of selection of these variables is twofold: first, only those are used for which information is available for about 200 or more of the 238 African societies listed in the *Atlas:* and second, from among those for which this type of data exists, a selection was made to include a diversity of variables covering structural aspects particularly important in Sub-Saharan Africa. The variables used are: Subsistence Economy (Dependence on Agriculture, Dependence on Agriculture and Animal Husbandry Combined, Sex Division of Labor in Agriculture); Political Structure (Jurisdictional Hierarchy, Succession to Office of Local Headman); Class Structure (Stratification of Freemen, Slavery); Settlement Pattern; Marriage, Family, and Kinship (Community Organization, Kin Groups, Marital Residence, Marriage Form, Family Form, Mode of Marriage); and Population.

Hypothesis

The hypothesis tested is: Possession trance is randomly distributed among Sub-Saharan African societies, and no particular societal characteristics are significantly correlated with the possession trance phenomenon. This is the null hypothesis. On the basis of statistical findings, a decision is made whether to accept or reject this hypothesis.

Methods

The following statistical methods are used:

1. A z value test (Bryant 1966) is used to determine the degree to which the 114 societies are representative of all 238 African societies listed in the Ethnographic Atlas.

2. Kolmogorov-Smirnoff chi square (Siegel 1956) and standard chi square tests are used to determine societal correlates of possession trance.

3. The Marsh Index of Societal Differentiation (Marsh 1967) is compared with the incidence of possession trance by a standard chi square test.

4. A tree-design technique (Lipschutz 1966) is used to develop a preliminary typology of societies.

FINDINGS

Similarity of Universe and Sample

Analyzing a selected group of 114 African societies raises the question of the degree to which the sample is representative of the "universe" of African societies.[1] The 238 societies for which adequate and available data exist in the *Ethnographic Atlas* are considered here to be the universe of African societies. The 114 African societies used in this analysis must be considered, not as a random sample of the universe of African societies, but as a sample based on the availability of information on the phenomenon in question. Although it would be highly desirable to have data that would permit random sampling, this is not possible given the nature of the studies on African societies at the present time. It is, however, important to know whether some justification exists for generalizing to all African societies conclusions or findings concerning the 114 societies examined here. A check on the geographic location of the 114 societies has indicated that they are scattered throughout Sub-Saharan Africa. Beyond that, a comparison is made

TABLE 1

COMPARISON OF UNIVERSE AND SAMPLE SOCIETIES
FOR 15 SELECTED SOCIETAL VARIABLES

SOCIETAL VARIABLE	UNIVERSE SOCIETIES		SAMPLE SOCIETIES		Z VALUE
	N	%	N	%	
Subsistence economy					
Dependence on agriculture	238	100	114	100	
Heavy (more than 46%)	207	87	95	83	−1.26
Low (45% or less)...............	31	13	19	17	
Dependence on agriculture and and animal husbandry combined ...	238	100	114	100	
Heavy (more than 25% from each)	60	25	30	26	+ .24
Low (less than 25% from either or both)	178	75	84	74	
Sex division of labor in agriculture	231	100	112	74	
Female predominates	123	53	64	57	+ .84
Other (male predominates; equal participation, absence of agriculture)....................	109	47	48	43	
Political structure					
Jurisdictional hierarchy..............	237	100	114	100	
Only local political levels	60	25	25	22	−1.06
1,2,3, or 4 levels beyond local level.....................	177	75	89	78	
Succession to office of headman.....	193	100	98	100	
Patrilineal heir	103	53	49	50	− .59
All other forms (matrilineal heir, election, appointment)	90	47	49	50	
Class structure					
Stratification of free men............	204	100	103	100	
No hereditary social classes	124	61	56	54	
Two distinct classes or more complex stratification	80	39	47	46	+1.58
Slavery	204	100	103	100	
Absent..........................	44	22	28	27	
Present	160	78	75	73	+1.21

45

TABLE 1—*Continued*

SOCIETAL VARIABLE	UNIVERSE SOCIETIES		SAMPLE SOCIETIES		Z VALUE
	N	%	N	%	
Settlement pattern	238	100	114	100	
Sedentary, permanent	215	90	99	87	−1.05
Migratory, impermanent	23	10	15	13	
Marriage, family, kinship					
Community organization	222	100	112	100	
Clan organization	83	37	43	38	+ .21
Other forms (demes, segmented groups)	139	63	69	62	
Kin groups	238	100	114	100	
Patrilineal	173	73	79	69	− .95
Other (matrilineal, double descent, cognatic)	65	27	35	31	
Marital residence	237	100	114	100	
Patrilocal	178	75	78	68	−2.48
Other (matrilocal, virilocal, avunculocal, etc.)	59	25	36	32	
Marriage form	238	100	114	100	
Polygyny	202	85	96	84	− .29
Monogamy or monogamy with occasional polygyny	36	15	18	16	
Family form	238	100	114	100	
Independent nuclear	132	56	63	55	− .31
Extended	106	44	51	45	
Mode of marriage	238	100	114	100	
Bride price or service	214	90	99	87	−1.05
Other (dowry, exchange, token) ...	24	10	15	13	
Population	217	100	104	100	
100,000 and over	103	47	64	62	+2.85
Less than 100,000	114	53	40	38	

NOTE: At the .05 level of significance, Z must equal 1.96 or higher. In the above table, the Z values significant beyond the .05 level are +2.85 for population more than 100,000 and −2.48 for patrilocal marital residence. For all other characteristics, no significant differences exist in the proportionality comparisons.

between the 238 societies of the African "universe" and the 114 societies of the "available sample," based on the 15 societal variables mentioned earlier.

Table 1 contains data on the distribution of the universe and sample societies, according to these variables. Using the formula $z = \dfrac{p' - p}{\sqrt{\dfrac{pq}{N}}}$ (Bryant 1966:112), z values have been obtained for proportionality comparison tests between the universe and the sample. A check of significance levels indicates that for 13 variables the sample does not differ significantly from the universe. Differences are significant for only two variables: population size and marital residence. It is likely, therefore, that generalizations discovered about the sample may be applied to the universe.

Correlation of Societal Variables with Possession Trance

Comparisons have been made between possession trance and the 15 societal variables used earlier in table 1. Table 2 contains the incidence of possession trance according to these variables. In each case, the standard chi square (X^2) is recorded, with its associated level of significance as well as the contingency coefficient (C). The variables are listed in descending order of chi square. Hence, the variables at the head of the table are those showing the highest degree of association with possession trance; and the degree of relationship declines rapidly toward the end of the table.

Only three variables are significantly related to possession trance (that is, the chi square is significant at or below the .05 level). The presence of slavery, a stratification system (of free men) of two or more distinct classes, and a population of 100,000 or more, each shows significant relationships to the presence of possession trance in a society. The contingency coefficient shows a relatively strong correlation of possession trance with slavery and stratification (.500 and .423 respectively), but a weaker one (.276) with population size.

Variables showing a significance level of .10 or less, though not as strongly related to possession trance as the three above, nevertheless could be considered as having a possible connection with the phenomenon. An

47

TABLE 2

Relationship between Possession Trance and Specific Societal Variables

Societal Variable	Total Societies		Societies With Possession Trance		Societies Without Possession Trance		Chi Square (X²)	Significance Level (p)	Contingency Coefficient* (C_adj)
	N	%	N	%	N	%			
Slavery	103	100	64	100	39	100	14.70	.005	.500
Absent	28	27	9	14	19	49			
Present	75	73	55	86	20	51			
Stratification of free men	103	100	64	100	39	100	10.11	.005	.423
No hereditary social classes	56	54	27	42	29	74			
Two distinct classes or more complex stratification	47	46	37	58	10	26			
Population	104	100	68	100	36	100	4.77	.05	.296
100,000 and over	64	61	47	69	17	47			
Less than 100,000	40	39	21	31	19	53			
Marital residence	114	100	75	100	39	100	3.36	.10	.239
Patrilocal	78	68	47	63	31	79			
Other (matrilocal, virilocal, avunculocal, etc.)	36	32	28	37	8	21			
Settlement pattern	114	100	75	100	39	100	2.81	.10	.219
Sedentary, permanent	99	87	68	91	31	79			
Migratory, impermanent	15	13	7	9	8	21			
Jurisdictional hierarchy	114	100	75	100	39	100	2.71	.10	.215
Only local political levels	25	22	13	17	12	31			
1,2,3, or 4 levels beyond local level	89	78	62	83	27	69			
Marriage form	114	100	75	100	39	100	2.36	.20	.202
Polygyny	96	84	66	88	30	77			

Monogamy or monogamy with occasional polygyny	18	16	9	12	9	23			
Community organization	112	100	74	100	38	100	1.96	.20	.185
Clan organization	43	38	25	34	18	47			
Other forms (demes, segmented groups)	69	62	49	66	20	53			
Family form	114	100	75	100	39	100	1.87	.20	.180
Independent nuclear	63	55	38	51	25	64			
Extended	51	45	37	49	14	36			
Dependence on agriculture	114	100	75	100	39	100	1.75	.20	.174
Heavy (more than 46%)	95	83	65	87	30	77			
Low (45% or less)	19	17	10	13	9	23			
Kin Groups	114	100	75	100	39	100	1.62	.25	.141
Patrilineal	79	69	49	65	30	77			
Other (matrilineal, double descent, cognatic)	35	31	26	35	9	23			
Succession to office of headman	98	100	62	100	36	100	1.58	.25	.178
Patrilineal heir	49	50	34	55	15	42			
All other forms (matrilineal heir, election, appointment)	49	50	28	45	21	58			
Mode of marriage	114	100	75	100	39	100	1.19	.30	.144
Bride price or service	99	87	67	89	32	82			
Other (dowry, exchange, token)	15	13	8	11	7	18			
Sex division of labor in agriculture	112	100	73	100	32	100	1.18	.30	.149
Female predominates	64	61	42	57	22	69			
Other (male predominates; equal participation, absence of agriculture)	48	39	31	43	10	31			

NOTE: *The Contingency Coefficients in this and other tables have been adjusted to range from zero to one.

examination of these variables indicates the following: possession trance tends to be somewhat more prevalent among societies with patrilocal residence, with permanent settlement patterns, and with political jurisdictional levels beyond the local level. Other variables relating to subsistence economy and to family, marriage, and kinship seem to have no discernible relationship to the possession trance phenomenon.

The strong association between possession trance and the presence of slavery and of stratification of free men indicates that possession trance tends to be present in African societies with fixed internal social status distinctions.

A Typology of Societies

A comparison of societies grouped according to fixed internal social status distinctions confirms even more strongly the above finding. For such comparison, the 114 societies were separated according to the slavery and stratification variables, using the "tree design" technique (Lipschutz 1966:176). As indicated in Figure 1, four types of societies emerge, as follows:

> Type I. Slavery present; stratification of freemen present (two or more distinct hereditary social classes).
> Type II. Slavery present; stratification absent (no hereditary social classes of freemen).
> Type III. Slavery absent; stratification present.
> Type IV. Slavery absent; stratification absent.

Because no information is available on stratification and slavery for 11 societies, the number of societies in the typology is reduced from 114 to 103.

Using these 103 societies, table 3 shows the distribution of possession trance within each of the four groups. It

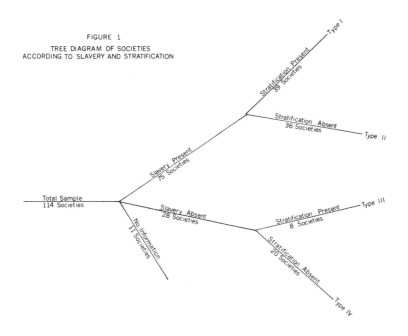

FIGURE 1
TREE DIAGRAM OF SOCIETIES
ACCORDING TO SLAVERY AND STRATIFICATION

is clear that in Types I, II, and III possession trance is much more likely to be present than absent. These are societies that have slavery and/or stratification. The reverse is true of Type IV. These societies are without slavery and without stratification, and the vast majority are also without possession trance.

Table 4 shows the incidence of possession trance among all the societies in Types I, II and III combined compared with societies in Type IV. For this table, chi square is 21.0, significant far below the .001 level. This unusually high value for chi square indicates a very strong association between fixed internal social status distinctions and the presence of possession trance.

TABLE 3

DISTRIBUTION OF POSSESSION TRANCE WITHIN
FOUR TYPES OF SOCIETIES

POSSESSION TRANCE	TOTAL		TYPE I		TYPE II		TYPE III		TYPE IV	
	N	%	N	%	N	%	N	%	N	%
Present	64	62	31	79	24	67	6	75	3	15
Absent	39	38	8	21	12	33	2	25	17	85
Total	103	100	39	100	36	100	8	100	20	100

NOTE: Chi square = 24.76. At three degrees of freedom, p <.001. C_{adj}=.622.

TABLE 4

DISTRIBUTION OF POSSESSION TRANCE AMONG
SOCIETAL TYPES I, II, III COMPARED WITH SOCIETAL TYPE IV

POSSESSION TRANCE	TOTAL		SOCIETAL TYPES I, II, III		SOCIETAL TYPE IV	
	N	%	N	%	N	%
Present	64	62	61	73	3	15
Absent	39	38	22	27	17	85
Total	103	100	83	100	20	100

NOTE: Chi Square equals 21.0. At one degree of freedom, this is significant considerably below the <.001 level.

Societal Differentiation and Possession Trance

The availability of an Index of Societal Differentiation for many societies permits a further test of the relationship found above. This index, developed by Marsh (1967), is an indication of internally differentiated roles and structures in a society, such that the greater the differentiation, the higher the index assigned to that society.[2] Differentiated roles and structures can be considered further refinements of status distinctions and a rough indicator of societal complexity.

Using this index, tests of the relationship between differentiation and possession trance have been made. Of the 114 societies used in this study, an index of differentiation was found for only 55 in Marsh's listing. Among these 55 societies, possession trance was present in 37 and absent in 18. This distribution is almost exactly the same as the distribution for all 114 societies (table 5).

TABLE 5

Possession Trance among all 114 Sample Societies Compared With 53 Societies with an Index of Differentiation

Possession Trance	Sample Societies		Societies With Index of Differentiation	
	N	%	N	%
Present	75	66	37	67
Absent	39	34	18	33
Total	114	100	55	100

Societies with indexes between 0 and 3 (relatively little differentiation) were compared with societies with indexes between 4 and 7 (relatively high differentiation), using a standard chi square test (table 6). The chi square found was 9.98, significant below the .005 level.

TABLE 6

Distribution of Societies according to Index of Differentiation and Possession Trance

| Possession Trance | Index of Differentiation | | | | | |
| | Total | | 0–3 | | 4–7 | |
	N	%	N	%	N	%
Present	37	70	12	48	25	89
Absent	18	30	14	52	4	11
Total	55	100	26	100	29	100

Note: Chi Square equals 9.98. At one degree of freedom, this figure is significant at the .005 level.

According to this test, possession trance is significantly more prevalent among societies with greater role and structure differentiation than among those with a lesser degree of such differentiation. This expands the previous findings of a positive relationship between possession trance and fixed internal social status distinctions among African societies to include a positive relationship with social differentiation and complexity.

CONCLUSION

Statistical Findings

On the basis of the statistical findings of this study, the null hypothesis suggested at the beginning must be rejected. In three tests, significant relationships between possession trance and specific societal characteristics have been found.

Among 114 societies, possession trance was significantly related to the presence of slavery and to the presence of a stratification system of freeman of at least two social classes. Among 103 societies, relationship of possession trance to either or both slavery and stratification was unusually strong. Among 55 societies, a significant relationship was found between the presence of possession trance and the degree of societal differentiation.

It seems clear, therefore, that possession trance is not randomly distributed among African societies, as the hypothesis stated, but instead is much more likely to be found among societies of a particular type, that is, those with fixed internal status distinctions and differentiation.

Areas of Further Analysis

In view of the strong findings indicated above, some

54

important questions arise. First, why is possession trance positively related to fixed internal status arrangements in societies? What aspect of life in such societies would encourage the change of identity phenomenon referred to here as possession trance? Is life more complicated, difficult, or restricted in these societies compared with groups without fixed status arrangements? Would any of these characteristics encourage the presence of possession trance, and for what reason? In short, is there a stronger relationship between some other aspect of society and possession trance than was found among the variables available for this study?

A second area of further study relates to the exceptions to the findings of this study. Specifically, among the 83 societies with fixed internal status distinctions, 22 societies (27%) do not have possession trance. Further, of the 20 societies with neither slavery nor stratification, three (15%) do not have possession trance. In total, 25 societies, or about one-fourth of the sample, do not conform to the statistical correlations found in this study. What accounts for these exceptions? Are there discrepancies in definitions and coding as applied to the different societies that would make for errors in classification? Or are there aspects of these "exception" societies that again correlate more strongly with possession trance than do the fixed status arrangements? In other words, is the fixed status arrangement merely an indicator of some variable or variables, with greater explanatory power?

The answers to these questions can only be speculated upon but not established from the data in this study. The statistically significant relationships found here, however, provide the justification for continuing to probe the subject. As a result, through an examination of the literature on some societies used here for statistical purposes, additional variables have been sought for greater understanding of the possession trance phenomenon and its place in society. A discussion of some of this work is presented in the following chapter in this volume.

1. No effort has been made to select societies according to culture clusters (Murdock 1967) or according to subsequent suggestions based on culture clusters (HRAF 1967; Naroll 1967; Murdock 1968b; Murdock and White 1969) because evidence is available (Greenbaum 1970) that no significant differences exist in the results using random samples or samples based on culture clusters for African societies in the *Ethnographic Atlas*.

2. Marsh conducted a test of his index by comparing it with findings of Carneiro and Tobias (1963) on evolutionary development. On the basis of this test, Marsh concludes (1967:332): "This suggests that our Index scores . . . are a valid measure of actual functional role differentiation in the Murdock sample of societies." Schaefer (1969) in discussing the Marsh Index states that his own research "indicates that his [that is, Marsh's] scale is significantly correlated with both Dr. Naroll's Index of Social Development and Dr. Freeman's Folk-Urban Variable Scale. Thus for a rough index of social complexity the Marsh data . . . is [*sic*] good."

REFERENCES

Abrahamson, Mark. 1969. Correlates of political complexity. *American Sociological Review* 34:690–701.

Ayres, Barbara C. 1967. "Pregnancy magic: A study of food taboos and sex avoidance," in *Cross-Cultural Approaches* (editor Clellan S. Ford). New Haven: HRAF Press.

Beattie, John. 1963. "Sorcery in Bunyoro," in *Witchcraft and sorcery in East Africa* (editors John Middleton and E. H. Henkers). London: Routledge and Kegan Paul.

Bourguignon, Erika. 1968. *A cross-cultural study of dissociational states: Final report.* Columbus: the Ohio State University Research Foundation.

————and Lenora Greenbaum. 1968. *Diversity and homogeneity: A comparative analysis to societal characteristics, based on data from the Ethnographic Atlas.* Occasional Papers in Anthropology, no. 1, Columbus: Department of Anthropology, the Ohio State University.

Bryant, E. C. 1966. *Statistical analysis.* 2d ed. New York: McGraw-Hill.

Carneiro, Robert L., and Stephen F. Tobias. 1963. Application of scale analysis to the study of cultural evolution. *Transactions of the New York Academy of Science* 26:109–207.

Chaney Richard P., and R. R. Revilla. 1969. Sampling methods and interpretation of correlation: A comparative analysis of seven cross-cultural samples. *American Anthropologist* 71:597–633.

Driver, Harold E., and Karl F. Schuessler. 1967. Correlation analysis of Murdock's 1967 ethnographic sample. *American Anthropologist* 69:332–52.

Fischer, John L. 1961. Art styles as cultural cognitive maps. *American Anthropologist* 63:79–93.

Greenbaum, Lenora. 1970. Evaluation of a stratified versus an unstratified universe of cultures in comparative research. *Behavior Science Notes* 5: 251–90.

Human Relations Areas Files (HRAF). 1967. The HRAF quality control sample universe. *Behavior Science Notes* 2:81–88.

Kuper, Hilda. 1947. *An African aristocracy*. London: Oxford University Press for International African Institute.

Lipschutz, Seymour. 1966. *Theory and problems of finite mathematics*. New York: Schaum.

Lystad, Robert A. 1958. *The Ashanti*. New Brunswick, N. J.: Rutgers University Press.

Marsh, Robert M. 1967. *Comparative sociology: A codification of cross-societal analysis*. New York: Harcourt, Brace and World.

McNett, Charles W., Jr., and R. E. Kirk. 1968. Drawing random samples in cross-cultural studies: A suggested method. *American Anthropologist* 70:50–55.

Meek, C. K. 1950. *A Sudanese kingdom: An ethnological study of the Jukun-speaking peoples of Nigeria*. New York: Humanities Press.

Murdock, George P. 1949. *Social structure*. New York: Macmillan Co.

———. 1967. *Ethnographic atlas: A Summary*. Pittsburgh: University of Pittsburgh Press.

———. 1968a. Patterns of sibling terminology. *Enthnology* 7:1–24.

———. 1968b. World sampling provinces. *Ethnology* 7:305–26.

Murdock, George P., and Douglas R. White. 1969. Standard cross-cultural sample. *Ethnology* 8:329–69.

Naroll, Raoul. 1967. The proposed HRAF probability sample. *Behavior Science Notes* 2:70–80.

Schaefer, James M. 1969. Personal communication.

Siegel, Sidney. 1956. *Non-parametric statistics for the behavioral sciences*. New York: McGraw-Hill.

Swanson, Guy L. 1960. *Birth of the gods*. Ann Arbor: University of Michigan Press.

White, Douglas R. 1967. *The societal research archives system*. Minneapolis, Minn.: University of Minnesota, Department of Anthropology.

Whiting, Beatrice B. 1959. "A cross-cultural study of sorcery and social control," in *Paiute socery*. Viking Fund Publications in Anthropology, no. 15, pp. 82–91. New York: Wenner-Gren Foundation.

Wolfe, Alvin W. 1969. Social structural bases of art. *Current Anthropology* 10:1, pp. 3–44.

2 : Possession Trance in Sub-Saharan Africa: A Descriptive Analysis of Fourteen Societies

Lenora Greenbaum

INTRODUCTION

The preceding chapter, in which a direct correlation between fixed internal status distinctions[1] and possession trance among African societies was established, raises some intriguing questions. First, what is the reason for the strong correlations found; why are societies with possession trance more stratified, complex, and socially differentiated than those without possession trance? And second, why are there exceptions to these findings; why do about one-fourth of the societies not fit the statistical correlations found?

By inspection, it is difficult to explain the connection between the structural variables and the possession trance phenomenon. There are some conclusions that cannot be drawn from these data, and these are worth noting. First because the statistical study is cross-sectional rather than longitudinal, we can make no determination of what happens regarding possession trance as a society changes from a simple to a complex one. Second, the relationship does not appear to be causal. Available evidence does not indicate that possession trance causes slavery and stratification or, conversely, that slavery and stratification cause possession trance. Were causality the explanation, it seems unlikely that so many exceptions would appear in the findings. Hence the search for intervening variables.

58

The assumption is made here that variables exist that have not been coded and counted and that relate both to status systems and to possession trance. Köbben (1967), Stuckert (1958), and Coleman (1964), among others, have indicated the need to search for additional variables to explain variations or exceptions in statistical results. Intervening variables are likely, therefore, to be important in answering both sets of the above questions.

+ The particular intervening variable suggested here as having greater explanatory value for the possession trance phenomenon is a *rigid social structure*.[2] The hypothesis is offered that in a rigid society, that is, one where the social structures deny the individual freedom for achievement and personal control over his daily life activities, possession trance is likely to be widespread. Conversely, under more flexible systems, possession trance is likely to be either absent or a rare phenomenon. The rationale is that, under rigid systems, simple decision-making is fraught with danger from internal and external social controls. Possession trance relieves the individual of personal responsibility in the decision-making process by temporarily changing the identity of a human being into that of a spirit. The medium, through whom the spirit speaks, and the petitioner, following the spirit's dictates, can thus solve the problem of meeting crucial daily life decisions without either intruding personally into the established order of things.

Following this reasoning, a second hypothesis is suggested: that in Africa rigid social structures and possession trance are more likely to be found among societies with fixed status distinctions. This would explain the strong correlations found. The exceptions, however, would result from the existence of societies with fixed social status distinctions that have a flexible social structure, permitting considerable personal control over daily life situations and personal achievement. In these groups, no need for possession trance exists, since individuals can take personal responsibility for decision-making.

Various researchers whose work has touched on changes of identity and possession trance as a social phenomenon have made some suggestive comments. Firth, in discussing societal rigidity as a situation that offers no outlets for abnormal behavior, states, "Institutional roles, such as that of the spirit medium ... may give people ample opportunity to redress their social balance" (1963:75). Prince, in a review of Lucy Mair's *Witchcraft*, indicated, "The diviner-witchcraft complex is a highly versatile mechanism for the manipulation of social forces in accordance with the wishes of the decision makers of the group hidden by a supernatural smoke screen" (1970:916).

Writing about religious cults using possession trance, Beattie has stated, "What is common to all the spirits or powers we have discussed is that they express, or may have originally expressed, new, formidable, and potentially dangerous kinds of power. The spirit cult appears to afford an acceptable way of coming to terms with such phenomena, with which ... there is no other obvious way of dealing" (1960:78). Nadel (1958:464), referring to mediums who work through the change of identity mechanism of possession trance, indicated that the unpredictable guidance from these spirit-inspired people is an important force for change since they can suggest reforms with no fear of disbelief or resentment on the part of the people at large. In addition, Field, writing about the Ashanti, specifically states, "The function of dissociation or 'possession' in priestly duties is to endow the priests' utterances with authority and to exonerate him from personal responsibility for them ..." (1960:76). These hypotheses cannot as yet be tested on a rigorous statistical basis because coded data on rigidity of social structures for large numbers of societies are unavailable. Analyses of a number of individual societies are undertaken here, however, as a preliminary exploration of these suggested relationships.

METHOD

Selection of Societies

Fourteen societies have been selected for brief description and analysis, as an initial judgmental test of the hypotheses. Following the typology of societies developed in the previous chapter, societies were chosen from each of the four types. Within each type, the approximate ratio of possession-trance to no-possession-trance societies was kept, with the results shown in table 1. Type III is represented by only one society, with possession trance; inadequate data on the two no-possession-trance societies of this type precluded adding one of them to this analysis.

The availability of good descriptive data determined which particular societies satisfying the above criteria were finally selected for this study.

TABLE 1

SOCIETIES SELECTED FOR STUDY

| | | SOCIETIES | |
SOCIETAL TYPE	TOTAL	With Possession Trance	No Possession Trance
Type I	5	4	1
Type II	3	2	1
Type III	1	1	0
Type IV	5	1	4
Total....................	14	8	6

Statistical Comparisons

Because of the small number of societies involved, statistical results following the descriptive analyses are formulated using Fisher's Exact Probability Test (Siegel 1956:96). It is recognized that these results cannot be generalized to a larger universe because of the nonrandom nature of the sample selection. They are presented primarily for their descriptive value in making some comparisons of variables for these fourteen societies.

FINDINGS

Descriptive Analysis

In describing each society, the following variables are briefly indicated: economy, political system, lineage arrangements, geographic mobility, stratification, and the religious system. A check is made on the coding of the presence of slavery, the complexity of the stratification system, and the presence of possession trance. In the definition of slavery and of possession trance, wide variation is possible in the extent and use of the particular structural form. For purposes of this study, the existence of any amount of slavery is accepted as indicating its presence in a society. The rationale is that the presence of slaves only in a chief's house or only among a very small proportion of the population indicates, nevertheless, a social acceptance of the phenomenon. As for possession trance, the requisites here are more stringent than those used to code possession trance in the previous chapter. Since the hypotheses of this study turn on the change-of-identity concept—the actual verbal instructions for decision-making from a spirit via a human medium—and general acceptance of the phenomenon by the society at large, these conditions must be met for the possession trance coding to survive in this analysis. As a result, those societies in which possession trance is occasionally reported but is not generally used for decision-making purposes or those where a trance or a loss of consciousness may be interpreted as spirit possession without any other manifestations of the spirit are reclassified as generally having no possession trance.

Finally, from the descriptive data, a judgment is suggested as to whether the society is considered to have rigid or flexible social structures. Admittedly, precise criteria for such determination have not been defined. This is a first attempt at a judgmental determination based only on the descriptive material found in the literature. As an aid in judging the rigidity or flexibility of a society, a formulation of ideology and practice in some important areas of social life is suggested, as indicated in table 2.

As an ideal type, a rigid society would have the follow-

TABLE 2

SUGGESTED CRITERIA FOR DETERMINING
SOCIETAL RIGIDITY OR FLEXIBILITY

AREA OF SOCIAL LIFE	RIGID	FLEXIBLE
Status		
Ideology	Nonegalitarian	Egalitarian
Practice	Ascription	Achievement
Political system		
Ideology	Autocratic	Democratic
Practice	Hierarchical	Federated or stateless
Residence		
Ideology	Fixed residence membership	Residence change available
Practice	Travel restricted	Travel encouraged
Religion		
Ideology	Fixed rites	Flexible rites
Practice	Central authority	Individual control
Group Membership		
Ideology	Permission needed for change	Freedom to move among groups
Practice	Fixed groups	Diverse and changing

ing characteristics: nonegalitarian, ascriptive status; an autocratic hierarchical political system; fixed residence and restricted travel; centrally controlled, fixed religious rites; and fixed group membership with changes only as permitted by higher authority. A flexible society would reflect the reverse pattern: egalitarianism with achievement-oriented status; a federated or stateless democratic society; freedom of travel and ease in residence changes; individual control over flexible religious rites; and freedom to join a variety of diverse groups. It must be kept in mind that this formulation is an initial effort at developing criteria for determining rigidity or flexibility. In the absence of any more rigorous methods, the fourteen societies in this study are judged on how closely they approximate the ideal types described above.

Type I

The five Type I societies selected are: Ashanti, Ganda, Mende, and Nyoro, all coded with possession trance; Hehe, no possession trance. Brief descriptions of each follow.[3]

Ashanti.—The Ashanti of Ghana in West Africa are an agricultural and trading society. Trading in slaves with the Europeans in past centuries resulted in great prosperity for the Ashanti. Craftsmen, specialists, and tradesmen abound in this group, as well as many small farmers. Many avenues for individual achievement exist. Travel is a necessary part of the large trading economy. The political structure consists of many decentralized though hierarchic bureaucracies loosely held together in a pyramidal organization. Slavery existed before British control of the area. Concerning individual achievement, Field states: "The point I have been trying to emphasize . . . is the absence of hide-bound rigidity. Class hardly exists; rank does exist but its attainment is the reward of individual merit. Institutions were made for man. Nothing is immune to criticism" (1960:26).

In the Ashanti religious system, many gods exist. Possession trance is a basic mechanism for transmitting the wishes of the gods and thus for decision-making in the society. It is interesting, however, that gods are viewed more as superhuman people rather than as mysterious supernatural forces. Hence, gods are expected to make mistakes, are not considered omnipotent, and are patronized as long as they seem to have some success in their decision-making assistance to people. Otherwise, they are abandoned for other gods. According to Lystad:

> From time to time, a god may achieve such a pinnacle of success that his fame spreads throughout Ashanti.... This has been particularly the case during...social upheaval, when many persons, socially or emotionally upset by changing cultural forces they cannot easily understand or master, have attributed their problems to the perverse activities of sorcerers. A number of shrewd gods have managed to create the impression that they can successfully identify and either kill or purge these demons, and their popularity has soared along with their bank accounts. (1958:167)

Coding: Stratification present.
Slavery present.
Possession trance present.
Social structures: flexible.

Ganda.—The Ganda are an agricultural people occupying central Uganda. The traditional form of this society is based on a hierarchy of people in authority and their subordinates. The king (Kabaka) is a despotic ruler exercizing the power of life and death over his subjects. Each village chief rules his village autocratically and likewise holds life and death powers over the villagers. In individual families, the father rules autocratically and is feared by his children. Personal relations generally are dominated by concepts of subordination and super-ordination. In this hierarchic society, generally, ascriptive status of its members is the norm. Personal achievement can result from service to more prominent, powerful people in the hierarchy. In a feudal sense, loyalty and service to a superior can result in improving one's own position. This type of achievement, however, is usually not available to people of the poorer strata. Although the political system is not supernaturally based, gods and spirits are appealed to for particular aid on a group or individual basis. Slaves are the captives brought into the society.

Geographic mobility is of a limited variety; a villager who is displeased with the misuse of autocratic power of his village chief can leave his village and join another where he feels the autocratic chief is somewhat more moderate. Generally, tyranny, feudal relationships, and hierarchical positions characterize this society. The basic form of the religion revolves around the possession trance phenomenon through the mediums in the society.

Coding: Stratification present.
Slavery present.
Possession trance present.
Social structures: rigid.

Mende.—The Mende of Sierra Leone are an agriculturally based society, in which two social classes predominate: slaves and freemen. At one time, slaves formed the principal wealth of a person or family. They largely are agricultural workers, on whom the society depends for its welfare. A hierarchy of chiefs form the political structure of the Mende, and tributes and fealty are exacted in a feudal manner. A large military organization exists, with the capture of men for slavery as its chief motivation. Households are patriarchal, with the head of the household delegating responsibility to its members.

Larger kinship groups are rather loose federations rather than strong lineages.

Achievement opportunities exist for a young man in several ways. When old enough, he can establish his own household; for a free man to be under the domination of another is considered humiliating. Although the leading positions in the society are held by hereditary ascription, education and training is nevertheless available for a man who wishes to improve his status and position. Secret societies are important as avenues of education and achievement. According to Little:

> Readiness to overlook even custom and precedent in favour of those who are "kind" to them is one of the reasons why it is impossible to conceive of many institutional aspects of Mende life in a rigid way. Even in respect to some of the more deep-seated items of their culture, the Mende give the impression of being eclectic, both in their way of looking at things and in their actual behavior. (1951:74)

Although diviners and secret societies are important in dealing with transgressions and illness, the question of possession trance in this society is a moot point. Dawson (1964:328) has indicated that some native doctors become dissociated while curing patients and patients with some illnesses are considered possessed and dissociated during illness, but specific manifestations such as the spirit speaking through the dissociated person are not indicated. On the other hand, Hofstra has stated, "It seems certain, however, that emotional movements, like prophetism of 'possession' bearing a definitely social character and for which, for instance, some of the Bantu tribes are known, do not occur among the Mende to any considerable degree" (1941–42:180).

Coding: Stratification present.

Slavery present
Possession trance coded earlier as present;
changed to absent.
Social Structures: flexible

Nyoro.—The Nyoro in Northern Uganda live in close settlements of small farms. Politically, the society is a centralized, feudal, hierarchical state, run by a hereditary ruler and a graded hierarchy of subchiefs. Social status is ascriptive, and inequality and hierarchy dominate all social relationships among the people. Slavery is universal, and even the poorest may own a slave. According to Beattie, "through the whole field of social relations, those of community as well as those of the state, we find this notion of ruling, of exercising authority over someone" (1960:9).

The paramount chief (MuKama) selects subchiefs as a result of personal service or favoritism. In the family, the father dominates the household and holds authority over his sons; wives are submissive and deferential.

Possession trance cults form the basic religious expression of the society. These cults use possession trance in handling problems of extended families and lineage groups, but have become more responsive to individual affairs more recently. In former times, the Nyoro were divided in 19 localized lineage groups each with its own important spirit. Each group had its own medium who would become possessed by the group's spirit. This spirit would care for the health, welfare, and fertility of the whole group. Furthermore, with new and unfamiliar pressures on the society as a result of exercise of European power, these possession trance cults now facilitate adaptation to change. Again, according to Beattie:

> traditional Nyoro modes of religious thought have shown themselves well able to adapt to the new and unfamiliar forms of power associated with the coming of the Euro-

peans. The Nyoro have interpreted these manifestations of power as implying a proliferation of new kinds of spiritual entities, with which the preexisting possession cult is quite fitted to cope. (1960:79)

Coding: Stratification present.
Slavery present.
Possession trance present.
Social structures: rigid

Hehe.—The Hehe, located in Tanzania in East Africa, are an agricultural society with some emphasis on cattle raising as well. In the traditional society, a paramount chieftain is the political leader, with undivided powers as judge, lawmaker, owner of wealth, leader in war, and so on. A tribal hierarchy of lesser chiefs and headmen also holds undivided power in their particular community. Groups of advisers selected on the basis of ability, however, assist chiefs at all levels in their judicial capacity. These advisers are very influential in the political structure and receive prestige but no financial reward for this work, except to be relieved of some public duties. Many people have slaves who were former war prisoners. The chief has additional slaves that are his alone.

The individual's public obligation is to pay taxes and perform some public work, such as roadbuilding or carrying loads. Otherwise, the authorities protect the individual's right to pursue his social and economic interests and protect his property, reputation, and activities in general. Geographical mobility is unrestricted, and changes of residence can be made at will. Religion is strictly a family affair; each man worships his own family ancestors. The chief's religious obligation is to pray to tribal deities. An emphasis on egalitarianism tends to discourage achievement in wealth and status far beyond one's neighbors. No possession trance is evident in this society.

69

Coding: Stratification present.
Slavery present.
Possession trance absent.
Social structures: flexible

Type II

Three societies chosen from this type are: Chiga and Nyima, with possession trance; Tallensi, no possession trance.

Chiga.—The Chiga of Western Uganda are an independent, peasant farming group and maintain a single class system despite sharp caste differentiations among neighboring societies. The social structure is a fissioning lineage system of patrilineal clans that change and subdivide without formal rules. No specific political leadership exists. Although the basic social unit is the patriarchal household, it often splits into independent units. Though land is owned by individual households, there is much geographic mobility without restriction. A total redistribution of the population can occur in a generation or less. Individual rights are respected within the household, and sons may set up separate households with the father's consent. Ownership of slaves is a sign of wealth. Few male slaves are kept. Female slaves who helped with the domestic work are more common.

According to Edel (1957:138), the phenomenon of possession trance is not very common, though some incidence has been reported. More common is the practice of sorcerers keeping spirits in horns. These spirits are cared for and fed. The sorcerers put the horns on their own heads and talk to the spirits, who might then answer back. No change of identity is involved in this practice, and the sorcerer does not become the medium through whom the spirit speaks.

Coding: Stratification absent.
Slavery present.
Possession trance coded earlier as present;
changed to absent.
Social structures: flexible.

Nyima.—The Nyima are a group of people who live in small individualized families, in nonlocalized clans, thickly settled on seven neighboring hills, in the Nuba mountains in East Africa. They maintain close but not necessarily amicable relations. Slave-owning is widespread. Geographic mobility is discouraged by the religious rites and beliefs and the age-grade organization.

Although there is no institutionalized political leadership among these people, the position of the rain priest, or *shirra,* approximates that of a paramount political leader. He holds his position by inheritance and divine right, and challenges to his authority are generally unsuccessful. His power extends over rain, health, and fertility for the whole society. The local shaman, on the other hand, is closer to being the local political leader. Several shamans coexist in the localities with different areas of control. They are the institutionalized purveyors of possession trance and resolve many of the individuals' daily dilemmas through this mechanism. According to Nadel, the Nyima social system is rigidly segmented into clans, and all human life is ascribed and dominated by the principle of descent. Through possession trance, the group can adjust and revise its supernatural mastery over the universe and enrich its "magic armory" (Nadel 1958:435).

Coding: Stratification absent
Slavery present.
Possession trance present
Social structures: rigid.

Tallensi.—The Tallensi are mainly an agricultural people in West Africa, living in amorphous type settlements with no central government. The boundaries and internal structure of the settlements change slowly but steadily to conform to the myriad of changing social relations of the people of the settlement. The chiefs have no political or administrative power, though they exercise some judicial and ritual functions and are an integrating force for uniting the community.

Individual social relations are fluid, with people belonging to many different groups and changing groups often. Individual initiative, ambition, and independence are important; and custom is neither rigidly adhered to nor an impediment to individual adjustments to life. Geographic mobility is unrestricted and often encouraged. People move about readily, sometimes for economic reasons and sometimes for curiosity and desire for new experiences. Fluidity of social structure and flexibility of social norms are typical of this group. Few slaves are kept, rarely more than half a dozen in any one settlement. Ancestor worship is the important religious belief and practice. But each family is responsible for its own achievement in agricultural success, and religious rituals and prayers are private affairs. The individual is personally responsible for the goodwill of his own particular ancestors.

Coding: Stratification absent.
Slavery present.
Possession trance absent.
Social structures: flexible.

Type III

The Zulu, coded with possession trance, are used as an example of a Type III society.

Zulu.—The Zulu are an agricultural and cattle-raising people of southeast Africa. In the traditional system, a strong political hierarchy exists. In theory, the king's power is not autocratic, and he rules with the consent of a tribal council. The king's councillors consist of members of leading families and headmen of smaller political jurisdictions, whose positions tend to be hereditary. A subordinate-superordinate power hierarchy of district headmen, village headmen, and subjects exists. Since the whole village feels responsible for any individual's transgressions, people are required to report wrongdoings to their superiors.

In actual practice, some kings become very tyrannical despite checks on their power. A widespread military organization exists; the whole society tends to be a military camp. Although trade and general travel is slight, girls and women often travel to bring food to their men in military service.

Religion dominates all aspects of life. The king is responsible for many centralized rituals. Ancestor worship prevails. Diviners using possession trance are often the main link between individuals and their ancestors; the ancestral spirits speak through the diviners as mediums.

Coding: Stratification present.
Slavery absent.
Possession trance present.
Social structure: rigid.

Type IV

Five societies chosen here are: Nuer, with possession trance; Amba, Kikuyu, Kung, and Turkana, no possession trance. Descriptions of these groups follow.

Nuer.—The Nuer of East Africa are mainly a cattle-raising people, with a fissionable lineage system similar to that of the Chiga. People belong to many segmented groups and may change from one lineage or clan to another without restraints. Little political unity or author-

73

ity exists. Chiefs have little real authority or power. The group has a sense of common equality. The individual has opportunities for achievement and can become rich, powerful, and important. Geographical mobility is likewise unrestricted; any man can found a settlement or lineage. Formal, hereditary, permanent chiefs are considered an unwise arrangement.

Religion is a dominant force in Nuer life. Belief in a "Supreme God" exists, along with belief in numerous lesser spirits. Possession trance seems widespread, with spirits making their wishes and demands known to the people, sometimes in cases of illness as well as other matters. It is interesting that these spirits are not regarded as great supernatural beings; they tend to be considered more as supermen, somewhat similar to the Ashanti view of possessing spirits. They are more capable than men and know more things, but they are not venerated as the "Supreme God" is. The spirits resemble men in their interest in good food and beer, and dancing. Spirits are very numerous, and only some of them become involved with men.

In addition, Evans-Pritchard has indicated that in recent times there has arisen a group of prophets who use possession trance for solving problems relating to external pressures from Arabs and Europeans. These prophets seem to have a unifying effect on the Nuer people.

Coding: Stratification absent.
Slavery absent.
Possession trance present.
Social structures: flexible.

Amba.—The Amba are an agricultural people in East Africa living in a series of villages with interrelated ties. No chiefs exist within the society. Authority rests in groups of older men who exercise generalized influence on the communities. These groups of elders do not form elite groups or develop autocratic powers. Human relationships are very important. Opportunities for individual achievement exist in the acquisition of wealth, power, and prestige. Personal factors, rather than age or birth, determine such achievement. Geographic mobility is unrestricted.

No evidence of possession trance exists.

Coding: Stratification absent.
Slavery absent.
Possession trance absent.
Social structures: flexible

Kikuyu.—The Kikuyu, located in Kenya, engage in agriculture and trading as major economic pursuits and rely on animals, especially goats, as an indication of wealth. The traditional society, prior to this century, had few outside influences and was not involved in trading with the Arabs for slaves or ivory. As the Routledges point out, "Kikuyu polity is local government run mad" (1910:195). Although the group is divided into 13 clans, some have a headman and some do not. Clans are not associated with particular locations. Whatever district organization exists is not very well defined. Great variation exists in the number of headmen in different districts. For military goals, a few homesteads will unite under a leader. The men will not follow another leader and, often, will not obey their own leader. No paramount ruler exists. In civil matters, the head of each household runs his household. Each household is the center of life for its members. Councils of different groups of people loosely keep some kind of order and maintain some ceremonies and responsibilities.

Trading markets are important; and men, women, and children all travel to various markets in the countryside. Wealth is highly regarded. It generally means greater esteem, but not a different style of living.

Kikuyu religion involves a belief in a supreme god for

matters affecting the whole group and ancestral spirits for daily life troubles. Elders officiate at some services. Medicine men also perform services. Although they interpret the spirits' messages, they do not resort to possession trance for their activities.

Coding: Stratification absent.
Slavery absent.
Possession trance absent.
Social structures: flexible.

Kung.—The Kung of southwest Africa are a nomadic hunting and gathering society, living in bands. Politically, each band is independent and autonomous. The leaders are skilled hunters and wise elders. Some are hereditary but have little real authority. No central authority exists, and there is little regulation of social life on a widespread basis throughout the society. Each family has great freedom of movement; no clan organization exists. Social control is maintained largely by custom. In religious practice, there is no organized worship, no ancestor cult, and there are no regular rituals.

Coding: Stratification absent.
Slavery absent.
Possession trance absent.
Social structures: flexible.

Turkana.—The Turkana of northwest Kenya are a cattle-raising people, very individualistic, and isolated from outside influences by natural geographic barriers. They are highly acquisitive, and their well being depends on many animals besides cattle, for example, sheep, goats, camels, and donkeys. Partly because of the needs of their animals and partly for social considerations, the Turkana have a great deal of geographical mobility. Migrations are individual rather than group endeavors, and neighborhoods are in constant flux. Politically, leaders arise spontaneously for raiding purposes; otherwise, there are no courts, councils, or tribunals. Public discussion is relied on for resolving disputes or handling of crimes. Through the acquisition of cattle, young men can achieve independence. Respect is shown for the individual opinions of everyone, including women and children.

Diviners who are successful can become leaders of territories. The diviners do not practice possession trance.

Coding: Stratification absent.
Slavery absent.
Possession trance absent.
Social structures: flexible.

Statistical Description

To summarize the results of the descriptive analyses of the fourteen societies above, some statistical tabulations and techniques are used. As has already been pointed out, the use of statistics here is not for purposes of statistical inference but as an efficient way of summing up and describing the essence of the findings in the literature.

Comparing the fourteen societies in terms of possession trance (using the coding of the previous chapter) and

TABLE 3

DISTRIBUTION OF SOCIETIES ACCORDING TO
STRATIFICATION AND POSSESSION TRANCE
(CODING OF PREVIOUS CHAPTER)

SOCIETIES	TOTAL	SOCIETIES	
		With Possession Trance	No Possession Trance
With stratification and/or slavery	9	7	2
No stratification or slavery	5	1	4
Total	14	8	6

NOTE: According to Fisher's Exact Test, p = .06.

degree of social stratification, (table 3), using Fisher's Exact Test, we find a correlation between these two variables, significant at the .06 level. Though this differs markedly from the unusually high chi square, significant well below the .001 level, found for all 103 societies in a similar comparison, it nevertheless shows some significant relationship for the group used in this study.

When the revised definition of possession trance is used, the results of Fisher's Exact Test show a correlation, significant at the .21 level (Table 4). This changes the relationship from a significant to a nonsignificant one for the fourteen societies used in this chapter. Some interpretation of this change will be made later on. For the present, it is interesting to note that the more-restricted definition of possession trance has reduced rather than increased the relationship with fixed status distinctions.

TABLE 4

DISTRIBUTION OF SOCIETIES ACCORDING TO
STRATIFICATION AND POSSESSION TRANCE
(NEW CODING)

| | | SOCIETIES | |
SOCIETIES	TOTAL	With Possession Trance	No Possession Trance
With stratification and/or slavery	9	5	4
No stratification or slavery	5	1	4
Total	14	6	8

NOTE: According to Fishers's Exact Test, p = .21.

Table 5 contains the distribution of the fourteen societies by rigidity or flexibility of social structures and presence or absence of possession trance, using the revised definition. In this comparison, Fisher's Exact Test shows a positive correlation between rigidity and possession trance, at the .01 level of significance. This

78

would tend to support the first hypothesis of this paper, that societies with rigid structures tend to have possession trance whereas those with flexible ones do not. Only two societies out of fourteen do not fit the hypothesis, and they will be discussed in greater detail later on.

TABLE 5

DISTRIBUTION OF SOCIETIES ACCORDING TO RIGID
OR FLEXIBLE STRUCTURES AND POSSESSION TRANCE
(NEW CODING)

SOCIETAL STRUCTURE	TOTAL	SOCIETIES	
		With Possession Trance	No Possession Trance
Rigid	4	4	0
Flexible	10	2	8
Total	14	6	8

Note: According to Fisher's Exact Test, p = .01.

Finally, table 6 shows a comparison of societies according to degree of social stratification and degree of rigidity. According to the Fisher Test, a nonsignificant correlation is found between these variables (p =.13). The second hypothesis of this paper, namely, that societies with fixed social status distinctions are likely to be rigid and those without these distinctions are likely to be flexible, does not seem to be confirmed by these data.

TABLE 6

DISTRIBUTION OF SOCIETIES ACCORDING TO RIGID OR
FLEXIBLE STRUCTURES AND STRATIFICATION

SOCIETIES	TOTAL	SOCIETAL STRUCTURES	
		Rigid	Flexible
With stratification and/or slavery	9	4	5
No stratification or slavery	5	0	5
Total	14	4	10

NOTE: According to Fisher's Exact Test, p = .13.

To summarize our findings, it seems that a positive correlation is likely to exist between rigidity of social structures and the presence of possession trance (as precisely defined here). On the other hand, it does not seem likely that a correlation exists between fixed social status distinctions and rigidity or flexibility of social structures.

CONCLUSIONS

The conclusions of this study—though tentative, given the nature of the data—are nevertheless quite interesting. Are they in conflict with the positive conclusions found in the previous chapter and based on a large number of societies? What can be distilled from the findings of this as well as the previous chapter? Is there some greater insight to be gained about the possession trance phenomenon from the research done here? And what direction, if any, should future research in this subject take? These are broad-ranging questions, and though they cannot all be answered entirely, there still are some judgments that can be made.

To answer the second question first, what has been learned from all this research? Perhaps the most significant item is that flexibility and rigidity of social structures seem to be important aspects of societies. In the past, these aspects have not received much attention in terms of precise definition and quantitative identification. Though this study did not attempt such precision, it did, in a general way, indicate that rigid societies seem to resort to possession trance on a society-wide basis, as hypothesized.

It would seem further that flexibility and rigidity are not directly related to the complexity of the society. Looking at table 6, we find that flexible societies predominate and account for ten of the fourteen societies studied. Interestingly enough, the four rigid societies all have some form of stratification. The flexible societies on the other hand are evenly divided between those with and those without some form of stratification. Looking at the figures another way, we can say that among societies with some form of stratification (nine altogether), more than half (five) were flexible. If, indeed, this is indicative of African societies in general, then it would seem that the complexity of a society does not necessarily create a constraining environment for the individual. Complexity may be accompanied by restrictive measures or may be, on the other hand, a means whereby freedom for the individual can be protected. A comparison can be made with the Western industrialized world, in which different nations with relatively similar levels of economic, political, and social complexity range in their internal structures from freedom and democracy to totalitarianism and repression. A similar range seems to exist among the more complex nonindustrial societies of Africa. However, all the simple unstratified societies studied (five) were flexible. On the basis of this information alone, it is difficult to say whether this is likely to be the case among all simple unstratified societies in Africa.

Turning our attention to the possession trance phenomenon, however, gives us another dimension for analysis. As has been indicated, when limiting the definition of this term to apply to a society-wide mechanism for decision-making that involved a change of identity through trance and a spirit speaking through a medium, the number of societies with possession trance was reduced from eight to six. Of these six with possession trance, four were rigid and two were flexible. All of the eight societies, however, that were without possession trance were also without rigidity. It might be, then, that possession trance is an indicator of rigidity. This may be true, at least insofar as its absence may indicate flexible structures in a society. Its presence, however, even in this specific definition, does not seem to assure rigidity. There are still two exceptions, that is, societies that are both flexible and have possession trance. These will be looked at presently.

From our analysis, we may be able to infer that simple unstratified societies in Africa generally tend to have flexible structures from two of our tentative findings: (1) all the unstratified societies (Type IV) evaluated in this chapter were rated as flexible, and (2) all except three societies of this type are without possession trance among those studied in the previous chapter. It would seem then that simple unstratified African societies without possession trance are most likely to have flexible social structures.

The converse, however, is not easily established. First, of course, it seems likely that complex stratified societies are not necesarily rigid, and, further, the presence of possession trance does not clearly indicate rigidity.

It is worth looking at the two exceptions mentioned, that is, societies with possession trance that are rated as flexible. These are the Ashanti (complex and stratified) and the Nuer (simple and unstratified). In both, possession trance fulfills the definition specified in this chapter. Both cases are, however, atypical in their evaluation of the possessing spirit.

Among the Ashanti, although the possession trance mechanism is used for daily life decision-making, there seems to be a great deal of flexibility in acceptance of the spirit's word. The Ashanti gods seem to be more man than god, and the possession trance mechanism does not seem to carry as much authority and power as among the Ganda or Nyima, for example. With regard to the Nuer, the circumstances again are somewhat unusual. The Nuer spirits are also more man than god; and though they inspire fear, they are looked upon as stronger or more knowing supermen rather than supernatural gods. In addition, some prophets using possession trance seem to be a relatively recent phenomenon, apparently a response to powerful outside hostile influences. Here possession trance is used only for dealing with influences external to the society and is not resorted to for daily life crises. It could be postulated that possession trance as used by these prophets entered the Nuer society because the people felt a lack of control over these external influences. This would, indeed, be similar to the role possession trance plays in rigid societies, where people resort to it because they lack control over their daily life activities.

Because of the unusual nature of these two "exceptions" to the hypothesis that is otherwise upheld by the available data, it would seem that further study is needed to determine how many such exceptional cases exist. Only after such a study, could some more definitive inference be made as to the presence of possession trance being a likely indicator of rigidity in a society.

An explanation is needed concerning the strong correlation between possession trance and fixed-status distinctions in the previous chapter and the effect of changing the definition of possession trance in this one. With a broader, more inclusive definition of possession trance, a great many more societies can be coded as having possession trance. These would include societies that are both rigid and flexible, as has been shown. Apparently, for occasional possession trance to be accepted in a society or for behavior or illness to be interpreted as possession trance without clear overt manifestations of the spirit, the society, generally, is of a more complex, stratified nature. The simplest societies, which all seem to be flexible in their structures, seem to have little need for spirits to inhabit people in a trance state.

When the definition of possession trance becomes more strict, the change in coding affects the more complex and not the simple societies. This is because complex but flexible societies may not rely much on this mechanism. Its presence in the society may be a residual from a former time when possession trance was more common and conditions were different; or, perhaps, it is a new phenomenon entering the society in response to some uncontrollable external pressure; or, indeed, it may have some unique explanation in the small locality of the society in which it is found to occur.

What seems likely from this study, however, is that societies in which possession trance is very heavily relied upon for daily life decisions and strictly adhered to because of the supernatural power of the spirits involved are probably societies that are stratified and rigid in their social structures.

Finally, in terms of further research in this field, it would seem that refinement, precision, and coding of the qualities of rigidity and flexibility in a society could provide some interesting insights into, and comparisons of, the nature of human societies. In addition, more extensive study of possession trance in its various specific manifestations in different societies could provide greater understanding of how people have chosen to solve the problems confronting them and how different cultures have utilized both possession and trance for their own needs.

This study further demonstrates the need to study exceptions to statistical findings in order to reach some deeper understanding of the mechanisms involved. Refinement in the definition of variables and examination of conforming as well as exceptional cases yields greater understanding and can revise statistical results in the research process.

And finally, it must be remembered that this study is a preliminary investigation of a few societies. The findings indicate that more extensive and intensive study along several lines is desirable to understand the possession-trance phenomenon more fully.

1. Fixed internal status distinctions is used here to mean the presence in a society of a stratification system of freeman or slavery, or both.

2. Some criteria for judging rigidity and flexibility of social structures are discussed later in this chapter.

3. Anthropologists find it convenient to write their descriptions in the "ethnographic present" although some of the features of social life they deal with may have changed in the recent past, or may be undergoing transformations now.

REFERENCES

GENERAL REFERENCES

Coleman, James S. 1964. *Introduction to mathematical sociology*. New York: Free Press of Glencoe.

Firth, Raymond. 1963. *Elements of social organization*. Boston: Beacon Press.

Köbben, A. J. F. 1967. Why exceptions? The logic of cross-cultural analysis. *Current Anthropology* 8:3–34.

Prince, Raymond. 1970. Review of: *Witchcraft,* by Lucy Mair. *American Anthropologist* 72:916.

Siegel, Sidney. 1956. *Non-parametric statistics for the behavioral sciences*. New York: McGraw-Hill.

Stuckert, Robert P. 1958. A Configurational approach to prediction. *Sociometry* 21:225–37.

ETHNOGRAPHIC REFERENCES

Amba

Winter, E. H. 1956. *The Bwamba*. Cambridge: W. Heffer and Sons.

Ashanti

Field, M. J. 1960. *Search for security*. Evanston, Ill.: Northwestern University Press.

Lystad, Robert A. 1958. *The Ashanti*. New Brunswick, N.J.: Rutgers University Press.

Chiga

Edel, May M. 1957. *The Chiga of western Uganda*. London: Oxford University Press.

Religion, Altered States of Consciousness, and Social Change

Ganda

Fallers, L. A. 1964. *The king's men.* London: Oxford University Press.

Roscoe, J. 1911. *The Baganda.* London: Macmillan & Co.

Southwold, Martin. 1965. "The Ganda of Uganda." in *Peoples of Africa* (editor J. L. Gibbs). New York: Holt, Rinehart and Winston.

Hehe

Brown, G. G., and A. McD. Bruce Hutt. 1935. *Anthropology in action.* London: Oxford University Press.

Kikuyu

Routledge, W. S., and Katherine Routledge. 1910. *With a prehistoric people.* London: Edward Arnold.

Kung

Marshall, Lorna. 1965. "The Kung bushmen of the Kalahari Desert," in *Peoples of Africa* (editor J. L. Gibbs). New York: Holt, Rinehart and Winston.

Shapera, I. 1930. *The Khoisan peoples of South Africa.* London: Routledge and Kegan Paul.

Mende

Dawson, John. 1964. "Urbanization and mental health in a West African community," in *Magic, faith, and healing* (editor Ari Kiev). London: Collier-Macmillan; New York: Free Press of Glencoe.

Hofstra, Sjoerd. 1941–42. The belief among the Mende in non-ancestral spirits and its relation to a case of parricide. *Internationales Archiv für Ethnographie* 40:175–82.

Little, K. L. 1951. *The Mende of Sierra Leone.* London: Routledge and Kegan Paul.

Nuer

Crazzolara, J. P. 1953. Zur Gesellschaft und Religion der Nuer. *Studia Instituti Anthropos* 5. Vienna: Mödling, St. Gabriel.

Evans-Pritchard, E. E. 1940. *The Nuer.* London: Oxford University Press.

Nyima

Nadel, S. F. 1947. *The Nuba.* London: Oxford University Press.

———. 1958. "A study of shamanism in the Nuba Mountains," in *Reader in comparative religion* (editors W. A. Lessa and E. Z. Vogt). New York: Harper and Row.

Nyoro

Beattie, John. 1960. *Bunyoro: An African kingdom.* New York: Henry Holt & Co.

Roscoe, John. 1923. *The Bakitara or Banyoro.* Cambridge: At the University Press.

Tallensi

Fortes, Meyer. 1945. *The dynamics of clanship among the Tallensi*. London: Oxford University Press.

——. 1949. *The web of kinship among the Tallensi*. London: Oxford University Press.

Turkana

Gulliver, Pamela, and P. H. Gulliver. 1953. *The Central Nilo-Hamites*. London: International Affairs Institute.

Zulu

Krige, Eileen J. 1936. *Social system of the Zulus*. London: Longmans, Green and Co.

3 : Social Change, Ecology, and Spirit Possession Among the South African Nguni

Judith D. Gussler

INTRODUCTION

The Southeastern Bantu have long held the belief that they maintain a close and important relationship with spirits and other supernatural forces, a relationship manifested from time to time by the manipulation of the behavior of certain individuals by spirits working either within them or upon them. Relationships to dead kinsmen are particularly significant and may reflect in the "other world" the major roles of kin ties and kin groups in the world of living men. Among the Nguni[1] Bantu, these men and women, "chosen" through possession by ancestors, have been powerful in both religious and secular matters. It is this phenomenon of spirit possession which is to be discussed here. Actually there has been a proliferation of possession beliefs and practices in Southeast Africa over the years, the most dramatic and best documented being those associated with the "illness" that is the call to divination. The cult[2] of diviners itself has been somewhat responsive to change, but has remained surprisingly viable up to the present time.

The Bantu societies of South Africa have been changing rapidly and in significant ways for more than 150 years. Establishing a "base line" for discussion of Nguni sociocultural change is difficult because of the number of powerful internal and external forces that have shaped both the configuration and cultural content of these social

88

systems throughout their recorded history. Nevertheless, this dynamic history gives the culture area some of its unique traits that have made it of interest to social scientists and historians. No doubt the most profound and shattering modifications of traditional patterns of living began after the defeat of the Zulu by the British in 1880. Then began the process of assimilating a very proud and independent "tribal" people into a modern nation within which they would have an increasingly inferior and dependent status.

The nature of this social change and its attendant stresses is reflected clearly in the expressive areas of behavior. In the beliefs and rituals associated with spirit possession, in particular, can be seen evidence of some of the major ethnohistorical changes in southeastern Bantu society of the past century and a half. That is not to say that the possession cults had a different face for every social situation. A look at some of the elements that have been retained for so many years is as revealing as a discussion of modifications. In this study I shall examine both the retentions and the modifications of possession behavior with regard to the individuals who become possessed. In other words, what *kinds* of people in the traditional and modern Nguni societies are recognized as possessed by spirits? What are the symptoms, explanations, and possible functions of possession behavior at both levels of change? How are the changes in etiology related to the wider acculturative situation? In addition to providing a structural context for possession behavior, I shall propose a possible biological (specifically nutritional) parameter for certain dissociational states in South Africa. I thereby hope to show how ecological factors may underlie and shape this particular sociocultural phenomenon. First, however, I must provide some relevant ecological, ethnographic, and historical background.

ECOLOGY AND ETHNOHISTORY

Groups of Bantu-speaking Negroes migrated into southeastern Africa during the seventeenth century. This part of the continent, bounded on the north by the Limpopo River and on the west by the Kalahari Desert, is savanna land for the most part—grassland with scattered trees and forests. Along the coastal lowlands are stretches of rain forest, but most of the land provides good grazing and is generally free from insect-borne cattle diseases. The arriving Nguni Bantu most likely found this region congenial to their mixed or semipastoral livelihood and settled down to garden and increase their herds. They were and are distinctively a cattle-people, possessing many of the characteristics of other such groups even though they depend to a large degree on their horticultural products. These are usually grown by women in garden plots.

They reckon descent strictly patrilineally, and the household generally consists of patrilineal kinsmen and wives from other exogamous patrilineal sibs. Among the Zulu, these wives must not be related to their husbands through any of their four grandparents. These households, or kraals, are also primary territorial units, being generally self-contained settlements scattered over the countryside at some distance from one another. Within the kraal, the various household members are of varying rank and status, the higher positions reserved for relatives by birth, the lower for "outsiders," that is, wives. The co-wives in a polygynous household are also internally ranked. The first married usually has some measure of prestige and authority, but occasionally a man will elevate a younger and perhaps more attractive wife to this position. Absolom Vilakazi notes that ranking in Zulu society produces rivalry and hostility between the women of the polygynous households; and since the rank that a woman establishes within the extended family is passed along to her children, they may become part of the competition for superior position very early. The emotional bond between a woman and the children with whom she lives in a separate hut is usually very close, whereas the father's relationship to the offspring tends to be that of disciplinarian and authoritarian. He may treat wife and children alike as subordinate minors (Vilakazi 1965:33).

Married women also must practice the custom of *hlonipha,* which refers to adherence to a strict pattern of avoidance and deference toward the in-laws among whom they dwell (Krige 1936:30). D. H. Reader suggests that *hlonipha* can be seen as an institutionalized and continuous reminder that the woman is "grafted" to her husband's kin group. Her success and well-being there depend upon the benevolence and good will of his kinsmen, both living and dead. Failure on the part of a wife to be properly respectful might result in the ancestors of the descent group causing her to be barren or miscarry (Reader 1966:210).

A new wife must also *zila;* that is, she must avoid eating, touching, or coming in contact with certain foods, articles, persons, and places (Vilakazi 1965:73–74). These taboos reinforce the peripheral position of female affines in the patrilineal household, since the prohibited items are often representative of the kraal itself. She must, for example, *zila* the cattle kraal, the cattle themselves, and the food products of the cattle, since the beasts are seen as belonging to, and representing, the ancestors. Among non-Christians there are proscriptions on the consumption of *amasi,* a curdled milk dish that is a very important dietary staple. Considered the "food of the household," *amasi* cannot be eaten by young wives until they have completed a period of abstention concluded ceremoniously (Krige 1936:383). A similar prohibition on eating meat is mentioned by Krige. *Amasi* is avoided

91

by females for seven days during their menstrual period, for some time after giving birth (Krige says two months), and for a year after the death of a husband.

Despite her structural relationships to her affines, a woman is expected to be a productive member of the household. The elaborate wedding preparations and ceremonies are meant to incorporate her into the husband's household, to break her ties with her ancestors and to establish new ties with the ancestors of her affines. She is introduced to the latter in a ritual during which the bride enters the cattle kraal where the shades of the ancestors dwell. Although henceforth she must strictly avoid this area, the wedding ritual is an important part of her integration (Reader 1966:206). The Zulu recognize, however, that these rites of incorporation are not always effective. If a married woman is bothered by her own patrilineal ancestors, further rituals may be undertaken to break the ties with them. It may be the woman's own kinsmen who perform these rites, and the young wife may be sent to live among them until the break is ritually complete. When the woman is properly grafted to her husband's kin group, her ancestral spirits will have very little influence on her life (Vilakazi 1965:90).

In addition to their structural inferiority, then, women are burdened with a ritual inferiority, in part because of their potential threat to the revered cattle. From a Western point of view the beasts of the Nguni have limited economic value. They provide milk for milk dishes like *amasi,* but milk production has been dropping significantly throughout the years (Reader 1966:38). Reader points out that most Zulu do not judge their cattle on milk yield anyway, and the best, healthiest (and presumably most productive) animals are those chosen as fit sacrifices for ancestors (1966:39). Cattle, however, are a self-reproducing and accumulative source and sign of wealth. They are used to establish and reinforce social relationships, as when a prospective groom and his kinsmen present the bride's family with *lobolo* cattle (Krige 1936:130). Yet the beasts are certainly more than an economic and social asset. Young men grow up caring for their family herds, and the animals become objects of concern and affection. Also, the cattle are, in a sense, considered as living links to patrilineal ancestors. This ritual significance of cattle is reflected in prohibitions on eating their meat. Generally, a man must have some ritual purpose for butchering and feasting on beef, as when someone becomes ill and a sacrifice is made to make peace with the afflicting ancestor. Beef, then, is not a regular part of Nguni diet, and poorer people with fewer cattle will have it only occasionally.

Women pose a threat to the ritual strength of the beasts. This partially accounts for the fact that among non-Christians women do not milk or touch the animals, and the contact of a menstruating female is especially dangerous (Reader 1966:37). Actually the deleterious effects of consuming milk during a menstrual period (at least in the form of *amasi*) are thought to strike both the woman and the cattle; the woman may be weakened and the animal may become thin and die (Krige 1936:86; Reader 1966:37).

The traditional social position of women is generally low, and that of men is high. Where women are weak, men are strong. Women are denied access to economic, legal, political, and ritual resources, save through male kinsmen; men make major decisions concerning the use and control of such resources. The Zulu have through the years emphasized the male role and masculine values. Virility and male strength are important in a nation of warriors and cattle men organized for warfare and conquest. The matter of strengthening men has long been of ritual as well as practical concern, and individual competition is encouraged (Krige 1936:108).

This stress of male virtues became particularly significant at the turn of the nineteenth century when the young Zulu Shaka took control of this previously obscure clan. He attempted to replace the political organization based on kinship bonds with a system of territorial ties that he himself controlled and directed (Murdock 1959:384). He then proceeded to establish the Zulu as a strong and terrifying war machine. Every young man after his rite of passage into manhood was expected to join other young men in the warrior "regiments." During his military service he was expected to remain a bachelor and live up to society's and Shaka's expectations of masculinity and bravery. Shaka was said, in fact, to harden the feet of his soldiers by marching them barefooted over beds of thorns; those who refused or hesitated were beaten, often to death (Ritter 1957:69).

Shaka and his warriors built a loose empire in Southeast Africa by conquering, killing, or putting to flight many of their neighbors. Whole societies disappeared, and refugees, banding together, formed new ones (van Warmelo 1937:149). Under the leadership of Shaka's successors, the Zulu empire was ended forcibly by the Dutch and British, whose numbers in South Africa had been increasing meanwhile. By the twentieth century the battles and skirmishes ended with the defeat of the Zulu by the British. The Nguni conquerors were conquered, and the process of subordination began.

It is not by any means possible to describe here the total effects of this defeat and the subsequent subordination on the Nguni Bantu. I must mention, however, some of the changes wrought by the growth and spread of white settlements, industrialization, and, briefly, Christianity. European-Bantu acculturation was in some ways truly deleterious for the Nguni. Many of their problems, of course, have grown directly from the racist acts and apartheid policies of the Euro-African government and

94

economy. Some problems, on the other hand, have arisen from the incompatibility of traditional Bantu social, economic, and ritual patterns with the modern industrial nation.

As the white colonists became more powerful and more numerous, they came to covet the good lands of the Bantu. In the familiar pattern the whites seized land from the blacks, forcing them into marginal areas. At the same time, the movements of the Bantu were severely restricted by their placement on "Native Reserves" in the 1920s and 1930s.[3] These acts directly influenced economic productivity, for both the traditional shifting agricultural and pastoral techniques required room for movement. The desire for many cattle, for example, has resulted in numerous rather than good animals. The poor quality of the beasts, combined with the destruction of the grass cover, within the context of the larger society that prohibits expansion and movement has resulted in the drop in milk production. The problem is intensified by the Zulu belief that burning off winter grass will help produce good young spring grass; the resulting practice of grass burning, says Reader (1966:30), destroys much of the good cattle fodder. Although milk production is low, the production of nonindigenous crops has increased. Maize from the New World was introduced early into South Africa, and many of the Nguni have come to depend heavily on it. The possible inplications of this type of diet are discussed in more detail below.

Although the Nguni have long considered farming to be women's work, some men have recently taken up the plow (Reader 1966:31). But plows, fertilizer, and new intensive farming techniques have only limited success on hilly, rocky eroded land—and little attraction for pastoralists. Many men leave the Bantu reserves altogether and work for wages in the mines and factories of industrial South Africa. Most women remain at home with the chil-

95

dren and the few remaining men. Needless to say, the day-to-day composition and functions of the patrilocal family have changed as a result of the migration of most able-bodied young men. Women on the reserves are now subject to neglect, as their men find the sophistication of city women more attractive than the simplicity of their wives (Vilakazi 1965:147).

The effects of Christianity have been uneven on Nguni society. Many Bantus have remained pagan, and some writers suggest that the orthodox white church, with its segregated worship and support of apartheid, is losing some adherents (Cole 1967:152).[4] Good accounts of the effects of Christianity on the Nguni society and religion have already been written by A. Vilakazi (1966) and B. Sundkler (1933), respectively, and I will not attempt to summarize their work. In any case, this discussion will deal primarily with non-Christian forms of possession with some reference to continuities of possession behavior in Christian services. It is sufficient to say that the religion of the Europeans with its emphasis on monogamy and individuality, changed the attitudes of many Bantu toward the role of men and women, the importance of kin groups, and the existence of ancestor spirits.

NGUNI SPIRIT POSSESSION

Against this cultural, social, and historical backdrop, the significance of dissociational states emerges. Some are not institutionalized, and symptoms do not result in special abilities or membership in a cult. E. J. Krige wrote of such a state in 1936 when she spoke of the "hysteria" that grips many young women during adolescence. This condition is believed to be caused by love magic made by would-be suitors (118). Again in 1959, a book written by a young medical missionary discussed the high incidence of hysteria among the Zulu. Many adolescents of both sexes "would one day begin to tremble and fall grunting, kicking and screaming to the ground, writhing and tearing their clothes" (Barker 1959:112). Or they may suffer pains, muscle convulsions, headaches, eye-strain, and have nightmares (113). In 1970 S. G. Lee, psychologist in South Africa, described his work with "cryers," women who have regular screaming fits, crying out or grunting for sometimes several weeks at a time (128).

Although all these states may not be clear-cut examples of dissociation, they suggest a general tendency toward such states, and an acceptance and perhaps expectation of dissociation. Below are descriptions of several such states, explained as spirit possession, which draw those possessed into some kind of group or cult participation. The differences in etiology and social implications between them are relatively minor, but they seem to have arisen at different times in response to different forces. In each case I shall describe first the state—symptoms, cure, and implications—and then the participants—their qualities and roles before and after possession.

Ukuthwasa

This possession-illness has a great time depth in South Africa, having been observed and recorded by some of the earliest European travelers and missionaries, including Callaway (1870), Shooter (1857), and Kidd (1904). A number of stereotyped symptoms announce the appearance of the disease in an apparently healthy individual, usually at a time of emotional crisis. He or she may experience loss of appetite or develop unusual food preferences. There are complaints of aches and pains in different parts of the body; the affected becomes morose and may go about constantly weeping, and he is plagued

97

by dreams ("He becomes a house of dreams" Callaway 1870:260). The dreams, too, are generally stereotyped. The most frequently occurring subject seems to be water, especially rivers and floods, and the dreamer may see himself being carried away by such a current. Dreams of wild animals and personal death occur as well, and some see crowds of people who may be threatening to harm the dreamer. Agitated, unable to sleep or eat, the man or woman may disappear altogether. After a time the individual returns, looking totally mad and disheveled after wandering about the land searching for roots and herbs seen in dreams. He may also have a snake draped about his neck, for snakes are believed to harbor the shades of ancestors. He becomes emaciated, his unanointed skin dry, and he is "incited by the spirits to leap over hedges and ditches, or even at times to bellow like a bull" (Krige 1936:301). Throughout this period of illness, which may last for several years, a number of diviners may be brought in to determine the cause, but the symptoms are not always immediately recognized as signs of spirit possession. The coming of convulsions, however, the use of snuff, the resulting sneezing and recurring yawning, belching, and passing of gas indicate that a spirit has entered the victim's body and wishes him to become a diviner. Some recent accounts describe how, during a fugue state, the possessed somehow finds himself at the household of an established diviner. The flight serves to establish both the diagnosis of the condition and identity of the person who will cure the condition and initiate the possessed into the ways of diviners (Lee 1970:135; Cole 1967:154).

The diagnosis of possession by an *Itongo* (ancestor spirit) is reinforced by the constant compulsive composition of songs and dances by the afflicted, an activity that may disturb the members of the kraal for many nights but that must be encouraged by their repeated hand-clapping in order to help the patient become well and develop the ability to divine. At this time, the man or woman who is ill *ukuthwasa*, that is, whose illness must be cured by initiation and training as a diviner, may become a novice under the tutelage of an established *isangoma* (pl., *izangoma*). But the training is costly, extensive, and hard, and the life of a diviner not easy; so the family of the possessed may decide to "bar" the spirit from entering their kinsmen. Such attempts usually result in failure, and the victim may never again be completely well (Krige 1936:304). In most cases the individual undergoes the long training for a new profession.

The length and nature of the initiation may vary according to the instructing *isangoma* but usually includes the use of water purification, emetics, and medicines in which to wash the patient-initiate. Many animals may be sacrificed to the afflicting spirits, too, decimating the herds of the patient or of his or her sponsors, who are usually concerned relatives willing to pay for the cure. Finally, the constant dancing and composition of songs is continued. Although the patient is already weak, he or she may be forced into long periods of dancing, usually in the company of others who have gone through the initiation; or the novice may simply be administered medicines until the possessing ancestor chooses to reveal its identity and agrees to allow the patient to get well (Krige 1936:305). During this period of the ritual, the novice may go into a trance and the *Intongo* "speaks" through his mouth. The spirit will most often be that of a deceased relative, who may have been a diviner himself in his lifetime (Callaway 1870:263, 270). The literature is unfortunately weak on the characteristics of the possessing spirit and its relationship to the possessed, but Vilakazi's material seems to suggest that many times an

99

individual's own patrilineal ancestors are responsible. A woman's dead agnates can afflict her even in her husband's kraal, as described above.

After the revelation, the pains of the afflicted may disappear, and he begins to learn and master the techniques of Nguni divination (Krige 1936:305). The culmination of this initiation is a feast and a test of the abilities of the new diviner. This ceremony serves to notify the public and other diviners of the new status of the man or woman once so grievously ill. Just prior to the ceremony a number of interested persons hide various objects about the kraal where the feast is being held, and the new diviner must find the hiding places without delay (Krige 1936:307; Cole 1967:154).

Once the initiation is complete, most new *izangoma* enjoy greater power and prestige than they did previously. They are now links between the living and their ancestors, and this relationship with the spirit world is constantly reinforced through regular propitiation and sacrifice (Krige 1936:309). Although the influence of the diviners on contemporary South African Bantu society cannot be accurately determined (some of their activities having been made illegal by the white government), they were in great demand in the traditional society. They were called to divine the cause of illnesses, find lost or stolen cattle, interpret omens, and smell out witches (Krige 1936:299). The smelling-out of witches is now prohibited because in this function the diviners had the power of life and death over other people. The *isangoma* also serves in a healing capacity when he cures and initiates someone suffering from the spirit-induced illness described above.

Although the ancestor spirits are the ultimate source of divining ability and power, the *isangoma* may not be in direct contact with the spirits (that is, possessed) while actually divining. He may, in fact, readily go into trance

100

during the rituals, but most divining seems to be accomplished through clever techniques such as "questioning." Divination through the asking of questions requires the practitioner to observe the reactions of his clients to certain statements he makes about the possible nature of their problem and in effect to tell them what they want to hear or are expecting to hear.

According to Callaway, the *izangoma* who utilize such methods do not have the full confidence of their clients, but this seems to be a widely used method, nonetheless. There have been *izangoma* said to have the "gift of divination" who apparently did not depend on client reaction to divine, and thereby gained the full respect of those in need of their services. There are some diviners who work through one or more familiar spirits, or, rather, the spirits supposedly work through the *izangoma* by revealing those things not apparent to the uninitiated. Krige suggests that the ancestor spirits possess the diviners during the rituals, but it seems from the literature that some of the possessed are merely fine ventriloquists; that is, they are not in trance. Another method of divination requires knowledge of the use and interpretation of a set of bones or sticks, rather than any particular mental gifts or aberrations, and is peripheral to the discussion of possession (Callaway 1870:327; Krige 1936:300).

The symptoms of *ukuthwasa* and the cult of diviners seems to have been remarkably stable for at least one hundred or more years. The early accounts of Shooter and Callaway sound very much like the recent ones of Barker (1959), Cole (1967), and Lee (1970), and throughout this extensive literature we see evidence of the most significant qualities of *izangoma*. Most frequently mentioned is the domination of the profession by women, particularly young married women (Lee 1970:144, for example). The material also suggests, however, that the great preponderance of female diviners is a relatively recent phenomenon. In 1857 the Reverend Joseph Shooter described the possessed patients as "prophets novitiates" and says only that the potential diviner "may be" a female (191). The Reverend Canon Callaway, who wrote somewhat later, mentions no predominance of either sex (1870). Nearly every writer of the twentieth century, on the other hand, comments on the great number of women who receive the "call." Furthermore, in Hilda Kuper's book on the Swazi, one of the Nguni societies, she notes that although the number of diviners is increasing, the number of men who become involved is decreasing (1947:165). The few men who do become diviners through *ukuthwasa* are generally described as thin, highly strung, neurotic—in other words, men who do not conform to the ideal image of masculine virtues. S. G. Lee elaborates on the apparent pathology of male *izangoma*. He says that they are generally young, unmarried at the time of their initiation, and have a definite "homosexual bent." They will generally be trained by female diviners, will don female clothing, and speak in "high-pitched tones." Lee also suggests that there is general recognition of the homosexual characteristics of these young men, since the marriage of a male *isangoma* called for "Rabelaisian comment" in that district (1970:143).

Despite possible mental or emotional pathology, especially in male diviners, *izangoma* are considered to be among the quickest, most observant, and most intelligent members of the community. That this is, indeed, the case has been stated by both Bantu and Europeans (for example, Callaway 1870:321; Kidd 1904:156; Lee 1970:149).

Amandawu, Amandiki, and Izizwe Possession

The real proliferation of dissociational states linked to

a belief in possession took place earlier in this century, and their spread, according to Sundkler, coincided with two severe epidemics of influenza and malaria (1961:23). Their growth also happened to coincide with the new Union of South Africa government's enactment of several policies that served to contain and subordinate the blacks. In the cases of *amandawa* and *amandiki* the cults are recognized by the Nguni as developing from external forces and in foreign places, and local tradition suggests that they came from the north or northeast. Those so possessed dance, bellow, belch, bark like dogs, and speak in tongues; the various cults are generally distinguished by the "language" spoken by the afflicted (Lee 1970:130). Actually, a person may have several spirits, or shades, in his body at once, each speaking its own language (Sundkler 1961:132). The possessing spirits in these newer cults are not ancestors, however, but the shades of the Swazi or Thonga, whom the Zulu previously had conquered, or, more recently, the shades of East Indians. Initiation into these cults is considered therapeutic, as with *ukuthwasa;* but even though initiation enables individuals to cure others so afflicted, it rarely brings special abilities such as divination (Lee 1970:130).

Izizwe possession is also associated with illness (although Lee says that physical discomfort may not be present), initiation-cure, and speaking in tongues. One of Lee's informants suggested that the possession behavior of *izizwe* differs from *amandiki;* in the case of the former, the individual moves and sways rhythmically, in the latter the individuals "sit like men" (1970:133). In any case, these forms of possession are generally less dramatic, severe, and debilitating than *ukuthwasa.* And, although the actual or imputed psychological and physiological changes of *ukuthwasa* are greater and longer lasting, the changes wrought to the lives of the initiated are also greater and, perhaps, more rewarding.

103

Zionism

The effects of Westernization on the Nguni religion can be seen most clearly in the Bantu Christian churches. The Europeans, of course, have attempted to convert the heathen Bantu from their ancestor worship to Christianity and have met with some success. However, many elements of the Bantu traditional religion have been incorporated into their Christian practices; even the types of individuals who are most active in the churches, and the behavior of these people, are very similar to those of the religious specialists in the possession cults. The Zulu Zionist churches, in particular, represent what Bengt Sundkler calls "new wine in old wineskins" (1961:238). The distance, he states, between the Zionist prophet and the traditional "witchdoctor" is not great. The Zulu must interpret Christianity in terms of their past cultural experience—in terms of revelation, possession, and psychic phenomena.

Sundkler has analyzed carefully the process of reinterpretation and syncretism of the two patterns of religious behavior, and draws a number of parallels between traditional and Zionist practices. Illness in the form of mental and physiological disturbances may lead, for example, to church membership rather than divining. The "somatic type" of these individuals is similar to that of the traditional diviners, since many are "thin, nervous, and highly-strung" and are bothered by dreaming. They may also cease eating certain foods like pork, which is "taboo" according to the teachings of the Old Testament (Sundkler 1961:350). Dreams are often of water, and subsequent ritual may involve water purification, as in the sacrament of baptism. Like the novice diviner, the new Zionist may suffer from insomnia and spend many nights composing songs and yawning. The Zionist, of course, is not thought to be possessed by ancestors or shades of foreigners, but to be "filled" with the Holy Ghost, who recommends to the possessed what special paraphernalia he should assume. The Zionist, like the diviner, is likely to join in loose organizations composed of individuals initiated by the same practitioner, and their activities are directed to some degree by him. Once initiated, the Zionist also engages in curing activities, often by the laying on of the hands, and is given to prophecy and revelation.

PARAMETERS OF NGUNI DISSOCIATIVE BEHAVIOR AND POSSESSION BELIEFS

To clarify the significance of the above descriptive material, a few general points should be made on such phenomena. First of all, two types of altered states of consciousness are common among the Nguni Bantu. The first, manifested in the illness *ukuthwasa* of the Nguni, appears to Westerners to be abnormal and pathological; the second, a ritual trance state, appears to be a reaction to intentional induction of dissociation by fasting, drumming, dancing, and so on. In most cases the Nguni attribute both states to spirits in the body of the trancer (for example, Krige 1936:301). Bourguignon emphasizes the "self-enhancing" and prestige-increasing aspects of possession, stating, with specific reference to Haiti:

> Where dissociation occurs and the gods are assigned the responsibility for such behavior, the social significance of the behavior is changed. (1965:54)

And again:

> I should like to argue that ritualized dissociation provides the self with an alternate set of roles, in addition to his everyday inventory of roles, in which unfulfilled desires, "unrealistic" in the context of the workaday world, get a second chance at fulfillment. (1965:57)

Such an explanation, with some modifications, helps clarify the function of possession trance among the Nguni, since there is general social recognition and acceptance of the possibility of spiritual forces affecting the behavior of men and women.

Sociopsychological Parameters

The advantage of looking at *ukuthwasa* and the other cults of the Nguni in terms of compensatory behavior is obvious on reviewing the position of women in those societies. They are raised being aware of their temporary residence in the kraal of their own kinsmen and of their secondary role in the patricentric cattle society. A young woman is often linguistically equated by her male agnates with cattle, which will be brought to them when she marries—she is referred to as "father's cattle." Vilikazi notes that a young girl who is being cautioned about her courting behavior is told, "Don't expose your father's cattle," or "Don't open your father's cattle kraal." A non-Christian Zulu with only daughters may refer to himself "as one who was not blessed with seed," for daughters cannot perpetuate the line (Vilakazi 1965:40). Nevertheless, the girl may have close emotional bonds to this family she must leave at marriage. Impending social and biological maturity of Nguni girls is often marked by fits of hysteria and accusations of love magic. Where the prohibition of cousin marriage exists, as it does among the Zulu, marriage means leaving the support of her agnates to live in a strange and possibly hostile household. When she does marry and take up residence in the patricentric kraal of her husband, she finds her position therein to be low. If there are co-wives with whom she must compete for the attentions of the mutual husband, the young wife may also be bored and restless. Few diversions are open to her, for a Nguni woman's place is at home, hoeing and caring for husband, in-laws, and children (Kuper 1947:165). She cannot opt to take up a career outside the home (in the traditional society), and she cannot inherit one from her father. (A man, for example, can inherit the profession of healer or herbalist from his father, but a woman cannot.) This social system, which incorporates both structural and ritual inferiority of females, produces extra stresses and problems for those who are bright, restless, and relatively ambitious.

But the Nguni do not argue with ancestors or attempt to deny their call when they possess their bodies. Possession of a married female by her dead agnates, for example, is one of the few circumstances that result in her returning to her natal home. The Nguni recognize the importance of attempting to sever the ties between women and their own ancestors, and this concern is institutionalized in the marriage rituals of incorporation and integration (see above). Vilakazi gives an interesting and revealing account of the marriage of *izangoma* in which there are actually two weddings, one for the woman, one for the diviner in her. This double marriage might be viewed also as implying recognition of the separateness and incompatibility of the two roles. The first is a regular wedding, with the usual ritual sacrifice and other ceremony. The second "wedding" is intended to replace the diviner's patrilineal spirits that reside on her shoulders with those of the husband's kin group. Both families make ritual sacrifices at this time. The husband's group tries to induce their ancestors to take control, while the wife's family attempts to lure away their ancestors with the gall bladder of a slaughtered goat. There is an additional stipulation that this goat must not be part of the *lobolo* that they received in compensation for their daughter (Vilakazi 1965:72).

In *ukuthwasa* and the role change associated with it can be seen a reflection of the structural opposition and juxtaposition of affines and consanguines, of their distinctiveness and interdependence through the exchange of women and beasts. Cult beliefs and practices also suggest that effective unilineal kin relationships here are not ended by death but are extended to include dead agnates. Within this system a woman may be seen to derive benefits from dead kinsmen who, unlike her living agnates, are unencumbered by practical social and economic concerns. Living kinsmen must not threaten the equilibrium and stability of the system of interdependence and exclusiveness of kin groups by encouraging unfeminine or "unwifely" or independent behavior on the part of women. Dead kinsmen and *ukuthwasa* possession loosen the structural bonds that restrict the roles and movements of women.

There are actually several ways in which *ukuthwasa* may cause physical separation of a married woman from her affines. First is the compulsive flight of the fugue state that often occurs in the illness stage of *ukuthwasa*. The woman who runs to the bush looking for snakes and herbs or who runs to the hut of a master *isangoma* may also be running away from a stressful situation. Second, as shown above, when a married woman is ill with *ukuthwasa,* afflicted by *her* ancestors, she is sent home until the proper rituals are completed. Third, traditionally the *isangoma* traveled about and divined where she was needed. Some women abandoned their prescribed female roles of wife, daughter-in-law, and mother and assumed the new role of diviner totally. Lee reports, however, that all the *izangoma* known to his informants remained with their husbands and that "their independence is psychological rather than spatial" (1970:149).[5]

The other non-Christian possession cults, in which possession is not by ancestors, do not seem to provide such a framework for independence. Zionism, on the other hand, has much the same effect. The assumption of Christianity itself tends to equalize the sexes and minimize the influence of the descent groups. And becoming a Zionist makes a Nguni woman even more independent. Lee quotes non-Christian leaders as saying, "Those damned Zionists steal our women" (1970:154). Within the church the women can hold positions of authority and respect not usually accessible to them outside it.

Ukuthwasa also reflects the opposition of the sexes. Women are nearly always at a disadvantage in their traditional relations to men. The fact that possession brings to women some of the prerogatives of men is brought out by the psychologist Lee. He speaks of aggressive and phallic symbols associated with this type of possession, such as the snake. Also, he says, "Meat and beer, masculine prerogatives in everyday life and rarely available to pre-menopausal women, are freely enjoyed by *izangoma*" (1970:151). This is reminiscent of Gluckman's description of "rituals of rebellion" that at one time occurred periodically in Zululand. The rituals were periods of behavioral license for women; they were allowed to don men's clothing, speak like men, and carry spears and shields like warriors. They could, Gluckman (1954) tells us, express dissatisfaction with their assigned roles in life without threatening the ultimate stability of the system. But these temporary, community-wide ritual role changes have ceased. The increasingly common role changes associated with *ukuthwasa* are noncommunal—individual—but longer-lasting. They are, nevertheless, functionally similar phenomena. In neither case is there a real attempt to alter the societal system of sexual roles and relationships. S. G. Lee administered thematic apperception tests to many Zulu women and found, indeed, that *izangoma* are more "masculine," more aggressive and ambitious in their goals and outlook than most other women (1970:150).

Possession among the Nguni certainly does "enlarge

109

the field of action" for women and provides additional sanctioned roles for them. Possession gives females a medium for expression of creative and intellectual ability. It does not do so *directly,* in the way suggested by Bourguignon (1965), for the behavior associated with the illness *ukuthwasa* and other dissociational states is relatively standardized and stereotyped. Among the Nguni the possession itself is only a sign or symptom of a wider, more profound change in the life of the possessed. During the greatest part of a woman's life as a diviner the spirits reside on the woman's shoulders, not within her. Most of the time, they are thought to be the source of her power without directly taking over her body.

The benefits of the *amandiki, amandawu,* and *izizwe* possession are usually more immediate and less enduring. They could provide a cathartic outlet for expression of confusion and conflict stemming from the stress of warfare, defeat, and disease. Possession by Thonga, Indians, and so on, reveals the distress caused by the defeat of the once powerful and feared Nguni, who now see themselves as plagued by a host of foreign ghosts. All of these possession activities may also serve simply as social affairs and brighten the usually dull lives of kraal women.

The participation of men in possession cults might also be explained in terms of benefits derived. In a society like that of the Nguni there are hardships for "unmasculine" men as well. In the past, of course, all young men were expected to be warriors—brave, virile, hardy. Even now, this is the ideal of manhood, and such an ideal certainly causes problems for the "thin, highly-strung" males, especially those with homosexual tendencies. The cult would give them a release for nervous tension, some standing in the community, and an ancestor-sanctioned substitute profession. Within the context of the cult, the homosexual or transvestite tendencies can be given expression, just as women can mani-

110

fest cross-sexual behavior, "and the gods [spirits] are assigned the responsibility for such behavior" (Bourguignon 1965:54).

For most of these men and women the decision to join the cult is not a conscious one. The matter, of course, is believed to be in the hands of the ancestors because individuals apparently have no control over *ukuthwasa* symptoms. When, in times of stress, a wave or "epidemic" of possession begins, it most likely first manifests itself in those "susceptible of psychic influences" (Kidd 1904:156)—the thin, the neurotic, the emotionally unstable, those with nervous twitches, hiccoughs, and so on. Secondarily, however, conscious or unconscious recognition of the benefits to be gained from cult membership would draw others without the "pathologies" to participate. Some of the major physiological changes probably could not be consciously induced, but not all symptoms have to be present for a diagnosis of *ukuthwasa*. Many such normal perople may have been drawn to the *amandiki* and *amandawu* activities as well, which might explain the relatively mild and undramatic symptoms of the related possession patterns and the relatively slight effect such possession has on the life of most of the participants.

This discussion, although it outlines certain explanations for the presence and prevalence of certain dissociational states among the Nguni Bantu, does not really explain the increasing domination of females in cult activities. It would seem, in fact, that, as the Bantu men are deprived of their traditional roles and power by the white society, such compensatory and tension-channeling behavior would be increasingly common among them. The crushing of Nguni militarism by the Europeans, however, may actually have reduced the pressures on the men who could not have measured up as warriors in the traditional society. In addition, the high level of technology and complexity of the Republic of South Africa open many new channels for expression and accomplishment, even for black men in the apartheid society. Many men are attracted to the cities, too, where there is greater anonymity and less pressure to conform in the traditional ways. Most women, on the other hand, still carry on in the traditional manner in the old roles, with the added problem of the absence of their men, who on returning from the cities may find their wives unattractive and dull. In the reserves, centers of conservatism, the female *izangoma* multiply. Most of the structural and ritual restrictions to which cult females apparently are reacting still exist in the reserve society. With the change of the old order, however, some of the problems of men have disappeared or been buried in the cities.

The significance of *ukuthwasa* possession within the context of Nguni society can be clarified by a brief comparative illustration. To the northwest of the Zulu are two groups of semipastoralists, the Venda and the Lovedu, on the fringes of the southern cattle area. (Unless otherwise indicated, the material below on the Lovedu is from Krige and Krige 1943; the information concerning the Venda is recorded by Stayt 1931.) Here disease and climate make cattle raising more difficult, and the local breeds of cattle are apparently less well adapted to the semitropics than those of the Nguni. Their beasts are neither economically nor ritually as important as those of the southeastern peoples. Milk is not a part of the Lovedu diet, and, in fact, few cows can be milked. The cattle-complex prohibition of women in husbandry affairs is not observed in this area. Despite patrilineal descent, patrilocal residence, local exogamy, and so on, the Lovedu women occupy a respectable position. They take advantage of their numbers in a polygynous household to bend their husband to their collective will; they have a great amount of control over marriage arrangements, which preferably involve a cross-cousin. The Kriges have suggested that one of the significant differences between the Lovedu and most of the other societies of southeastern Africa is the importance of the mother's side of the Lovedu family; an individual's mother's family has economic, ritual, and social significance for him (1943:79).

The ritual separation of women and cattle does not exist among the Venda either. Women may actually possess, herd, and milk cattle, although physical contact with the animals is avoided during menstruation. In addition to patrilineages, functioning matrilineages are found, and the latter are of particular significance in the ancestor cult (Murdock 1959:288). In both of these groups gardening is more intensively pursued than among the Nguni: it involves both men and women, and work units may include patrilineal and matrilineal kinsmen. Here the organization of larger gardening groups is facilitated by cousin-marriage. Among both the Venda and the Lovedu a bride's in-laws may be a parent's sibling and spouse and, therefore, relatively sympathetic to the position of their daughter-in-law. There is no strict separation of male and female roles, and men are not expected to be warriors and models of strength and virility.

Although certain illnesses may be diagnosed as possession in the northwest, the "hysteria" and extreme physical and behavioral changes are absent. Weeping, loss of appetite, convulsions, and fugue states are not characteristic of possession in this area. The Lovedu and Venda also show greater continuity of personality while in a dissociational state, and those possessed are often responsive to social pressure (Krige 1943:243). Related, perhaps, to this lack of personality discontinuity is a lack of social discontinuity or change in social status related to possession behavior. The classic shamanistic theme of "rebirth," which reflects the complete involvement of many Nguni in their profession, is missing in the northwestern initiation-cure and cult. For the Nguni woman, especially, there is a definite breakaway from familial roles and responsibilities and extrication from her husband's kin. To the north, on the other hand, cousin marriage is permitted and some of a woman's in-laws may be consanguineal kinsmen. From the woman's structural position the exclusiveness and opposition of affines and consanguines does not exist; she and her husband will have certain ancestors (though not unilineal) in common. Venda and Lovedu brides may also have almost daily contact with their natal families in the course of agricultural activities.

In these societies possession may simply be a means of winning material benefits and attention from one's husband and affines, whereas in the southeast possession obviously has greater implications. It means the undertaking of a new profession—and a most demanding one—and a new way of life. The *isangoma* is, in a sense, truly "reborn."[6] There is no barring the Nguni spirit without endangering the health of the possessed, and the established relationships with spirits often result in unusual powers and abilities.

In the northwest, among the Lovedu and Venda at least, the social position of the possessed may change relatively little. Prestige may be increased, and, certainly, the cult dancing affords relief from home drudgery; but only rarely does the individual reveal divining ability as a result. Here the afflicted are primarily dancers, not diviners or shamans, and they retain their primary statuses at home. These cult members are amateurs, who, for the most part, are participating in organized social affairs. The Nguni cult members, after *ukuthwasa,* are professionals, engaged primarily as individuals in serious and socially significant enterprises.

Ecological-Biological Parameters

The following material is intended to supplement, not supplant, the discussion above and is actually a different level of analysis. This analysis deals specifically with the symptoms of *ukuthwasa,* the stereotyped, dramatic signs of possession illness that have been continuous throughout the recorded history of the Nguni. I shall argue that ecological change, subsistence practices, and traditional social patterns have combined to produce certain nutritional deficiences that in turn produce some of the physical, physiological, and behavioral changes associated with *ukuthwasa.* I shall provide a theory suggesting the convergence of these biological and sociocultural conditions in the development and perpetuation of the patterns of possession behavior and include a model to illustrate the integration of these factors. The causes and nature of nutritional deficiencies known to be endemic among the Nguni are described below.

Pellagra: Symptoms and Causes.—Pellagra is a deficiency disease whose symptoms include "diarrhea, dermititis, and dementia" and in some extreme cases death (Spies et al. 1962: 625). The relationship between this condition and a heavy dependence on maize in the diet has long been recognized, but until the 1920s toxic substances or spoiled grain were thought to be the major causes. Although the exact mechanisms are still not entirely clear, more recent research has determined that negative properties of maize, not positive ones, are pellagragenic; without certain nutritional supplements a maize diet may result in pellagra. Maize lacks both niacin, or nicotinic acid, and tryptophan. The first is a vitamin that is essential for healthy metabolism, the second an amino acid that the body converts into niacin.[7] The amino acid must be obtained from food protein, but zein, the maize protein, lacks tryptophan (Gillman and Gillman 1951:432; Spies et al. 1962:624). The disease pellagra, induced primarily by a niacin-tryptophan deficiency, actually is often compounded by the lack of other essential nutrients, including thiamine and riboflavin (Taylor and Pye 1966:275).

A diet deficient in these nutrients results in a state of chronic malnourishment, compounded among many Nguni by chronic undernourishment, which produces in some individuals a low or "markedly depressed" basal metabolism (Gillman and Gillman 1951:38). The symptoms of pellagra may not be obvious in these people for some time; however, acute malfunctioning can be precipitated by nearly anything that affects homeostasis, such as sudden temperature changes, physical illness, or emotional stress.

One author suggests that this chronic condition can exist in individuals throughout their lifetimes, with the acute condition (marked symptoms and malfunctioning) "superimposed" on the chronic base. The classic example, he continues, is the emergence in the spring of the acute signs of deficiency disease in pellagrins. The author warns that the disappearance of the acute symptoms are often mistaken for cure (Jolliffe 1962:8). Even if the change in seasons does not produce the symptoms of pellagra, "the organism may nevertheless be so sensitized that a slight change in metabolism following a chill, gastroenteritis, anesthesia or any other trivial stimuli, may be all that is needed to allow pellagra to emerge fully" (Gillman and Gillman 1951:56).

A perpetual lack of niacin and tryptophan in a diet, compounded, perhaps, by deficiencies of thiamine and other vitamins, may produce symptoms that include both physical and behavioral change. The onset of acute pellagra is manifested, for example, by skin rashes and lesions of varying degrees of severity. In some extreme conditions hyperpigmentation occurs, followed by the peeling and scaling of the dry tissue as in the case of severe sun damage (Gillman and Gillman 1951:65–68). Gastric disorders are also commonly associated with pellagra. They range in severity from indigestion and excessive acidity to diarrhea, to acute gastroenteritis, which may cause death.

The mental disorders and changes in behavior associated with this condition are numerous and nonspecific. They have been described by such terms as anxiety states, hysteria, neurosis, and neurasthenia, all of which may be related to a variety of conditions and causes. Some of the behavioral and mental symptoms repeatedly described in the clinical literature are, on the other hand, certainly relevant to this analysis.[8] Some of the major changes associated with pellagra may be summarized as follows:

1. Emotional disturbances. Pellagrins have reported that while ill they are easily frightened and are generally vaguely anxious and apprehensive. A number of them have reported an unreasonable fear of death, and this specific anxiety is reflected in dreams of death. The victims often speak of being bothered regularly by frightening dreams about a number of subjects. Some of them also express a fear and dislike of groups or crowds of people. Victims of pellagra often are irritable, easily angered, and may be unable to control their rage effectively when disturbed. Very commonly, pellagrins become sensitive and easily offended. They may lack voluntary control over their reactions; they often overreact to a situation, become quite depressed, cry easily and with little provocation.

2. Changes in cognitive and intellectual functioning. Spies et al. (1943:129) report for many victims of this deficiency disease a "general slowing of cognitive functions." Some individuals may suffer from poor memory or clouded consciousness.

3. Other common symptoms include neuritic pains, numbness in the extremities, burning sensations, dizziness, shortness of breath sometimes expressed as a fear of suffocation, headaches, loss of appetite, and insomnia. In some severe and advanced cases muscular spasms and

117

convulsions, hallucinations, and delirium may occur (Spies et al. 1943:125–30).

Many of the people who suffer from pellagra are diagnosed as neurotic or somehow emotionally disturbed. Some diagnosticians point out that a poor diet is just one common aspect of general social and environmental stress for some segments of certain societies, and these stresses may produce emotional instability even before pellagra develops (Spies et al. 1943:132).

A number of these symptoms show a remarkable parallel to the institutionalized illness *ukuthwasa*—the gastric disorders manifested in excessive gas and belching, the drying of the skin (the skin of the possessed, says Callaway, becomes "dry and scurfy" (1870:259), strange pains and sensations with no obvious organic cause, loss of appetite, and insomnia. Both the possessed and the pellagrin often seem to be morose and anxious and cry easily, and anxieties are expressed in the quantity and content of dreams.[9] Furthermore, both pellagra and *ukuthwasa* are said to be precipitated by a crisis of some sort, either physical or psychological.

Pellagra, like *ukuthwasa,* is endemic in South Africa. The diet of the Nguni has caused pellagra to be a common source of distress among them. Beef, of course, is not a regular part of the diet, for cattle are butchered and consumed only sporadically, on ritual occasions. Milk and milk products were staples of the diet in the past, but milk production has dropped because much land control has shifted to the whites, resulting in overgrazed reserve lands. And, as described above, the Bantu's desire for many animals has resulted in poor techniques of husbandry and inferior stock (Reader 1966:38). More significantly, even when milk is available, the consumption of *amasi* is restricted by a number of taboos because it is believed to be a weakening food. Women, in particular, must forego eating it while menstruating, after marriage, and after the birth of a child (Krige 1936:101, 383). There are also times during which the ritual position of women is particularly dangerous or her social position tenuous (as when she is being incorporated into her husband's family) or crises threaten. In terms of the discussion of pellagra, the great number of female food taboos appears especially significant. The postpartum *amasi* taboo seems particularly dysfunctional, since the niacin requirement of pregnant and lactating women is greater by about 2 or 3 mg. per day (Jolliffe 1962:893).

Other types of meat and poultry are consumed from time to time, but fish are avoided because they are equated with snakes to some degree, and snakes are associated with the ancestors. These food sources of niacin, then, are not consumed in sufficient quantities to maintain health; and the milk, high in tryptophan but low in niacin, cannot in itself provide the minimum requirements for healthy metabolism. The Nguni dependence on maize, however, is very great, and for some people this food alone may supply as high as ninety percent of the total calories (United Nations 1953:50). The Nguni generally use maize either whole or ground, and few nutrients are apparently lost in processing it; on the other hand, supplementary ingredients, like yeast, which might provide the needed niacin, are usually not added to the meal. The Nguni diet is broadened by the use of yams, manioc, pumpkins, millet, wild greens, and so on; but the availability of these foods varies with the area, season, and socioeconomic level. Therefore, there are not only gross dietary deficiencies of certain specific nutrients like vitamins A and B (thiamine, niacin, and so on), but in many cases the entire caloric intake is very low, often below two thousand calories per day (Gillman and Gillman

119

1951:41). This type of diet produces the pellagra symptoms and is also, perhaps, responsible for some of the symptoms of possession-illness.

Furthermore, the incidence of pellagra and *ukuthwasa* among the South African Bantu reveal some striking parallels. For example, both occur regularly among the Nguni, particularly among the lower classes and the rural traditionalists; and both the possessed and the pellagrin are more likely to be women than men. The possession cult is predominantly female, of course, but there is some evidence suggesting that females are also more susceptible to the nutritional disorder. Furthermore, laboratory studies have indicated that it is more difficult to induce a significant niacin deficiency in males (Goldsmith 1958:482). Although there is no evidence in the literature of a seasonal pattern as to the occurrence of the possession-illness as there is with pellagra, it does tend to strike in waves or "epidemics." Finally, both conditions have been on the increase in this century with a presumably related intensification of the segregation and subjugation of Bantu peoples under white rule, the loss of good grazing land, and the increasing dependence on maize.

It is possible, of course, to view the cause and incidence of the two conditions as parallel rather than as intersecting or overlapping phenomena. That is, both conditions may exist among the same populations but with different etiologies. *Ukuthwasa,* for instance, exists among the marginal and poor because these hysterical reactions to the stresses of their existence may result in higher status and greater wealth, and the symptoms are more common among women because of their low position in a male-dominated society. The diviner's role would improve the position and increase the power of these women and the few men who become involved. Pellagra, on the other hand, is endemic among the poor because of their generally inadequate diet and among women in particular for a variety of reasons. There may be more female pellagrins because of female physiology and female food taboos. Also, in the white-dominated industrial society, the female is of less importance as a source of labor and does not receive the food that some mines and industries furnish for their male employees. Most likely, in South Africa all of these factors combine to produce more female than male victims of pellagra.

I am not suggesting a simple and direct cause-and-effect relationship between pellagra and *ukuthwasa*. There are cases of the nutritional syndrome diagnosed and recognized as such with no indication (at least in the available literature) of possession in the same individuals. And some of the symptoms of pellagra, such as a characteristic pattern of skin lesions, have not been mentioned in descriptions of possession-illness. It does seem significant, however, that so many of the people most susceptible to *ukuthwasa* probably are undernourished and malnourished and therefore potential pellagrins. Furthermore, to suggest that *ukuthwasa* and pellagra are simply parallel conditions does not explain the similarities in the symptoms. This, then, is the relationship that may, in fact, exist between these two phenomena.

In traditional Nguni society many people live on an inadequate maize diet that results in a chronic deficiency condition reflected in a "depressed" metabolic pattern. Certain types of people are under additional stress in this highly structured, male-dominated society, especially women and weak or poor men. Some stimulus may cause this stress to climax in an "emotional crisis" that disturbs the metabolic equilibrium and precipitates certain symptoms of pellagra (see fig. 1). The condition may be further compounded by severe emotional stress and loss of appetite. Erik H. Erikson (1963:44) describes from his clinical experience several similar occurrences of neurotic

121

Figure 1

BIOCULTURAL PARAMETERS OF <u>UKUTHWASA</u> POSSESSION·ILLNESS
AMONG THE NĠUNI OF SOUTH AFRICA

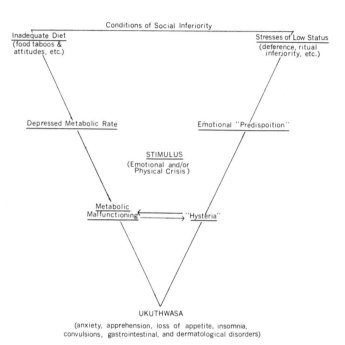

breakdown that apparently reflect an interaction between biological, psychological, and social factors. He suggests that these "combined circumstances . . . are an aggregate of simultaneous changes in the organism ([such as] exhaustion and fever), in the ego ([such as] breakdown of ego identity), and in the milieu." Sudden traumatic change in one or more of these processes may actually intensify the problems of adjustment to the others in the precipitation of breakdown. In the case of emerging *ukuthwasa*, change in the milieu may produce psychological stress that in turn aggravates the organic (metabolic) malfunctioning. Physical distress may also intensify the problems of emotional adjustment. Such a crisis might occur, for example, when a woman marries and takes up residence in the kraal of her in-laws; any psychological stress caused by this social change, combined with the new food taboos the bride is expected to observe, could precipitate acute organic malfunctioning and related behavioral change.

The stereotypy of *ukuthwasa* symptoms, then, may be a result of acute malfunctioning due to specific nutritional deficiencies. When ancestor possession is diagnosed, many ritual sacrifices are made, and most established diviners therefore have a regular supply of beef through all of the ritual feasts they conduct. The initiation-cure of the *izangoma* may actually alleviate the condition by (1) removing the cause of stress through improvement of a low social position or unhappy situation, and (2) improving the economic condition, and thus most certainly the diet, of the individual who has taken up a new profession.

CONCLUSION

Ukuthwasa and the resulting role of diviner have been remarkably stable patterns for many years, and their continuity of form reflects the conservatism of certain aspects of Nguni society, such as emphasis on the male role and relationships to living and dead kinsmen. The perpetuation of stereotyped symptoms may, as I suggest above, be partially due to their physiological basis. On the other hand, *ukuthwasa* may also reinforce some traditional patterns. Every time someone becomes ill through possession, it could be interpreted as evidence of the viability of the ancestors and the importance of kinship.

As new problems have arisen for the Nguni from exter-

123

nal sources, new cults have arisen in response. And although the symptoms are somewhat similar to *ukuthwasa*, the local etiologies are different and indicate the source of the stress. Apparently possession by aliens is mostly a feared condition and only occasionally brings special powers and benefits. An exception might be the Zionist prophets, who gain prestige and sometimes wealth. These people, however, have made certain adjustments to the new order in terms of their life style. On the other hand, even if more and more Nguni make this adjustment to the Christian Separatist churches, with their blend of the traditional and the new, it appears likely that some of the old ways will prevail.

1. The Nguni are several groups of semipastoralists who live, for the most part, below the Limpopo River in southeastern Africa. Their Bantu dialects are distinguished by "click" consonants assimilated during contacts with Khoisan-speaking Hottentots. The best known and best described are the Zulu. Although there are numerous differences between the Nguni groups and subgroups, the Zulu will be taken as representative. Others include the Swazi and Xhosa (van Warmelo 1959:45).

2. "Cult"is defined here as a group of individuals sharing certain religious and magical beliefs and goals and participating in common related rituals. The organization of most of these Bantu cults is loose and informal.

3. In his 1966 book, D. H. Reader refers obliquely to some of the effects of land "controls" on traditional subsistence pursuits (pp. 29–36).

4. Vilakazi, however, suggests that only some of the intellectuals are leaving the church. He does not indicate that there is a return to paganism among the people in general (1965:101).

5. Some of the mobility of the *izangoma* may have been hampered by the restrictions and controls of the white government. The data are not available, though, to show to what extent the compulsive acts of the possessed conform to the laws of a new wider society that does not recognize the influence of ancestor spirits.

6. The theme of "rebirth" is repeated throughout the cure and training of the Nguni *isangoma*. The term *ukuthwasa* itself is from the Nguni word for the new moon; the moon is "reborn" regularly. It has also been suggested that the occurrence of water in ritual washing, dreams of rivers, and so on during initiation is an example of the Freudian concept of water-birth association (Lee 1950). The cleansing in the river that is often part of the ritual would be an act symbolic of the rebirth, a public announcement of status change. *Ukuthwasa* ritual is comparable to a rite of passage with respect

to the public recognition and acknowledgment of the initiated. The absence of this theme in the cure of the Lovedu and Venda is evident in the literature.

7. Approximately 60 mg. of tryptophan converts to 1 mg. of niacin. However, one source suggests that the proportions of conversion will vary according to total diet pattern and individual physiology (Pike and Brown 1967:365).

8. These descriptions were compiled from observations of white and black patients in the United States.

9. Lee also describes the anxieties and dreams of a number of women suffering from a condition he compares with *ukuthwasa*: "The crowds of dead people [in dreams] undoubtedly symbolize the ancestors, and usually are indicative of a quantum of guilt anxiety in the patient. . . . Death symbolism itself is very frequent in dreams, the subject often being threatened with interment in open graves by . . . crowds of people" (1950:17).

REFERENCES

Barker, Anthony. 1959. *The man next to me*. New York: Harper & Brothers.

Bourguignon, Erika. 1965. "The self, the behavioral environment and the theory of spirit possession," in *Context and meaning in cultural anthropology* (editor M. E. Spiro). New York: Free Press of Glencoe.

Callaway, the Reverend Canon Henry. 1870. *The religious system of the Amazulu*. Publication of the Folklore Society 15. London: Trubner & Co.

Cole, Ernest. 1967. *House of bondage*. New York: Random House.

Erikson, Erik H. 1963. 2d edition. *Childhood and society*. New York: W. W. Norton & Co.

Gillman, J., and Theodore Gillman. 1951. *Perspectives in human malnutrition*. New York: Grune & Stratton.

Gluckman, Max. 1954. *Rituals of rebellion in South-East Africa*. Manchester: Manchester University Press.

Goldsmith, G. A. 1958. Niacin-tryptophan relationships in man and niacin requirement. *American Journal of Clinical Nutrition* 6:479–86.

Jolliffe, Norman. 1962. "The pathogenesis of deficiency disease," in *Clinical nutrition* (editor Norman Jolliffe). New York: Harper & Brothers.

Kidd, Dudley. 1904. *The essential Kafir*. London: Adam and Charles Black.

Krige, E. J. 1936. *The social system of the Zulus*. London: Longmans, Green and Co.

———. 1938. The place of the north-eastern Transvaal Sotho in the South Bantu complex. *Africa* 11:265–93.

Krige, E. J., and J. D. Krige. 1943. *The realm of a rain-queen*. London: Oxford University Press.

Kuper, Hilda. 1947. *An African aristocracy*. London: Oxford University Press.

Lee, S. Gilmore. 1950. Some Zulu concepts of psychogenic disorder. *Journal for Social Research* 1:9–18.

———. 1970. "Spirit possession among the Zulu," in *African mediumship*

Religion, Altered States of Consciousness, and Social Change

and society (editors J. Beattie and J. Middleton). New York: Africana Publishing Corporation.

Murdock, G. P. 1959. *Africa*. New York: McGraw-Hill.

Pike, Ruth L., and M. L. Brown. 1967. *Nutrition: An integrated approach.* New York: John Wiley and Sons.

Reader, D. H. 1966. *Zulu tribe in transition*. Manchester: Manchester University Press.

Ritter, E. A. 1957. *Shaka Zulu*. New York: G. P. Putnam's Sons.

Shooter, the Reverend Joseph. 1857. *The Kafirs of Natal and the Zulu country.* London: E. Stanford.

Spies, T. D. et al. 1943. "Emotional disturbances in persons with pellagra, beriberi, and associated deficiency states," in *The role of nutritional deficiency in nervous and mental disease* (editor Stanley Cobb). Baltimore, Md.: Williams and Wilkins.

Stayt, Hugh. 1931. *The Bavenda*. London: Oxford University Press.

Sundkler, Bengt G. M. 1961. *Bantu prophets in South Africa*. London: Oxford University Press.

Taylor, Clara Mae, and O. F. Pye. 1966. 6th edition. *Foundations of nutrition.* New York: Macmillian Co.

United Nations, Food and Agriculture Organization. 1953. *Maize and maize diets: A nutritional survey*. Rome: FAO.

Vilakazi, Absolom. 1965. *Zulu transformations*. Pietermaritzburg: University of Natal Press.

van Warmelo, N. J. 1937. "Grouping and ethnic history," in *The Bantu-speaking tribes of South Africa* (editor I. Schapera). London: Routledge and Kegan Paul.

126

II

Field Studies

4 : Spirit Mediums in Palau: Transformations in a Traditional System

Anne P. Leonard

INTRODUCTION

Palau, an island culture in the western Pacific, provides an interesting example of how the traditional functions of classical spirit possession trances, and of trancers themselves, can diminish as a culture undergoes rapid change. During the past century Palauan culture has been subjected to strong exogenous forces that have produced fundamental changes, many of which have been eagerly accepted by the Palauans. At the present time the culture reflects a curious blend of traditional and foreign value systems and institutional structures. These result from the imposition on the culture, often by administrative fiat, of three foreign and vastly different sets of institutions.

Palauan reactions to successive occupations by first the Germans, then the Japanese, and finally the present American administration form the basis for the changing uses of supernatural aid in coping with problems. The traditional use of trancing spirit mediums is only one aspect of this change, but one that plays an interesting role in Palauan culture today.

Several excellent accounts of Palauan society, including descriptions of spirit mediums, have been written, by Barnett (1949) and Vidich (1949) in particular, and these will be referred to where appropriate. However, the following descriptions and conclusions are based primarily on data provided by Palauan informants during the course of fieldwork conducted in the Palau Islands and among Palauans in Saipan in 1966.

PHYSICAL SETTING AND COLONIAL HISTORY

In order to better understand present Palauan culture a brief description of the physical setting and a colonial history of Palau follows.

Physical Setting

The Palaus are a series of lovely and picturesque islands in the Western Carolines. They are located between 7 and 8 degrees north latitude and 134 and 135 degrees longitude. In 1965, the year before fieldwork was conducted, the total population was 10,663, with 4,665 people on Koror, the island that is the administrative center of the area, and 4,524 on Babeldoab, the largest island of the group, located just north of Koror. Smaller populations live on the islands of Angaur, Peliliu, and Kayangel (Eighteenth Annual Report to the United Nations: 2–3).[1]

The Palaus have a hot, moist, tropical climate. They consist of high, limestone islands set within a large lagoon and support an adequate variety of plant and animal life.

Palau falls within the general area known as Micronesia, which includes the Marianas, the Marshalls, the Gilberts, and the Caroline Islands of which the Palaus are a part. Palau has a distinct whole culture of its own —that is, it is not part of a larger culture, or even of a cluster of cultures in the Carolines. Its traditions, language, and social organization are quite distinct from those of Yap, for instance, Palau's nearest neighbor in Micronesia.

Colonial History

Three colonial powers, each of which has left its imprint, have held sway over Palau since the end of the last century. A fourth power, the Spanish, had contact with Palauans but had little impact on their culture. A brief history of these foreign "contacts" is helpful in understanding modern Palau.

First, while the Spanish held claim to the Marianas and the Carolines from the sixteenth century to the end of the nineteenth, they made little effort to administer any of the Caroline Islands; and there were no consistent contacts between Palauans and outsiders until the mid-nineteenth century when whalers, copra traders, and missionaries began to visit Palau. Following their ambitions for a Pacific and Far East empire, the Germans became interested in Micronesia and bought all of the islands, except Guam, from Spain at the close of the Spanish American War in 1899. The Japanese occupied the islands during World War I and received them from the Germans as a League of Nations mandate at the end of the war.

Both the Germans and Japanese occupied the Palaus during their tenures in Micronesia and made vigorous efforts to impose their particular colonial policies on the Palauans. However, the Germans did not attempt to change traditional culture patterns as much as did the Japanese. Under the Japanese, Koror was a large administrative center, and the Japanese had considerable success in developing a modern economic structure there to serve the needs of the Japanese military. Palauan labor was integrated into the Japanese economic system, and Palauans became used to urban life on Koror and to Japanese life styles and consumption patterns.

American forces occupied the islands during World War II, in 1944 and 1945. In 1947 the Marianas, the

Marshalls, and the Carolines were placed under United Nations Trusteeship, with the United States as trustee. In 1951 the United States Trust Territory of the Pacific, as it is now called, was removed from the administration of the United States Navy and placed under the Department of Interior, where it remains today.

Palau felt the effects of World War II severely—the Palaus underwent bombardment and occupation, and the Japanese city on Koror was destroyed. The Palauan economy never recovered from the departure of the Japanese at the end of the war. This is due, in large part, to the difference between Japanese and American policies. The Japanese had made vigorous efforts to change the old social system of Palau and to urbanize and integrate Palauans into the Japanese economic, military, and social orders. They developed Palauan agriculture and fishing for export and worked phosphate mines on Angaur. Initial American policy, in contrast, was aimed toward returning Palau to a self-sufficient village economy, to the degree possible, and toward reestablishing the traditional society. There has never been an attempt to integrate Palau or Palauan labor into the American economic system. This change greatly curtailed the availibility of money wages and imported goods to which the Palauans had become accustomed under Japanese rule. Their primary source of outside, or American, money now is government employment. Changes in colonial policy have had far-reaching consequences for Palauans, which will be discussed presently. Although American policy has been modified in some respects in recent years, its aim according to the latest report to the United Nations is still to make the Palauans self-sufficient and self-governing.

Palauans have been generally hospitable to outsiders over the centuries and have shown a willingness to learn about other people and places. They are willing to travel and work outside Palau, and they never resisted foreign rulers as did the people of the Marianas and Ponape, in the Eastern Carolines. However, up to 1966, it was the policy of both the Japanese and the Americans, each for their own particular reasons—primarily military—to discourage visits by outsiders. In the past few years this situation has changed and the trust territory is now open to tourists, with jet service from Hawaii to Okinawa. New hotels have even been built on some of the islands, but Palau is still a side trip for the visitor.

TRADITIONAL PALAUAN CULTURE

Following is a brief survey of Palauan culture as it functioned traditionally, with references to how cultural patterns have changed. Some aspects of traditional culture have disappeared and some changed subtly in function, but many aspects of the traditional culture remain intact.

Subsistence Occupations

Over the centuries Palauan subsistence has depended on the farming of taro and tapioca plants, along with raising pigs and fishing around the reefs. In addition, wild plant foods are abundant: coconuts are especially important—or were until the advent of the coconut beetle. Subsistence is basically easy. Traditionally, farming the taro was, and remains, the women's occupation, and the men fished, built houses and canoes. Since the Japanese occupation, many Palauans have worked for money wages. Wages earned working in government jobs, for the American administration, play an important part in the Palauan economy today.

Clan Organization

Palauan society is stratified by two classes, nobles *(meteet)* and commoners. Membership in these classes was and is determined by clan membership. In addition, there are various ranks and titles held by kinship groups that give status in society.

Each person belongs to what may be termed a localized, matrilineal clan, called a *kebliil*. The *kebliil* is exogamous. Each *kebliil* has a traditional homesite, and members of the *kebliil* will give the traditional homesite as their home whether they live there or not, or whether anyone still lives at the traditional homesite.[2] A number of clans, or *ar kebliil* will be associated into a larger group called a *klebliil*. All members of the same *klebliil* trace their descent to a common mythological ancestor, but marriage within a *klebliil* is permitted.

His matrilineage within the clan *(kebliil)* is very important to the individual Palauan because the order of these lineages determines succession rights to the various titles of the *kebliil*. The *kebliil* is the most important unit in the social system because it controls the land, titles, and Palauan money of its members.

In the old days each *kebliil* had a totem—a fish or bird, or such, that was sacred to it. A person could not eat the totem of his *kebliil* or of his father's *kebliil*. In addition, each village had to observe the totem of the highest ranking *kebliil* in the village.

Economic Organization—Wealth and Power

Wealth in Palau consists of land and Palauan money (and American money today). These are controlled by the clans. Palauan money consists of pieces of ceramic or glassware, red and black—the red more valuable than the black. The history and exact composition of this money is problematical.[3] Each piece of money has a special story and a particular value to Palauans. This money is held by the clan elders and each clan guards its money, keeping it put away except for special occasions when a piece or two may be displayed as a matter of pride. For example, there is a special ceremony for a woman after the birth of her first baby. At this time she will display a piece of her clan's money hung around her neck like a pendant. This money is used as payment for various services and becomes especially important at the death of a spouse when all obligations between the two clans involved have to be settled up. Women have a parallel money exchange, but their money is made of tortoise shell. Usually Palauan money is exchanged only after a great deal of negotiating and hard bargaining by the elders.

Although descent is traced matrilineally, control and power is in the hands of the men; more particularly, those holding the proper titles. The main preoccupation of men in Palau who are in a position to do so is the manipulation of wealth and titles. This manipulation is based on a system of exchanges between clans linked by marriage. In essence a woman works, providing food (raising taro) and services for her husband's clan, and in return, the husband pays to her clan (represented by her oldest maternal uncle, or her brother) sums of Palauan money (and now sometimes American money) on certain specified occasions. The money received by the woman's clan permits her brothers to be married and to pay their obligations to their in-laws. A father must compensate for his children's "services" to his clan in much the same manner. If a father cannot or does not wish to meet the payments due his child's clan, he may "throw away" his child—

return it to the responsibility of the child's clan. This involves loss of prestige on the father's part, however.

Palauans constantly attempt to place themselves and their children in favorable exchange positions within the society. One method of accomplishing this aim is through the Palauan custom of adoption. For example, often a sister will adopt a brother's child, thus placing the father in the position of receiving money for his child from his brother-in-law rather than having to spend money for the child. This exchange system, along with frequent marriages (and other sexual liaisons), divorces, and adoptions make Palauan kin relationships very complicated and difficult for the outsider to understand. The Palauan clans and their concomitant system of exchange are still a strong social force in Palauan society today.

Family and Marriage

Sexual intercourse and a large number of liaisons before marriage were and are the norm for Palauans. Traditionally, such behavior was institutionalized through concubinage in the men's clubs. People generally made several marriages in a lifetime, as circumstances and advantage dictated. Often a final marriage would begin at middle age. People would be ready to settle down, perhaps feeling that they had little more to gain by changing sexual partners. Such "promiscuous" behavior is still a characteristic of Palauan society in spite of opposition by Christian missionaries and the outlawing of the concubinage in the men's clubs.

Palauan institutions have never favored a strong nuclear family or strong and lasting emotional ties to any one person. Children have always been trained to be ready and able to live amicably in any household into which they might be placed.

Nonkinship Groups

As stated previously, Palauans belong to noble or commoner classes according to their clan ranking. In addition to class and clan groupings clubs for men and women were very important in the past. The men's clubs were especially important because much political and social life centered around them.

Each village would have several men's clubs, each with a membership that cut across clan and class distinctions. Boys joined these clubs when they reached puberty and went to live in the clubhouses. It was through the clubs that boys were educated into Palauan manhood. The clubs served religious, social, political, and military functions. All ages were represented in each club, though internally they were divided into age groups.

Each clubhouse was served by a number of young women who would come from outside that village. These women were selected by their home districts on the basis of beauty and lineage to serve as servants and concubines in the clubhouses of other districts. This was considered to be a great opportunity for the girl selected. She was expected to try to gain the affection of as highly placed a man as possible with a view to either making a good marriage or at least obliging a man to pay her clan a valuable piece of Palauan money. Thus this custom was yet another way in which the Palauans manipulated the system to gain wealth and prestige for the clans.

This aspect of Palauan life was the first to be attacked by missionaries, as might be expected. "Concubinage" was outlawed very early, but the same attitudes toward the function of women remain today. Young women are encouraged to form alliances with men who might be able to bring money into the clan. Children born of such liaisons are clan members with no stigma attached.

Today, it is considered a mark of prestige by some to have a "white" baby (as it was to have a "Japanese" baby formerly). Therefore, American men on Palau are sought after by Palauan girls. Money payments may result from such liaisons, although the significance of these payments is not the same for the donor as for the recipient because of differing cultural backgrounds.

The Japanese changed the structure of the men's clubs from being vertically organized by age groups to being horizontally arranged. Under the Japanese the men were divided into three groups: a young men's organization whose members generally worked for the Japanese outside their home villages, a middle-aged men's club whose members worked at home, and the "retired" men's group (Vidich 1949:71).

Women had a parallel set of organizations, titles, and money that were subordinate to those of the men. Today, men's and women's clubs exist, but their functions are primarily social in nature.

Political Organization

In former times, Palau was made up of a number of independent villages and hamlets that formed alliances and pledged their support to the chief of the strongest village. Wars were fought and alliances switched. Village rank was determined by the amount of Palauan money a particular village controlled, and this amount could vary with the fortunes of war. Thus power and position were based ultimately on military success. With the advent of outside control and the elimination of intervillage warfare, however, these positions became fixed into approximately the structure that exists today: a number of hamlets within an area combined into municipalities, and these municipalities grouped to form the two main political divisions of Palau—North Palau, with its high chief, Reklai, and South Palau, with its high chief, Ibedul. Each clan has a chief, and the clan and the chief are ranked as are the chiefs of the two main political divisions. Thus the Ibedul outranks the Reklai.

The traditional system of social control was authoritarian. The dictates of the village and clan chiefs had to be followed. However, rule was not autocratic, as in some parts of Micronesia—the Marshalls, for example, where the chief owned all the land and could remove people from the land at his pleasure. In Palau, control of the land remained in the hands of the clans. To quote John Useem:

> Power was distributed unequally and along hierarchical lines, yet it was not linear but circular. Legitimate authority was an attribute of offices and not the private property of persons. While paramount chiefs outranked other title holders, their right to rule was circumscribed. No chief could act without the approval of other title holders. In theory, the order of rank was changeless; in reality there were numerous cases in which it was changed. Inheritance rules set the order of succession to titles but did not guarantee anyone the right to positions of authority. Those in line of succession to titles had to prove their qualifications for office and those in office had to demonstrate a reasonable ability to govern. (1949:25)

Social Mobility

As can be inferred from the foregoing, traditional Palauan society was not as rigidly stratified as it might first appear. Rankings could change. It was difficult, but not impossible, for a commoner to achieve status—through adoption into a higher clan or, for a few, through holding the office of official spirit medium. In addition, special recognition was given to a man who, by his own cleverness, amassed great wealth. Such a person was called a *merau*, and he could come from

139

a lower clan—a "self-made man," as it were. Palauans today who have made a success working for American money, outside the traditional system, might be considered in this category. In short, Palauans esteem wealth and power and cleverness in achieving these, even outside their system of inheriting wealth and position.

Religion and the Supernatural

In the old days Palauans believed in a set of hierarchically placed gods, each with a title. There were the high gods of all Palau, the gods of villages, and the gods of the clans. Today, although there are gods of villages and larger areas and gods of the clans, the hierarchy is incomplete. However, many of the old myths have been preserved through the efforts of anthropologists and of Palauans who have taken an interest in preserving knowledge of their traditional culture.

According to several informants, the gods of the clans, or *chelid a blai,* "gods of the house," are female, whereas the gods of the villages are male. The worship of the clan deities was the responsibility of the clan chiefs. Barnett states that each clan had a god and goddess with titles corresponding to the clan titles (1949:202). In addition to clan deities the spirits of the clan dead were important. They had to be propitiated, for they could punish members of the clan for various infractions or slights—such as, for example, if a clan member had, even accidentally, eaten the sacred clan totem animal. These spirits of the clan dead were able to communicate with living members of the clan through dreams and were consulted about various family matters. For example, their blessing was asked at the dedication of a new house. Before the housewarming a dead relative might enter a living member of the family through a dream and tell him about special medicines for sickness in the new house. These practices are still extant. Clan gods and spirits do not possess people, however.

Gods of the village or higher ranking gods were represented by a "medium" who held a title and office and who was confirmed in office by the chief and/or the village council. This traditional medium still functions to some extent today and will be described in detail presently.

In addition to the priests of the gods and ancestors and the traditional mediums, there were specialists in magic and divining. There were various specialized rites involved in canoe-building, house-building, and so on, described by Barnett (1949:208). Several types of religious festivals, which were large social gatherings, were held from time to time, but these are no longer observed. Palauans still consult various mediums, diviners, and magicians.

Present-Day Religious Beliefs

The old religious structure of the Palauans has largely disintegrated, although many elements of it survive in everyday life today. Vidich (1949:60) suggests a plausible reason for this breakdown in the knowledge of the structure of the old religion. Early in this century the Germans began a systematic removal of the old "shamans," or mediums, from office. Because these were the "experts" in the old religion, though these offices were later filled again, the continuity of knowledge was lost; and now it is hard to find anyone well versed in the old religion. This is a reasonable explanation. In their highly structured traditional society not all Palauans had equal knowledge of all aspects of their culture. There were experts on house-building and the rites associated with this, on magic, on knowledge of Palauan money, and so on. This, doubtlessly, was also the case with the old religion; full knowledge of it was available only to specialists. However, it could also be that Palauans never had a really integrated system of beliefs.

Most Palauans today claim to be Christians or belong to a nativistic religion developed in this century called *Modekngei*. The Palauans have been missionized successively by the Catholics, beginning with the Capuchins in the latter part of the last century, a German Lutheran group dating from the 1930s, and the Seventh Day Adventists, invited in during Japanese times. After World War I, Modekngei developed, incorporating many old beliefs together with some Christian ideas, and was presented as the only truly Palauan religion by its leaders. At the present time informants estimate that about 60% of the Palauans profess to be Catholics, 30% Modekngei, and the remaining 10% are divided between the Protestants and the Seventh Day Adventists.

Most Palauans do not appear to have any firm or consistent commitment to any one religion. They do look for supernatural explanations of various events, however—deaths and illnesses, for example—and they still practice magic of various sorts.

POSSESSION, TRANCE, AND MEDIUMS

In the following section as many as possible of the practices and beliefs associated with trance and possession in Palau will be discussed. This includes definitions of terms; descriptions of the mediums and their functions in society; of Modekngei as a force in Palauan society; of possession, trance, and illness; of betel as a possible trance-inducing agent; and, finally, some comments on the Palauan personality and its attitudes toward the supernatural.

Definitions and Palauan Terms

In the terminology developed by Bourguignon in her study "World Distribution and Patterns of Possession States" (1968), the Palauans have a supernaturalistic explanation of trance states as opposed to a naturalistic one. They believe that trance is caused by a spirit or god entering or possessing the individual and taking over his being. The key elements of such possession in Palau are trembling, dissociation, and amnesia—that is, the person does not recall what he said or did while he was possessed. Thus, only possession trance is known in Palau; no trance linked to other explanations was encountered.

Palauans, at least older ones, also believe that the entry of evil spirits into the body can cause sickness, but trancing is not associated with this idea—this is possession, not possession trance. Cures for illness themselves do not involve trance, although diagnosing the supernatural cause of an illness may.

Possession trancers in Palau act as agents for contacting the gods and spirits of the dead, hence the term "medium." Not all mediums in Palau use trance, but because no one Palauan term was discovered that refers to mediums in general, it is more convenient to use the English term.

The closest to a general term for the office of "traditional" medium is *kerdelel chelid*. One informant translated this term as "standing between god"; another as "god's chair," a rather free translation. *Chelid* means "god." The Palauan-English dictionary (McManus 1964:55) gives the term *kerdel*, meaning "flame," or "landing place." The dictionary also gives the terms *kerrodel*, "landed"; *kerrodel a chelid*, "possession by a spirit"; and *kerrodel dil*, a "medium." This last term was given by informants as the title of the medium at Ngetkip. The term *korong* used by Barnett (1949:205 ff) for the shaman, or medium, is the same as the title of the medium at Ngchesar. Some informants said *korong* refers today to one who chews a lot of betel nut. In any case, *kerdelel chelid* seems to be a generally accepted term among older informants. Younger informants use the term *tengellel a chelid,* or "descending of the god," to mean medium, which is also acceptable, though it refers to the event rather than to the person. That is, the *kerdelel chelid* prepares himself for the *tengellel a chelid,* or descending of the god.

There is another term that should be discussed at this point—*odong.* This term refers to the signs of being possessed. When the god enters, the medium becomes *odong. Odong* may also refer to the signs of the god leaving at the end of a possession ceremony. Or, to put it another way, *odong* refers to the symptoms of trance that indicate the god has entered the person. Whenever a person is acting hysterically, people may ask "Is he *odong?"* (possessed).

The Modekngei religion has its own mediums, which will be described, but they do not go into trance. In Modekngei, the god, or gods and spirits of the dead, do not possess people. They speak by a strange, whistling noise that the medium, or leader, then consciously "translates" to the people.

Possession trances occur within the context of traditional beliefs; that is, the mediums for the traditional village gods act as vehicles for the gods to communicate with the people. Since it is primarily within the context of the traditional mediums that trance occurs today, our attention will be focused on these. Because a slightly different type of possession ceremony did occur in the recent past, as a part of funeral ceremonies, however, a brief description of this behavior follows.

144

SPIRIT MEDIUMS IN PALAU

The Sisch

Informants have stated that in the recent past (within the memory of the informants) the spirit of a dead relative could possess a living person under special conditions, causing a trance-like state. This situation occurred as a part of the old-style funeral ceremonies called the *sisch*. The *sisch* ceremony was observed on the third day after death. A special group of old women was secluded in the house during the period between death and before the *sisch*. On the third day a special bouquet of brilliant flowers was prepared. In this bouquet were two new buds of the coconut, which looked like ears. The base of the bouquet was wrapped in a special cloth and set on a special mat. The *bladek,* or spirit of the dead person, was believed to be in this bouquet. The nearest female adult relative of the dead person whispered the name of various gods who might have caused the death into the "ears" of the bouquet. Meanwhile, the other women were chanting *korngi a ngarkari,* "he took you," or just *korngi.* When the name of the god responsible was whispered, the bouquet started turning slowly around, "dancing." (One older informant said he had seen this happen in several *sisch* ceremonies, but had never seen the spirit enter a person.) At this point, sometimes it happened that the spirit of the dead person would leave the bouquet and "climb the body" of a close female relative. This most often happened when the relative was someone especially beloved of the dead person—the mother, for example. The woman trembled and swayed, but did not speak or make any noise. She remained seated while the spirit caused her to "dance" like the bouquet. This trance lasted about seven or eight minutes. Some women immediately returned to normal, and others laid down afterward. (For a detailed description of the old funeral rites, see McKnight and Obak 1960:15–16). The

145

sisch custom is no longer followed. Today the term *sisch* refers to a funeral feast.

Characteristics of Traditional Mediums

Village and municipality gods are all males. Each hamlet has a tutelary god, or *chelid belu*. In the past there was a medium with a special title who served the god of each village. Not all these offices are filled today, however. Several villages share the same god, and, in the case of Melekeyok, one municipality has two gods. In former days the sharing of the same god among several villages served as a link of friendship, but not as a strong political affiliation. It is said that members of villages so linked would not kill each other in war.

Although information is incomplete, table 1 lists the municipalities and hamlets of Palau, with the information that was obtained concerning the presence or absence of a "traditional" medium today and the name of the god and the title of the medium, where possible, for each. Table 2 indicates the medium's age, sex, and method of selection. From the latter table, it can be seen that there are still a number of traditional mediums in Palau today and that the majority of them are old men. It should be noted, however, that not all people holding these titles are actually practicing today.

It seems evident that through time and among different villages there has been variation in the manner of selecting the mediums, in their sexes, and in some of their techniques of trance. In some villages the medium can properly only be a man. In Ngerkeseuaol and Ngerchelong, which one informant specifically described, the medium is always a man. These villages, in the old days, had a "wife of the god" in addition to the medium, but she did not act as a medium. This woman belonged to the same *kebliil* as the medium, and the god selected

146

TABLE 1

LIST OF PALAUAN MEDIUMS BY LOCATION AND TIME PERIOD

PLACE NAMES	NAMES OF THE GOD	MEDIUM'S TITLE	SEX OF MEDIUM 1966	Recent Past
North Palau				
Melekeyok	Olekeyok	Ruar		M
	Uchelrubesang	Mlechei[1]	F	
Ngeburch				
Ngeruliang				
Ngemelech	Odalmelech	Seraruleyang	M	
Ngerang				
Ngerubesang	Uchelchelid (Uchelrubesang)[2]			
Kayangel	Uchelschehal	Kuul		M
Ngerdilong				
Ngerdims				
Ngerchelong	Ngirangerechelong	Sachalhoy	M	
Mengellang				
Ollei				
Ngeiungel				
Ngebei				
Ngriil				
Iebukel				
Ngerau				
Ngaraard				M
Ulimang				
Elab				
Ngebuked				
Ngkeklau				
Chol (or 01)	Ngiramukuul[3]		M	
Ngiwal	Ngirungor	Remechal		M
Ngercheluuk				
Ngermechau				
Ngchesar	Ngirngchesar	Kerong		M
Ngchesar				
Ngereuikl				
Ngeraus				
Ngerkesou				
Ngergesang				
Ngersuul				
South Palau				
Koror				M
Ngeramid				Unknown
Ngerkeseuaol	Echeodel[4]	Rechedsomel	M	
Ngerchemai				
Iebukel	Echeodel[4]	No medium		
Ngermenganged				
Ngerbeched	Uchelchelid (Uchelrubesang)[2]	Mlechei	F	

TABLE 1—*Continued*

Place Names	Name of the God	Medium's Title	Sex of Medium 1966	Recent Past
Ngerkbesang Ngerdmau Urdmau Ngerutoi Ngetbang	Sakelkui	Ngirkebai	M	
Ngeremlengui Imeong Ngermetengel Ngerutechel Ngchemesed	Uchererak	Yechadera edukel	Unknown	
Ngetbang Mechebechubel[5] Ngetbang	Medechibelau	Ngiraked		F
Imeliik Medorm Ngchemiangel Elechui Ngerkeai Imul	Tungelbai	Rengechel[6]	M	
Airai Ngetkip Ngerusar Irrair Oikull Ngchesechang	Medechibelau Obak el Sechel	Ngirikiklang Kerrodel dil	M F	
Peliliu Ngesias Ngerdelolk Ngerkeikl Ngerchol Teliu	Ngirabeliliou Echeodel[4]	Beromel	M	
Angaur Ngerbelau Ngermasech Rois				

1. Mlechei is the medium for both of these gods today.

2. Two names for the same god.

3. Became the god of Modekngei.

4. Ngerkeseuaol, Iebukel, and Peliliu have this god in common, but there is no medium in Iebukel because this is only a "resting place" for the god.

5. Home of the famous Modekngei medium described on pages 163–65.

6. Name, no title known to informants.

her by dropping betel nut in front of her as she sat with other people in the house. She slept in a special sacred part of the house, at the end opposite the hearth, reserved for old people and the sick. The god came to visit her at night, and made his presence known by whistling. Today, the term "wife of the god" refers only to women mediums. Barnett states that these "wives of the god" were not supposed to marry mortal men and that there were also transvestite mediums who acted as "wives of the god" (1949:206).

There are several hamlets in which the medium has been a woman, with a title, for generations. For example, Melekeyok has a female medium whose title is *Mlechei*. Ngetkip, in Airai, also has had a female medium for several generations. As mentioned above, these mediums are considered to be wives of their respective gods. In Ngerbeched, there is also a man's office and the title *Dingelius*, "friend of the god," but he never acts as a medium. He comes from a low clan and helps the medium in her activities, acting as a kind of informant.

The selection of mediums of one sex or the other seems to be traditional. Most villages have men, but some traditionally have women. Both highly ranked villages such as Melekeyok, home of the Reklai (chief of north Palau), and poorer hamlets, such as Ngetkip, in Airai, have female mediums. The hamlet Ngerbeched, on Koror, has a female medium also; thus, they are not confined to the island of Babeldoab. In short, there is no apparent rationale or pattern to the choice of the medium's sex. It may be that, traditionally, a particular god preferred mediums of one sex or another. For example, Melekeyok and Ngerbeched have one god in common, and the mediums for this god in both cases are women. Ngerkeseuaol and Peliliu share a god and have (or had) only male mediums (Iebukel had the same god, but no medium)

(See tables 1 and 2). There are also implications in the preceding data that each god had two official representatives, a man and a woman, with only one of them serving as a medium. This dual set of offices fits the general pattern of Palauan social organization. Information, however, is too scarce to form a final judgment in this matter.

TABLE 2

DISTRIBUTION OF PALAUAN MEDIUMS BY
SEX, AGE AND METHOD OF SELECTION

	Total	SEX*			AGE			METHOD OF SELECTION†					
		M	F	N	60+	40–60	–40	N	A	B	C	D	N
Traditional mediums holding office today	12	8	3	1	6	1	1	4	5	2	1	. . .	4
Those traditional mediums of recent past for whom some information was obtained	8	3	2	3	1	. . .	. . .	7	1	1	. . .	2	4

*M = male; F = female; N = no information

†A = Selection by god from a special clan
B = Selection of medium by council of elders; must be from special clan.
C = Office inherited, but not specified how.
D = Two villages no longer have traditional mediums, but anyone can become possessed by the god and act as a temporary medium.

Mediums, whether men or women, are normal members of their society; they marry and have children. No transvestite mediums were discovered in the present study.[4] One man affected the manners and dress of a woman, but he was considered to be ill—mentally unbalanced—and had no special connections with the gods.

Methods of Selecting Traditional Mediums

There is some variation in the method of selecting the medium. It is a common pattern for the medium to be selected by the god from the members of a particular *kebliil* (see table 2). Though in some cases this is the highest-ranking *kebliil* in the village, in others it is a lower-ranking one. Members of the special *kebliil* are prone to having "strange experiences": premonitions, fits of crying, sudden shouting and/or fainting when some bad thing has happened, and so on. In two cases, at least, Ngetkip and Ngerdmau in south Palau, this might happen to a woman who has married into the family; that is, an affine could be chosen as a medium. This is interesting because marriage does not change one's clan affiliation. People can tell whom the god has selected by the signs of possession trance that that person displays. After the death of an old medium, the new medium-to-be will suddenly speak in the voice of the god. He will become *odong* (possessed). He, or she, may say in the voice of the god, something like, "Do you not recognize me?"

Sometimes a person may show signs of possession but will not want to become a medium. For example, this happened to the wife of a man of the Ngeremlkii clan of Ngetkip. (In Ngetkip the medium must be a member of the Ngeremlkii *kebliil* or be married to one, and her assistant must come from this clan also.) In the middle of a big celebration on the occasion of the completion of the new *bai* (men's house), this woman who was married to a member of the Ngeremlkii suddenly became possessed. Although a very quiet and shy elderly lady, she suddenly went from the women's end of the *bai* to the other, where some visiting dignitaries were seated, and took a red cloth from the neck of one of the visitors. She began waving this cloth, jumping up and down, and trembling. People asked if she was going to become a medium, since she was married into the proper clan. Her husband, however, had become a Protestant and did not want her to be involved in the old religion. He rocked her in his arms until she quieted down, and, evidently, she has not been troubled again in this way.

A different pattern of selection exists in Ngerkeseuaol, where the medium is chosen by a group of the old chiefs and old women of the village. Once elected, the new medium will begin to experience possession trance if he has not done so before.

Since the medium has a title and an income from the fees paid for his services, it is tempting to suppose the office is often given to one person or another for political reasons. In one case, for example, the medium's title is held by the chief's younger brother. In Peliliu the present medium is the chief himself. In Ngerbeched, where the medium is a woman, her title is second only to the highest-ranking woman's title, which is held by the head-woman of the highest-ranking clan. The medium must also come from this clan.

Apparently, in the past, in some areas, the medium could be anyone the god selected, even a person of low rank. Ngiwal and Ngchesar, on the island of Babeldoab, are probably in this category. It is interesting to note that in these two villages today anyone, by chewing much betel, may become possessed by the god and make predictions. There are no longer any official mediums for these villages. In this situation the office of medium could serve as a channel to wealth and influence for one of low rank, subject, however, to the approval of the chief.

Whatever the method of selection, the traditional office of medium was a position of power, and doubtless mediums could influence the decisions of the chiefs. Once in office it might be difficult for a chief to remove a medium who opposed his policies. However, the office, where it is functioning today, is generally under the control of the chiefs and the high clans. Today it never functions as a counterweight to the chief's power, but rather, mediums tend to support the chiefs in their policies.

152

Two Contemporary Mediums:
Rechedsomel and Kerrodel Dil

In order to illustrate some of the variations and similarities in trance techniques of the "traditional" mediums, the procedures of two mediums practicing today will be described. Both of these are mediums of some repute. One is a man, the medium of Ngerkeseuaol, the other, a woman, the medium of Ngetkip.

In Ngerkeseuaol, the medium, whose title is *Rechedsomel,* was chosen by the old chiefs and old women of the village. He serves the whole village in an official capacity and also helps individuals and families. In an individual case, however, the god does not possess him; rather, he is consulted as a practitioner of magic. For example, if someone has been robbed, he may ask the medium to find the thief and punish him in some special way, perhaps by making him "act crazy," so everyone will know who it is. The medium gives his answer then and there, without going into possession trance. He promises that the thief will be caught but cannot say exactly when. The medium is paid in money—American money—which is placed on the special mat the medium has in front of him.

Often, groups representing the village in some matter, or some special group in the village, will arrange a meeting with the medium. They may consult him before going on a journey to get his protection, or to get his prediction on the outcome of some venture. In this case the group will prepare a special basket of betel nut and leaves. This is the god's basket and must be carried in a certain way. There must be no tobacco mixed with the betel on this occasion. When they enter the house, the leader takes the basket to the medium. The members of the group line up and begin to talk. They sit cross-legged with their feet tucked in their legs, yoga fashion. Their backs are

153

straight, and they must be very respectful. They keep their eyes on the medium.

The medium sits in the same fashion, but leans forward on his arms. His arms are straight, with his palms flat on the floor. At first his head is down and his eyes look down, or are even closed. As the people begin to talk, explaining what they want, he makes low moaning noises. Then his arms begin to tremble. He raises his head, his eyes roll up. He then speaks in the voice of the god. The god asks, "What do you want? I am very busy up here [in "heaven" where gods live]." This is said in a rather impatient and gruff voice. The god of Nger-keseuaol is *Echeodel*, which means "old," and in this case he appears rather stern. There is no elaborate attempt to act out a personality, however. There is no assistant. The answers are given directly in the ver-nacular. The god stays until all the questions are answered, which is usually not longer than thirty minutes. When the god leaves the medium, the medium is dizzy and sleepy; but the people do not permit him to sleep until he has returned to himself. They pour water on him and massage him until he has done so; then they let him sleep.

The medium does not follow a special diet and follows the same taboos in regard to food that the whole village observes. His ceremonies occur in his house, at the sacred end, called the *eldeng*. This practice is also followed elsewhere, for example, by the medium in Ngerdmau, who also holds his ceremonies in the *eldeng* of his house.

The medium in Ngetkip, a small hamlet in Airai, is an old woman whose title is *kerrodel dil*. She gives both public and private consultations and uses possession trance in both types of ceremonies.

As is the custom in some other villages, this medium has a special small house in back of her living house, called the *ulengang*, where she goes when the god possesses her. Under the *ulengang* are the special sacred stones associated with the god. These stones, together with the *ulengang*, form the sacred area called the *ileakllolled*, the place where the god lives when he is in the hamlet.

When a special delegation wishes a consultation with the god, arrangements are made beforehand. In the case of a group consultation, the medium is alerted in advance. In Japanese times, the men of Airai and surrounding municipalities engaged in canoe races. Before the construction of the Airai canoe was completed, the men asked the medium to make it a winner. She told them to bring it to her when it was finished and leave it overnight in the sacred place before the race. They were also told to bring her the winner's flag when the race was over. They received all these instructions from the god, while the medium was possessed. Their boat won the race.

People also come to the medium to ask for protection on journeys and for predictions on the outcome of medical treatment. Informants say that when a person comes to see her, he brings a red cloth that acts as an amulet against misfortune. This red cloth is usually kept by the individual in a high and safe place, but it may be taken out and worn on the arm in times of danger. The cloth is returned to the individual at the end of the ceremony of divination. This custom is an old one in Palauan culture. In former times the "amulet" was a kind of stick that was considered to be an actual piece of the god. The Palauan term for this sacred aid is *mengkerengel*. It must be kept up high, so that it is never stepped on or over, for this would show great disrespect to the god. Such disrespect could be severely punished by the god.

Those seeking her assistance approach the medium and sit in front of her. She is seated, facing them, with a special mat in front of her. She has an assistant, who sits to her right but across from her, next to the clients, to help them ask the questions and to interpret the answers. This assistant also prepares her betel mixture for her. The medium is now ready for the descending of the god.

She begins by speaking in a normal manner, but gradually showing signs of possession trance. She starts to tremble and to speak faster. She becomes more eloquent than usual, although she uses the vernacular and has no special language. She chews more betel than usual. The betel mixture, as with the medium in Ngerkeseuaol, must contain no tobacco. The medium spits the betel juice out in different directions. One recent client said that she had saliva running down her mouth without her seeming to be aware of it, which made her appear to be crazy. She perspires freely during the trance. Her eyes gaze straight ahead and look "strange." They sometimes become red, but there are no tears in them. She has no special gestures, nor is there anything unusual about her breathing. She is not called upon to demonstrate her possession by showing that she can endure pain.

Several informants stated that some mediums, and this one in particular, speak the opposite of what they mean in answering their clients' questions; the client mentioned above stated that in this case it is the question and not the answer that must be couched in opposite terms. In any case, the custom of saying the opposite of what is meant is fairly common in Palau, not only in this context, but also in putting a curse on someone or working magic against someone.

When all the questions have been answered, the god leaves the medium. The possession may last twenty or thirty minutes in the case of a group consultation, and less time in the case of a family or individual. When the god is finished, each client takes back his red cloth and leaves. After the clients have left, the medium will shout loudly, once or twice, what sounds like "Oi!" She will then lie down and go to sleep. This sleep lasts about ten minutes, and when she awakes, she does not remember what she said during her trance.

The client who had visited this medium recently said the trance lasted about seven or eight minutes in his case and that the medium rather quickly returned to normal. He had come to get protection for his daughter who was ill and had to go to Guam to obtain medical treatment. The medium predicted that the treatment would be a success and that she would have a safe journey, which turned out to be the case.

This medium is paid for her services also. The client described above gave her $5.00 in American money on his first visit. When his daughter returned safely and well, he returned to see the medium again. At that time he paid her another $5.00.

The medium follows no special diet nor does she fast before a ceremony.

Possession trances are not always prearranged. The god may possess the medium at any time, without warning. He or she will shout loudly and then start speaking in the voice of the god. This occurs when something unusual happens or some taboo has been broken. One informant described an incident in Ngetkip, which occurred in German times, when he was a boy. Two important men had quarreled. Later, during a dance, two of the dancers, girls of about 12 or 13, suddenly died. The medium suddenly started shouting that the girls had died because of the quarrel. The people gathered around her and believed what she said. Although they spoke ill of the two men, no one did anything to them. However, at the girls' funeral, the *rubaks* (chiefs and elders) met and settled the quarrel. It was decided that people must be careful not to let such a thing happen again.

Functions of the Traditional Mediums

In the traditional culture, mediums served several important functions. They were an important link with the supernatural beyond those links supplied through the family and clan gods and spirits. They had political power. For example, as the representative of the god, the medium was consulted as to the best time for going to war and sometimes even advised the people whether to go to war or not. The medium could also serve as a peacemaker to settle internal quarrels, as in the incident just described for Ngetkip.

Because he was paid for his services, his position could bring considerable wealth to the medium. Much Palauan money circulated through this office. It could be a channel to wealth and power for a poor, even a low, clan individual, depending on the method of selection in his village. It should be remembered, however, that in any method of selection, the medium was apparently still subject to the approval of the chief. Yet, the office of medium was powerful, and there were undoubtedly instances when a chief might have wished to have one medium replaced by another who was more amenable to his policies. Nonetheless, although the mediums might counterbalance the chiefs' power, they were basically part of the traditional power structure. It would seem unlikely that the office of medium was ever used to affect any basic social changes.

In this century the traditional mediums have lost many of their old functions, so that even when the office is filled today, its occupant is often inactive. Only those mediums who have some success in helping individuals and families with their problems and in predicting for groups the outcome of events (especially sports events), function today; and these, too, will probably gradually die out.

When the Germans occupied Palau and the Palauans lost their nominal political independence, the medium's political power was curtailed. The Germans began removing the old "shamans" from office, apparently with the cooperation of some of the chiefs (Vidich 1949:60). The Christian missionaries also immediately attacked the mediums, but their greatest challenge came from the development of Modekngei, a new "Palauan" religion.

Modekngei

During changing times and conditions from the beginning of this century, use was made of supernatural manifestations to support changes in Palauan society. A new religion, Modekngei, developed. Originally, Modekngei made use of possession trance ideas, but these diminished in importance quite early, perhaps because Modekngei leaders were opposed to the traditional mediums. Modekngei developed mediums of its own who used techniques quite different from those of the old spirit mediums. Modekngei had two aspects: on the one hand, it tried to supplant the old religion, and on the other, it opposed the new ways being imposed on the Palauans by the Japanese. The importance of Modekngei has diminished in recent years, partly because American policy has not been as directly inimical to the traditional social order as was that of the Japanese.

Although possession trance is an old technique in Palau for contacting the supernatural, it served as only one method among many. A variety of strange behaviors were interpreted as special contacts with the gods, even though these contacts did not necessarily lead to official positions. It was possible for a man to build a reputation and a following based on such supernatural contacts. In times of stress, recognized mediums and others would be more likely to have supernatural experiences. Such times are ripe for new movements to develop, for people are looking for signs and portents to tell them what to do. One such period in Palau occurred just before and immediately following World War I. At that time, the German administration was deliberately trying to break the continuity of the old traditions by forbidding the mediums to practice. Many were put into the prison on Yap.

During this period an abortive movement was headed by a man named Rdiall (or Ardiall), who set himself up as a herald of future changes in the Palauan way of life. In 1905 he built a nontraditional frame house near Ngkeklau, erected a flagpole near the house, and began to till the soil—a most un-Palauan thing for a man to do. Although of low rank, he was able to gain a following through his shamanistic activities, but his movement had died out by the time the Japanese arrived in 1914 (Vidich 1949:83). He did, however, set a pattern for the later development of Modekngei.

The history of the Modekngei cult has been described in some detail by Vidich (1949) and Barnett (1949). Modekngei, which means "get together," was founded by a man named Temudad, who came from a rather high-ranking *kebliil* within the hamlet of Ol in Ngaraard. (Actually, though he had been adopted into this *kebliil*, he was born into a low-ranked clan.) He was employed by the Germans as a constable, and spent some time on Yap. When the Japanese came, he enrolled in a carpentry course in Koror. There he met two men who were to become very important in his movement: Ongesii and Rengul. In 1916 he had his first "seizure," possibly epileptic, and related that he had "contacted" the village god (*chelid belu*) of Ol and that this god had given him special powers to change foods that were taboo. At times he appeared to be "possessed," according to informants cited by Barnett (1949:216). He told the people they could now eat bananas, which had been taboo in that area. When he ate bananas and did not suffer for it, the people were amazed, and his reputation was established. He was then joined by Ongesii and Rengul.

The movement grew and spread, gaining the support of many of the old chiefs (but not the high chiefs), and came to be considered a political threat by the Japanese. Temudad died in the 1920s, and the movement was then dominated by Ongesii, who was a strong organizer rather than a visionary.

Under Ongesii the movement took a more nativistic turn; foreign songs and foods were forbidden, for example (Barnett 1949:219). The main features of the movement at this time were curing with various concoctions of leaves, large gatherings to collect money for the gods, and the establishment of various functionaries in each district. Ongesii did not go into trance. A number of elements from Christianity were fused with old beliefs, although Modekngei was presented by its leaders as the only true Palauan way. Some strange events were arranged; for example, on one occasion Ongesii made the spirit of a dead boy play his harmonica. However, possession trance did not play a part in Modekngei observances. According to all informants on the subject, the god spoke to the leader in whistling noises, which the leader then interpreted to the people.

Today, of course, fact has merged with legend in the minds of Modekngei adherents. Temudad, the founder, is now considered semidivine, sent by God to lead the Palauans. It is his spirit that directs the movement, communicating by whistling noises with the present leader. The movement is antiwhite and antiforeign in orientation.

Modekngei was opposed by the high chiefs and those

Palauans who identified with the Japanese administration. Modekngei's main centers were those areas farthest from the Japanese centers: Ngaraard, Ngerchelong, Ngerdmau, Ngeremlengui, Ngetbang, Aimeliik, and Peliliu. It was also opposed by the old mediums, because from its inception, Modekngei leaders undermined the position of these mediums. They were said to be evil, making much money at the expense of poor Palauans, and it was claimed by Modekngei leaders that they worked black magic against people. Those opposed to Modekngei, on the other hand, made similar charges against the Modekngei leaders. Basically, the Modekngei leaders were trying to take over the functions of the traditional mediums, such as curing and the making of predictions. It is significant that those areas that are strong centers of Modekngei today no longer have functioning traditional mediums.

The Japanese began investigating and prosecuting Modekngei leaders in the 1920s. Both Temudad and Ongesii were jailed for a while, at that time. These activities culminated in 1937, when Ongesii was tried and sent to prison on Saipan, where he died after the Americans came. The movement went underground; Rengul became the leader, a position he still held in 1966. Just before and during World War II, Modekngei reached its peak of influence among Palauans. Immediately following World War II, after the arrival of the Americans, Modekngei reached a low point, and very few people would admit to belonging to the movement. Modekngei has never recovered its former momentum. This is at least partly due to the differences between American and Japanese policy. The Japanese had tried to convert clan lands into private property, undercutting the power of the old chiefs, and to limit the old money exchange system; but the Americans returned clan lands and made no direct attack on the old social system. Because the old chiefs no longer felt so threatened, they abandoned their support of Modekngei. Another possible factor in Modekngei's decline is that because Americans are generally Christians, the Palauans may have felt that they should associate more closely with Christianity. The Japanese had made no attempt to teach Palauans anything about Buddhism or Shinto, but had, rather, encouraged Christian missionaries.

In any case, perhaps one-third of the Palauans belong to Modekngei today. Much secrecy surrounds this religion, however, and it was not possible to get much information about present-day practices and beliefs.

A Famous Modekngei Medium

There is one famous Modekngei medium in Ngetbang. Many stories were told to the author about Modekngei mediums who could contact the dead, but these stories could all be traced back to this woman. She is apparently not a "leader," but acts simply as a medium for consultations.

One client described his consultation with her. This man is not a Modekngei, but a Protestant. His daughter had died in Guam, and the family suspected that her death was due to the magic of a particular "medium" in Ngiwal. It took him six months to arrange a consultation with the medium. On the day set for the consultation, he, his wife, and one son arrived after dark. When they went in the house, the medium gave them a red pillow that she placed in front of them "like a table." While she was doing this, a whistling noise started in the lefthand corner of the room, behind them. It gradually drew closer to the medium and grew louder. The medium said, "That is your daughter calling you." The client wondered if this were true. The son had written out the questions in English (this happened about 1961) on a piece of paper, which he placed on the pillow. The medium was able to answer these questions, or rather, to translate the whistling of the dead daughter, even though she, the medium, did not know English. This convinced the client of her authenticity. The daughter, through the medium, confirmed the family's suspicions about her death: she said that she had died of heart disease caused by the medium in Ngiwal. The client asked the daughter whether she knew that her older brother was in the American army in Germany. She said that she did and that she stayed with him most of the time. She said that she wanted her father and brother to quit drinking hard liquor and smoking and, interestingly enough, to attend Protestant services. She told them not to go to Modekngei mediums too often because they might then stop believing in the Protestant religion. She concluded by saying "good-bye" to her brother in English. The medium was seated and spoke in a normal tone of voice during the entire meeting.

References to other mediums who may be Modekngei were found in conversation; one has been mentioned for Ngiwal. In Kayangel there is a woman from the highest clan who, it is said, can stop typhoons by beating the ocean with a special paddle held traditionally by her family. There are no longer traditional mediums in either of these places, and both have long been centers of Modekngei.

Present Distribution of Mediums— Traditional and Modekngei

The amount of direct foreign contact and control and the existence of Modekngei are, no doubt, the most important features in the distribution of traditional mediums today. Koror, the district center under both the Japanese and Americans still has at least two practicing mediums, however. Also, although northern Babeldoab and Kayangel have long been centers of Modekngei, there are still a few traditional mediums there. In Koror, hamlets vary in their affiliations. Ngeramid, for example, is strongly Modekngei and has no traditional medium. Other localities are more mixed in affiliations. Many Catholics and Protestants do not hesitate to patronize mediums. Peliliu has a traditional medium now—the chief—but was influenced by Modekngei at one time. The chief of Angaur said that he was, and had been since 1915, a Christian, and did not know anything about traditional mediums in Angaur. Nearly all of Angaur is Catholic. Other sources indicated that perhaps there are mediums in Angaur, but that they operate in relative secrecy.

Other Contacts with the Supernatural

As indicated previously, mediums other than those officially recognized can go into possession trance today. In Ngiwal and Ngchesar no one holds the title of medium any longer. However, the local god might possess anyone in the village, thereby making that person a sort of temporary medium. If one wishes the god to enter him, he can chew a quantity of betel nuts and eat no other food. This will make him get "hot"; he will begin to tremble and the god will enter. In this state the "medium" can predict the outcome of a baseball game, for example. The person so possessed will say the opposite of what he means. This behavior no longer leads to appointment as an official medium in these municipalities. This type of possession was not found in any other area in Palau, however, during the course of fieldwork.

There are still other people who have strange experiences in predicting the future, but who have no official status in this capacity. Such people, who are known for their premonitions, are regarded with awe by the

165

Palauans, and anything they might say is carefully interpreted. Several instances may be cited from field notes.

Not long ago, a group of Palauans were sitting and talking; one woman, noted for such experiences, suddenly fell back. She then sat up and said to another woman, "Why is your father crying?" The second woman did not know what she was talking about; but later when she was walking down the path to go home she found her father crying. A special friend of his had died in a neighboring village, and he had stopped to compose himself before coming to tell the others.

During the German occupation in Ngaraard (a center of such behavior, evidently) there was a man "to whom the gods came." When this happened, he would wander through the village. He would not speak, but would act out things or draw pictures of coming events. For example, it is said that toward the end of World War I he made two flags, one German and one Japanese. He put up the Japanese flag before anyone knew the Japanese were coming. When they arrived, the flag was there. On another occasion, he drew a picture showing very thin people with knives, and, in less than a year, there was a food shortage in Palau. Once he did speak. When the father of the informant who told these stories was to make a trip to Japan, there was a large going-away party for him. This man to whom the gods came began to cry in the middle of the party. He said, "Let us all cry," but would not explain why he had said this. The informant's father died while he was in Japan. This man did not come from a special clan and held no title, but the people of Ngaraard believed he was like a "professor" and that he could foretell the future. He died during Japanese times.

In addition to cases such as the above, Palauans have their share of "ghost stories": mysterious strangers who appear in the dark and walk beside a person, then disappear; strange and sudden deaths caused by magic, and so on. These always make for interesting conversation and serve to supply explanations for unusual events.

Palauans do not seem to have any elaborate set of theories or explanations of the causes of possession trance, such as exist in some societies. It is generally felt that the spirits of the dead retain an interest in this world, especially in their own families and clans, and that therefore they must not be offended. The same is true for their gods, for Palauans still know something of their old gods, even though the structure of their old religion is gone. The gods are often present, so people must be careful not to offend them. Possession trance is one way of contacting the gods, but it is not the only, nor probably the most important, one today.

Illness and the Supernatural

It is still firmly believed by many that offended gods can cause illness and insanity. Although the idea of spirit entry causing illness is a common one in Micronesia, Palauans do not usually explain illness in this way. The idea is not absent, however, for there are instances of illness associated with spirit entry. An example, according to an older female informant, is illness that causes fever and delirium. The patient may even get up and walk around in a trance-like state. This could be due to a spirit entering the body; and if the patient fights taking medicine, it is because the spirit resists being driven out. She also said that sometimes a male spirit will become interested in an attractive woman and enter her, causing illness.

The reverse case, a goddess entering a man, can also happen, according to other informants. A man may become "possessed" by a goddess from the sea. When this happens, he acts like a woman; at the same time

167

he is enabled to catch a lot of fish and will want to go fishing all of the time. It will make him very nervous if he cannot fish. In the old days people would not keep seashells in their houses—it would be an invitation for such sea goddesses to come in and cause trouble. In the particular case described, the man's wife became sick. The goddess caused this illness because she was jealous of the wife. The people at the hospital could not help the wife, so the family called in a magician who gave the husband some medicine that made him sick at first, but cured him. He also gave some ointment to the wife, but once the husband was cured, his wife got better also.

There is a distinction between trance states and insanity. Insanity is not considered to be caused by spirit possession. A person who acts strangely because he is possessed by a god is not considered insane. Of course, it is sometimes hard for Palauans to judge whether a person is "crazy" or is showing symptoms of possession. Such cases have to be proved one way or the other over time, and are judged individually. A person who behaves strangely, but whose behavior turns out to have some relevance to future events as they occur, will be considered to have special contacts with the gods rather than to be insane.

Palauans recognize a number of categories of mental illness. One kind of insanity, called *delboi a reng* or *delboi (a rengul)*, occurs if a person has offended some god, and the god "breaks his heart"—makes him insane as a punishment. This type of insanity is not severe or disabling; the affected person is just rather strange at times. Seizures, such as in epilepsy, are caused by the gods also. The term is *besangelel (a chelid* is understood), which means "slapped by a god."

Sometimes a medium or magician can cause a person to become insane, as in the case of the thief described earlier. A common form of insanity caused by magic is *kebelung*. A person who is *kebelung* withdraws from people and refuses to speak. A person who talks irrationally and wildly most of the time is *melebeseyaol*. He is like a person who is very drunk. The behavior of a person intoxicated by liquor is associated with trance-like behavior. A drunken person is not considered to be possessed, however. *Eltelaol* is the usual term for drunkenness.

Betel: A Possible Trance-inducing Agent?

There is one more factor to be considered in the study of trance in Palau: the possibility of the use of trance-inducing drugs. The only agent used by Palauans that might fall into this category is the betel nut. The betel mixture, as used in Micronesia, consists of the nut of the areca palm *(Areca catechu)* sliced in half and lime prepared from coral, wrapped in the leaf of the betel pepper plant *(Piper betel)*. This mixture is put into the mouth, and the resulting cud is chewed. The saliva turns bright red and is expectorated from time to time, although some of it is swallowed. The mouth and teeth are stained, but the staining can be removed by brushing the teeth. Betel is used over a wide area, from southern India, across southeast Asia, and into the Pacific islands.

Some chemical interaction must occur when all of these ingredients are combined, but the exact products of this interaction have never been actually analyzed as far as can be determined. Chemical analysis shows no one agent in the ingredients of the betel mixture that can be considered as a primary trance-inducing agent[4] (Hayman 1965).

The vast majority of Palauans are inveterate betel chewers and are never far from their betel containers. The continual chewing of betel does not appear to interfere with their daily activities, any more than smoking cigarettes might, but the physiological effects of betel have not been throughly investigated anywhere as far as can be determined.

Although the use of betel is an important element in the trance ceremonies in Palau, almost all evidence indicates that as a rule it is not used to induce trance. For example, in Ngerdmau the traditional medium did not use betel nut at all in his possession trance ceremonies. (The holder of the title as of 1966 was not active in office.) Indeed, there are other areas in Micronesia where betel is chewed, but it plays no part in trance. For example, according to informants, the Carolinians of Saipan—that is, descendents of people who settled in Saipan from some of the small islands of the western Truk district—still have a few mediums who go into possession trances. The Carolinians in general are very fond of betel; but when the spirits come to the mediums, they demand coconuts and perfume, not betel.

The possibility that betel can be used to induce trance cannot be eliminated entirely, however. Informants from Ngiwal and Ngchesar said that a person can induce trance by fasting and then chewing a large quantity of betel rapidly. Other informants indicated that chewing a great quantity of betel after not chewing it for a while can make one dizzy and "drunk" and that taking a little sugar will overcome this. Also, the effects of betel evidently vary with different individuals.

Variations in the proportions, kinds, and qualities of ingredients might also be important factors. The author was told that more lime in the mixture makes it more effective. It has already been noted that tobacco is forbidden in the god's special mixture, although it is sometimes mixed with betel for everyday chewing.

Betel is apparently not used in Modekngei rites and was, indeed, outlawed by Modekngei leaders at one time, without much success.

Much certainly remains to be learned about the effects

SPIRIT MEDIUMS IN PALAU

of betel. For present purposes it can only be said that betel is probably not the primary agent in trance behavior in Palau. However, further study needs to be made of the lives, reactions, and habits of the trancers in Palau before the various physiological or psychological factors can be properly weighed.

The Palauan "Personality": Adaptability and Anxiety

During this century pressure on the old-style mediums has come from the government authorities, from the Christian religion, and from Modekgnei. Many of their old functions have been usurped by other religions, and they no longer serve important political functions within their villages. In spite of these changes some old style mediums still practice and are consulted, along with Modekngei mediums and other diviners and magicians, for their diagnostic and prognosticating abilities. The fact that Palauans seem to feel the need to consult many different supernatural agents is most certainly a reflection of the uncertainties and anxieties they feel in their attempts to adapt to the vast changes that have occurred in their social environment.

Palauans are not typically introspective or solitary. They do not seek religious experiences for their own sake. They are not interested in trance experiences as such, but only seek aid from the supernatural as a guide in their activities here on earth. This may explain why possession trances have declined so quickly in importance. Palauans never had a deep emotional attachment to such experiences; they considered them to be one of many ways of finding out how to further one's own interests or to discover the reasons for one's misfortunes.

Of all of the people of the Carolines the Palauans have been the most willing to learn new ways and have proved most adaptable. Palauan adaptability and competitiveness have helped them succeed in many areas. Palauans today hold many jobs in the administration in Palau and on Saipan, the administrative center of the trust territory, and many Palauans work on Guam. Jobs with the administration or on Guam offer members of low-ranked clans opportunities they could not have had at home to enhance their positions and to bring money to their clans.

This success has a concomitant psychic toll, however. Many Palauans seem to feel anxious and insecure and to seek some sort of assurances for their actions wherever they can find them. Rorschach and TAT tests given to Palauans in the late 1940s indicated that Palauans felt great anxiety, a sense of inferiority, and have great difficulty in making decisions (Barnett 1961:15 ff).

Much of Palauan adaptability and anxiety has its roots in traditional Palauan culture. Although traditional Palauan society might appear on the surface to have been rigidly structured, in its operation it required great adaptability in the individual. Children were taught from early childhood to be able to adjust to new households and not to form too many close personal attachments. At the same time, Palauans were adaptable for a purpose: they shifted locations and groups to enhance their opportunities for obtaining the things most valued by their culture—wealth, position, and power. Palauans were under pressure to compete for these things, and the exchange system under which wealth and power were achieved required considerable flexibility, adaptability, or deviousness, along with a surface amiability.

At the same time individual security depended on membership in the *kebliil*. It was the most important and stable unit of Palauan society, providing protection and care to its members, even as their lives were ordered according to clan interests. Traditionally, to be without clan membership is to be outside Paulauan society, with no access to land or the means of obtaining basic necessities. Today, the individual knows still that his clan will look after him.

The foregoing pattern carries over into the present time, with an additional factor—a "generation gap." Young people go wherever they can get good jobs: to Koror, Saipan, or Guam. When these people have children, they are expected to let grandparents or other relatives "adopt" the children. Thus, Babeldoab villages appear to be filled with old people and children. The young people live and work elsewhere and send money back to the family. The most stable unit in Palauan society is still the clan. It is even more important today, because for all practical purposes, many of the other traditional institutions, such as the men's clubs and the old religious structure, are gone. Today, individual Palauans may sometimes resent their clan obligations and, at times, try to evade them. However, clans remain strong and serve, perhaps, as the most important factor in holding Palauans together as a people, even when they are away from home.

Palauans have always measured their own worth against the achievements of others rather than through internalized standards. In the traditional culture, roles and statuses were clear cut, and relationships with other people were formalized so that the individual knew what was expected of him in different situations. Today, however, Palauans have had their sense of the value of Palauan ways severely attacked by the advent of three powerful foreign cultures. In addition to this, they are faced with new and more fluid situations that they find difficult to evaluate. Even under the Japanese things were simpler, according to some older informants. Even though Japanese rule could be harsh, the Palauans knew exactly what was expected of them. However, it is a tribute to Palauan drive and ability that the shocks they have

173

suffered in this century have not defeated them or made them try to withdraw from the present situation, but instead have made them try to turn the situation to their advantage.

Today, there are three generations of Palauans—the very old, who learned some German and German culture; a sizable generation that absorbed a good deal of Japanese culture and language (Japanese movies and music are still very popular in Palau); and the younger generation that has learned the English language and American ways. One older informant said that even people who grew up under the Japanese rule believed in the old gods and magic, but that the younger generation who have been educated by the Americans no longer know, or believe in, the old ways. "Modern" beliefs will no doubt continue to encroach upon the old Palauan system. The traditional mediums are not being replaced, and at the time of the author's visit in 1966 there did not appear to be any resurgence of Modekngei. Palauans have not found any one religion or set of answers for their needs. Indeed, it does not appear to be their "nature" to do so. In spite of their anxieties and, perhaps, their indecisiveness, they are too eclectic or pragmatic to "put all their eggs in one basket," so to speak. Success is their criterion for judging new ideas or ways of doing things.

In the past five years change has been proceeding even faster. Since the author's fieldwork, in 1966, a large contingent of Peace Corps volunteers has entered Palau, teaching English language and American ways, directly and indirectly. The area has been opened up to tourists, and transportation has become easier to obtain. The twentieth century is moving in on Palau faster than ever, and it is to be expected that the old ways, perhaps even the clan system, may finally break down under this impact.

Certainly it is worth watching to see how Palauans meet these further challenges. Observation of their ability

174

to live with rapid changes in institutions is a study very relevant to all men of the twentieth century.

SUMMARY

Palau is an interesting example of rapid, overwhelming cultural change. Changes in the traditional use of possession trance are but one facet of the entire culture change.

Palau was traditionally a stratified society in which interpersonal relationships were more or less formalized. However, individuals within this society were expected to strive to achieve wealth, position, and power. Although titles and statuses were inherited, such inheritance was not guaranteed. One had to do considerable maneuvering, through an elaborate system of exchange, to achieve and keep wealth and status. Ranks and wealth were not fixed eternally, but could change: therefore, a premium was placed on cleverness and ability to adapt.

The old Palauan religion had a system of hierarchically placed gods, similar in structure to Palauan society. In addition, ancestral spirits and ghosts were important. Operating within this system was the traditional spirit medium. This was a man, or woman, whom the appropriate god would enter in a possession trance to speak to the people. In this state, the medium could diagnose the causes of misfortunes or illnesses and predict the outcome of various events. Through the god, he could influence political decisions, such as going to war. The office of spirit medium was a powerful one, politically and religiously.

Under the impact of the German, Japanese, and American administrations in this century, Palauan culture has undergone many changes. The influence of the old-style medium has declined. Political control has been taken over by colonial governments and those Palauans who support them. The structure of the old religion has broken down and has been, in part, replaced by a new native religion, Modekngei, and to some extent by imported Christian religions. Today, where the traditional medium functions he is an agent—one of many—for contacting the supernatural to answer questions for Palauans who want help and assurances about various events in their lives.

Traditional mediums still use possession trance, but the exact way this state is induced and proceeds seems to vary from one medium to another. They do not use drugs to induce possession trance. In theory it just happens to the proper person for the office, whether he is selected by a council or directly by the god.

Not many people in Palau today are possession trancers, and those that practice this activity are nearly all old people, more of them men than women. The importance of possession trance as a supernatural device has declined rapidly in this century with the decline of the old office of spirit medium. It would seem that possession trance, as an experience, has not been of critical emotional value to the Palauans, and it has found no new niche in the institutions of the Palauans of today.

1. The total population of Palau in 1970 was 12,525, with distribution proportionately the same; figures from the Office of Territories, Department of the Interior.

2. Data are confusing. Useem (1949:13) says the most important and stable unit is the *blai*, "household," which has a traditional homesite. Informants stated that the *kebliil* is the local clan—one that has its home in a particular place, while the *klebliil* is made up of *kebliils* from all over Palau. Barnett (1949:201) says each clan had a traditional homesite. The term *blai* is of interest because the gods of the clan are called *chelid a blai* or "gods of the household."

3. A few references for those interested in the history of Palauan money are: Roland W. Force, "Palauan money: some preliminary comments on material and origin," *Journal of the Polynesian Society* 68, no. 1 (1959); Douglas Osborne, *Archeology of the Palau Islands: An intensive study* (Honolulu, Hawaii: Bernice P. Bishop Museum Press, 1966); Robert E. Ritzenthaler, *Native money of Palau*, Milwaukee Museum Publication in Anthropology, no. 1 (Milwaukee, Wis., 1954).

4. There was one medium, a man, now dead, who may have been a sexual deviate, but only scanty information was obtained.

5. For a summary of what could be discovered from the literature about betel, its ingredients, physiological effects, and distribution, I am indebted to Mrs. Mildred Hayman for her paper, "A survey of the use, distribution, and physical properties of the betel nut (*Areca catechu*)" (1965). Dr. Richard Evans Schultes, Head of the Harvard Museum of Economic Botany, who is the ranking authority on psychotropic plant substances confirms that there are no hallucinogenic agents in the betel mixture. He states, however, that there are instances in the literature where "trances, dreams, visions, and so forth are induced by plant preparations in which no hallucinogenic substances are known to exist" (personal communication, 1972).

REFERENCES

Barnett, H. G. 1949. *Palauan Society*. Eugene, Ore.: University of Oregon Press.

———. 1961. *Being a Palauan*. New York: Holt, Rinehart and Winston.

Bourguignon, Erika. 1968. "World distribution and patterns of possession states," in *Trance and possession states* (editor Raymond Prince). Montreal: R. M. Bucke Memorial Society.

U.S. Department of State. 1964–65. *Eighteenth Annual Report to the United Nations on the administration of the trust territory of the Pacific Islands*. Statistical Appendices. Washington: Government Printing Office.

Hayman, Mildred. 1965. "A survey of the use, distribution and physical properties of the betel nut (*Areca catechu*)." Working paper no. 3, Cross-cultural study of Dissociational States. Columbus: The Ohio State University, Department of Anthropology.

McKnight, R., and A. Obak. 1960. "Taro cultivation in Palau." Anthropological Working Papers, no. 6. January 1960.

McManus, Edwin, S. J. 1964. "Grammar and dictionary: Palau-English and English-Palau." Unpublished.

Useem, John. 1949. "Report on Palau." Coordinated Investigation of Micronesian Anthropology, no. 3. June 1949.

Schultes, Richard E. 1972. Personal communication.

Vidich, A. J. 1949. "Political factionalism in Palau: Its rise and development." Coodinated Investigation of Micronesian Anthropology, no. 23. June 1949.

5 : Apostolics of Yucatán: A Case Study of a Religious Movement

Felicitas D. Goodman

INTRODUCTION

Mexico, the largest of the Mesoamerican states, covering 758,259 square miles, has been an independent country since 1821, when it broke away from the crumbling Spanish empire. Its double heritage, Spanish and Indian, very much determines the physiognomy of modern Mexico. But though the Spanish, dominant society has a single origin, the Indian side is characterized by a bewildering diversity, in that each region manifests the characteristics of the indigenous tribe.

Thus it is also in the case of Yucatan.[1] The Yucatecan Peninsula was and still is the country of the Maya Indian (see Redfield 1941). It is here that part of the classical Maya civilization flourished. And, although the Spaniards arrived centuries after it had collapsed, the sedentary Maya population stubbornly resisted their advance and then their domination: there was a bloody uprising as late as 1761 (Reed 1964). The present political division of the peninsula into the states of Yucatán, Campeche, and the Federal Territory of Quintana Roo is the result of yet another uprising of the Maya peasantry against their *Ladino* (Spanish, dominant society) overlords and the Mexican state that they represented. This was the Caste War, which started in 1847 and did not really end until the beginning of this century. Even today, Yucate-

178

cans feel allegiance not to *La República* (that is, Mexico) but to *La Peninsula,* or *Yucatán.*

The same language, with minor dialect variations, is spoken all over this territory: Yucatecan Maya. In contrast to many other Amerindian languages, Maya seems to be in no imminent danger of being obliterated. At present (1972), it is even being used in radio advertising. However, the ability to speak Spanish carries prestige, and it is the language of all official business and public transactions, including church services.

In the following discussion, historical Yucatán will be considered the larger society of which the village of Utzpak* and its Apostolic congregation form a part.

Power, Class Structure, and Prestige

Historical Yucatán, that is, the states of Yucatán and Campeche, and the Territory of Quintana Roo, covers 139,810 square miles and has, as of the 1960 census, a population of 832,437 inhabitants. In theory, its politial system, determined by the liberal Mexican constitution, is republican. Power rests in the hands of elected and appointed officials, and the transfer is by constitutional means. The cultural belief about status is egalitarian, status being accorded by achievement.

The social reality is, of course, considerably more complex. Yucatán, in fact, harbors two societies: the very rich, historically the heirs of the Spanish conquerors, and the others. The former have ascribed status and, in keeping with their economic strength, possess a disproportionately high concentration of political power. In this study, we will do no more than recognize the separateness of this caste and will concern ourselves with *the others.*

This part of society divides roughly into two strata,

* Not its real name.

179

the urban and the rural, with some mobility possible between them. The peasant's son can become a trader (a well-developed role before the Conquest), a university student, a priest, a minister, or a teacher; or he can assume a number of roles provided by the (limited) development of industry, especially tourism. However, in the order of seriousness from the least to the most, the following factors may hinder passage from the rural into the urban sphere: a Maya surname (although not an Indian phenotype), illiteracy, peasant manners and dress, and insufficient knowledge of Spanish. Considerable cleavage between the two strata is indicated, at the behavioral level, by the discrimination, condescension, and paternalism on the part of the urban segment and by the defensiveness, withdrawal, and ambivalence of the rural peasant.

Economy and Wealth

The backbone of the Yucatán's economy is the cultivation of corn and beans. Henequen, an industrially used fiber, is still important, despite its declining role in the world market. In addition, there is cattle-breeding, honey and wax production, and, of increasing significance, the tourist industry.

Beginning in the 1940s, industrial goods of considerable attractiveness and prestige have become increasingly available in the peninsular markets, in the stores of Mérida, or from local traders who buy through the various free ports, especially Chetumal. Yet a large part of the peasantry has no possibility of earning the necessary cash to acquire a satisfying portion of these goods, mainly because the increase in trade has not been accompanied by a comparable growth in industry that would provide the necessary jobs. Simultaneously, there has been a decline in the traditional employment opportunities. On the henequen ranches, a two-days-a-week schedule is the rule. In the spring of 1970, the state governments tried to force the large ranches to pay a minimum wage to the farmhands. According to Utzpak informants, many ranchers reacted by dismissing their help and converting to cattle. Also, the Maya peasant, lacking training and experience in Euroamerican methods of money management is not able to take advantage of economic opportunities actually available, such as bank credits from the Banco Agrario at low (4%) interest rates for purchasing seeds. The Maya householder continues to work *a su cuenta* (self-employed), preferring to consume what he produces and neither borrowing money nor repaying debts. Thus, because of the growing population (Utzpak had 3,433 inhabitants in 1960; 5,232 in 1970), more land should be cultivated; yet the ejido² land lies fallow. The majority of the peasants do not own land except for the plots on which their homes stand, which includes the *sembrado* (household garden). The owners of large tracts of land are urban, although not necessarily absentee, landlords. Thus both inside the henequen belt and outside of it (where Utzpak is located), the peasant is caught between increasing felt needs and shrinking opportunities for local wage labor.

Neither has Yucatán, on the peasant level, participated in the "Green Revolution" that is spreading in Mexico proper, with its intensified cultivation and diversification of crops. As Utzpak informants tell it, agricultural agents, trained elsewhere, are at a loss about how to help peasants faced with an exhausted soil in an area where not even the plough can be introduced due to the geology: a Maya farmer works the humus that collects in the holes eroded into the limestone shelf that is Yucatán. Nothing is done either on the community or state levels to combat the diseases of poultry and hogs that every year decimate the smallholder's stock.

Thus, in more and more peasant families in Yucatán,

181

so it is said, *¢'aal* is practiced. This means that for a family meal there is *one* hardboiled egg to which each one may touch his *tortilla*. Or, as one informant put it, "If they have to *buy* corn, what will they do for beans?"

Under these circumstances, the exchange of goods between the urban centers and the villages is unbalanced. Merchandise flows toward the population centers outside the cities, but the peasant can sell little produce, since there is no industry to process it. The most important contribution of the villages to the economy of the larger society is people. Young girls go to Mérida or even further to work as housemaids; men, to labor on the roads and in the forests. Boys and some girls attend school in the provincial centers such as Motul, then go on to Mérida, which houses the University of Yucatán, and eventually seek employment elsewhere in the republic, preferrably in the capital.

It follows that there is a great deal of movement of people on the highways and byways of Yucatán. Young peasant couples usually travel to the market together. Older men travel alone; in addition to business concerns, they are frequently on errands originating in their religious lives. Women travel on different occasions, keeping kin relations active, taking their young children with them, and doing their shopping. Peasant women often undertake, alone, extended trading trips, involving transportation by bus, hiring horses to reach outlying villages, or hiking over jungle paths. The more a woman is involved with city ways, the more she assumes a pattern of dependency, expecting her husband to take her on trips (for example, to her mother's house for delivery). Even higher on the social scale, the expectation is for a woman to have a female companion. Change of residence is freely available, and neolocal is preferred over patrilocal and matrilocal residence.

Religious Structure

The religion of Yucatán is Catholic, with its fixed rites and central authority. Since, according to the Mexican constitution, state and church are separated, Prostestant missionizing has been going on for some time without hindrance from the authorities. The Presbyterians, for example, came to Yucatán before World War I. Once a person has left the Catholic church, he roams quite freely among the many Protestant groups. This mobility is not restricted to the men; in many instances the woman takes the initiative and joins a Protestant group, and the husband often, but not always, follows. Before coming to the Apostolic church, a number of members had contacts with such groups in Yucatán (although not all represented in Utzpak) as the Baptists, Jehovah's Witnesses, Latter-Day Saints, and Presbyterians.

The Advent of Pentacostalism

Pentecostalism is the single most important Protestant movement in Latin America in the twentieth century. Its rise has been so spectacular that Lalive d'Epinay (1968), in discussing its evolution in Chile, speaks of it as the Pentecostal explosion. In Mexico, the movement is represented by various churches, among them the Church of God, the Pentecostals, and the Apostolics. The latter differ mainly in their greater emphasis on the unitary aspect of the Trinity.

The start of the Apostolic church in Mexico goes back to 1914 to Mexicans who brought the movement with them from the United States. In 1964 (Gaxiola), the church had over one thousand ministers working in various parts of the country. Missionizing in the southeastern district, which comprises the peninsula of Yucatán, was begun in 1959, by an evangelist from Guadalajara named Oscar Gill. In 1970, there were seventeen established congregations on the peninsula, and several more have been started. (We may thus say that the growth of the Apostolic Church in Mexico has been every bit as rapid as elsewhere in Latin America, and it promises to have a similar evolution in Yucatán.)

Mechanism of Propagation

The Apostolic church in Yucatán spreads along the highways. In addition to the three cities of Mérida, Campeche, and Chetumal, fourteen villages had active congregations. All of these villages were on the highway. In contrast, when the minister from Holcá (on the highway), which had a Pentecostal congregation, together with some of his congregation members attempted to evangelize in Tibolón (accessible only by jungle path), they were driven off by violence. The daughter of a congregation member from Utzpak, married in Tibolón, was threatened with arson if she would allow a service to be held in her home.

After an initial, more-or-less accidental contact has been made between the evangelist and a few innovators (that is, persons who shift from denomination to denomination in search of a more satisfying religious experience) from some rural area, the new members are recruited predominantly along the arteries of the kinship network and within the villages: the success of the movement in the towns of Yucatán is negligible by comparison. This is interesting, first, because Lalive d'Epinay attributes part of the success of the Pentecostals in Chile to the fact that they appeal to the rootless, migrant population (in Utzpak all but two of the male members were born and raised there); second, Wolf (1966) and others feel that for the peasant, dyadic contracts—that is, two-

184

sided, personally based relations outside the kin group—are more important than kinship relations beyond the nuclear family; and third, because Redfield contends of the Maya (1941:211) that even on the village level there is "a disappearance of institutions expressing cohesion in the great family." On the basis of this pattern of propagation of the Apostolic church, we may be able to say that here is a new institution expressing cohesion in the "great family," which as a structure thus must be assumed to be latently available.

Speaking in Tongues

The central behavior of the Apostolic worship service is speaking in tongues. In the following I should like to summarize research results detailed elsewhere (Goodman 1969 *a,* 1969 *b,* 1971, 1972), that refer to this behavior. Speaking in tongues, or *glossolalia* (from Greek *glōssa* "tongue" + *lalia* "speech"), is an act of vocalization in trance. It is actually a behavior complex, consisting (and learned in this sequence)[3] first of all of a mental state in which a person is dissociated from ordinary reality— that is, he is largely unaware of what is going on around him. He does not perceive many ordinary stimuli, such as strong light, heat, sounds, or discourse directed at him. Instead, he has experiences not verifiable by an observer, such as pressure on his chest, floating, disappearance of persons around him, and so on. In physical terms, he is hyperaroused; his body works more intensely than under ordinary conditions, evidencing an accelerated pulse and heart beat, exaggerated perspiration, salivation, tear flow, flushing, and various patterns of motion.

Second, there is vocalization, that is is, glossolalia proper. This vocalization is superimposed on the hyperaroused state—in other words, it is learned while the person is dissociated. It has a very distinct pattern that does not vary from language to language: persons speaking various English dialects, Portuguese, Spanish, or Maya, all display the same pattern in this vocalization. A simplified description that concentrates only on what is relevant here follows. At the onset, a unit utterance of glossolalia—that is, a vocalization pattern (a sequence of syllables) uttered without a longer pause between its parts—is heard by the listener as being in the medium range of the usual range of the particular person's speech. It then rises to a peak that is perceivable as louder and more intense, often simply very fast[4] as compared with the rest of the vocalization or containing vowels and consonants that take more effort to pronounce than those that preceded (the *e* in eel, for example, takes more effort to form than the *a* in accompany). Finally, the utterance decays in dropping of the voice, but much faster and to a lower pitch and intensity than it does at the end of a sentence; in fact, the end of a glossolalia utterance is sometimes hardly audible.

Third, after the glossolalia has been uttered, most persons do not immediately return to ordinary reality. They remain on something like a platform; they are not as hyperaroused as before, but appear rather somewhat disoriented, their speech possibly a bit disturbed, sounding as if "squeezed" or drawn out (with overlong vowels), their recall of memory material halting. An important psychological correlate of this mental state is a considerable depression of inhibitions, making people say or do things that they would not if they were not in this altered mental state.

Finally, a dissolution of this residual hyperarousal takes place, and the person returns to ordinary reality. Very little of what an observer knows has taken place is remembered by the person who has been in this form of dissociation. He may not remember that he uttered anything, he recalls none of the movements the observer has recorded, and he does not know how much time has elapsed since the start of the episode. He does, however, remember the perceptions mentioned above, such as pressure on the chest and so forth.

The Apostolics believe quite generally that this "baptism of the Holy Spirit" will make them feel happy, relaxed, and full of hope. This agreement is probably due to cultural conditioning, which is a powerful force for shaping experience.

If we now draw a generalized pattern of the glossolalia utterance itself, we see a unit wave, with its medium onset, peak, and drop. I suggest that what happens during hyperarousal dissociation is that the person relinquishes a measure of cortical control over his own behavior. When he then superimposes the vocalization on this dissociated state, the brain structure that has taken over control forces its own processes upon the vocalization and gives it its particular form. In analogy to the deep-structure–surface-structure model suggested by transformational grammarians for ordinary language behavior, I propose that the hyperarousal trance acts as the deep structure for the glossolalia behavior. This altered state then invests the utterance with its cross-culturally uniform intonation pattern.[5] The intonation patterns (basic speech melodies) of ordinary languages are unique and vary greatly, as Hockett (1958:34) also points out. How speech melody affects Mayan, a tone language, is amply illustrated by Blair and Vermont-Salas (1967).

The vocalization behavior of the glossolalist is subject to change over time. We might say that in addition to the micropattern seen in the individual utterance, namely, that of a single wave, the evolution of the glossolalist's behavior also represents a wave. In most cases, he first learns to dissociate (although quite a number of people acquire the hyperarousal and the vocalization skill almost simultaneously.) This might be called the onset. He then

superimposes the vocalization. In the beginning this vocalization shows evidence of tremendous effort: it is usually very loud, of high intensity (perceived as the person
pressing the sounds out), and extremely fast. For a while,
he can maintain this level of energy discharge, which
is correlated with great euphoria and seems to make possible the dissolution of even considerable anxiety. This
is followed by a lessened intensity of the trance state,
when the utterance appears "stereotyped," that is, it
is repeated over and over in exactly the same form. But
later, usually within six months or so, it is no longer
possible to reach such high levels. The glossolalia utterance changes; the sounds that constitute the utterance
need less energy to form, the individual consonant-vowel
groups follow each other at greater intervals, that is,
speaking is slower, the unit utterance becomes longer,
and there are fewer utterances in an episode. Still later,
the glossolalia may become very short, just a phrase or
two. Quite often, only the dissociation can be achieved,
which in turn is merely of the level of the residual arousal
following the glossolalia described above.

The question now arises of how this attenuation is
interpreted on the emotional level. In other words: how
do people cope with having a cherished experience, as
it were, slip through their fingers? In the congregations
that I have studied, I have seen a number of different
responses. Some people take the drop in intensity of the
trance in their stride: they have had the experience; it
has fulfilled its function of identifying them with the group;
it has expressed their commitment; it has given them
the exhilaration of having participated in the baptisms
by the Holy Spirit; they have gone to the very pinnacle
of religious fulfillment. There is nothing that compels
them to demonstrate over and over again that, indeed,
this is so, and the demand was never made in any of
the sermons that I ever heard.

Some others become indifferent. The ecstasy has been tasted, it has faded, and new possibilities are explored; the person drifts away to other movements. But there is still another group, for whom the hyperarousal has brought an unexpected boon: it has freed them of severe anxieties. Attenuation for this group will have serious repercussions, in my opinion, in direct proportion to the magnitude of the anxiety suffered before experiencing the release produced by the trance. Some among them may blame themselves: the loss of ability to speak in tongues is interpreted as punishment for some transgression. Or their panic may become so intense that they will try through every means possible to recapture what they possessed before. In Yucatán I saw various attempts to accomplish this; and since they pertain to my discussion, I will briefly summarize them here.

There was a man in the Yucatecan congregation, called Emilio,[6] who tried to recover the previous intensity of his trance experience by pressing his arms against his chest, by offering very lengthy, extremely loud prayer, and by using various motion patterns that he probably identified as having occurred in his previous trances (they had not); he justified all this to the congregation as flowing from an overwhelming urge to pray for the sick.

In the second instance, that of Lorenzo, the minister, the panic was occasioned by a fear of relapse into "the ways of the world." He had a history of relapses and had conquered the last and very serious such episode by learning the trance behavior. The trance represented for him an insurance against a recurrence. When the intensity of the trance behavior began to wane, the threat of backsliding, a totally intolerable prospect for a minister, must have loomed very large indeed. He escaped into fanaticism and rejected the congregation that might become a witness to his failure.

Finally, in two other instances, the men involved,

189

Anselmo and Peregrino, pushed themselves, apparently by intense and prolonged prayer and concentration, into renewed hyperarousal. However, instead of returning to the level at which glossolalia normally occurs, they strayed into a new level, a hallucinatory experience, which my data prove to be of even greater intensity.

Normally, such psychological reactions would not extensively disturb the life of the congregation where they take place. For example, in the congregation that I studied in Mexico City there were members who had been converted forty years ago and others for whom speaking in tongues was a recent and new experience. Thus, there were glossolalists present in every stage of evolution, and individual attenuation experiences had no repercussions at the societal level. On the basis of theoretical considerations, however, it is conceivable that the majority of the members of a group might learn the trance behavior simultaneously, or nearly so. In this case, there would be a summation on the group level with each person reinforcing the behavior of all others. The following is the presentation of just such a case, which I had occasion to observe in Yucatán. Having already determined that the unit glossolalia utterance represents a wave and perceiving the evolution of the behavior in the individual over time as evidencing a similar pattern, I feel that the current data can best be presented as following the same course, which in my opinion, the events actually did.

COMMUNITY AND CONGREGATION

The Community

Utzpak is the terminal point on one of a number of highways penetrating outward from Mérida into the peninsula. By Redfield's (1941) criteria, it is a village, although a large one, with more than five thousand inhabitants according to the 1970 census. The majority of the population are Maya, and the rural way of life predominates. However, the regular bus connection with Mérida, the merchandise in the stores, the recently completed permanent market hall, the movie theater, and the children's clinic, all available because of the existence of the all-important paved highway, provide more contact with urban ways than would be available in the villages that can be reached only by footpaths through the bush.

Since the community lies outside of the henequen belt, there is more opportunity for the men of the village to find employment on the ranches, and thus, poverty is not as intense as in some of the communities to the west of it. There are 240 cattle ranches within the area, most of them with small holdings. The principal crops are maize and beans, predominantly produced by the householders for their own consumption.

The cleavage of the peninsular society into the *very rich* and *the others* is quite evident on the village level also. The few very rich have only tenuous ties with the village, even though some of them have roomy private homes there. Among the others the more affluent group is city-oriented. Their homes are square, constructed of stone and mortar, with tile floors and electricity. Some of the families possess television sets and cars. The men wear dark pants, white shirts with ties, and shoes; the women wear dresses. The children finish the local grade school and are sent on to school to Motul, or to Mérida. The lower stratum has oval mud-and-wattle houses, with dirt or, at most, cement floors. The men wear *alpargatas* (sandals) and white pants and a white jacket, which is a costume derived from the earlier peasant garb. Many of the women prefer the native embroidered dress, the 'ipil, to the Western-type clothes. Their children drop out of school after the second or third grade.

The majority of the people of Utzpak are Catholic.

According to the 1970 census, there are only about three hundred Protestants in the community, most of them Presbyterians, some Baptists, Pentecostals, and most recently, Apostolics. The very rich are Catholics, as are the destitute families without homes of their own. The Protestants represent a cross section of the lower and middle strata.

The Apostolics Come to Utzpak

In 1959, a Mexican evangelist coming from Guadalajara, named Oscar Gill, made some initial contacts in Mérida. One of the women he converted was Consuelo. Even at this early stage, the kinship system became operative. Consuelo's daughter-in-law was from Utzpak. It was her kin group there that furnished the initial converts of the community. They were joined by some neighbors and more relatives, and by the early summer of 1969, nine kin clusters[7] were represented in the congregation. By midsummer of 1970, of the 31 new members, only two joined from outside the already represented kin groups, and they promptly began their own clusters. Of the sixteen baptized on August 1, 1970, a single young girl was from outside the already existing clusters, and she did not persist with the congregation.

Of those who had started clusters in the above sense, six men and three women were available for interviews in 1969. Of the six men, five had a history of membership in, or at least intensive contact with, other Protestant groups before coming to the Apostolics, and all three women had had considerable knowledge of Protestantism. Other members of the clusters have no such history. Economically, the congregation is a cross section of the majority of the community, exclusive of the very rich and the destitute. All of the members are native Maya speakers.

From its inception late in 1959, the Utzpak congregation showed only sporadic growth. It was not until the arrival of Lorenzo, the new minister, early in the summer of 1969, that its membership began to increase at an accelerating rate. Why this happened is explained by the type of preacher this minister represented.

The successful ministers all over Yucatán, the leaders of growing congregations, had several characteristics in common. They were passionately committed to the belief that the Second Coming of Christ was imminent, and that this would result in the destruction of everything except the Apostolic church; that both baptism by water and speaking in tongues, indentified with a baptism by the Holy Spirit, were indispensible for entering into heaven or for participating in the Kingdom of God to be established with the Second Coming, but that speaking in tongues was incomparably more important than baptism by water. They were quite conversant with village ways. They themselves, however, represented the city both in background and in way of life. Thus they brought urban sophistication into the village churches. This was desirable, the peasant congregations felt, although there was considerable ambivalence toward city ways and accouterments. The popular ministers were also efficient in inducing the altered state of consciousness, leading to glossolalia. Lorenzo incorporated all of these traits.

At the time he took over as minister, the Apostolic congregation of Utzpak possessed a church building, as well as a schedule of fully structured church services. Yet it was practically moribund. Its preceding minister, who had left to attend some courses at a Bible Institute, was the exact opposite of Lorenzo. He was born in a Maya bush village. He did not demand tithing of his parishioners, always a sore point in the Maya congregation; he knew the Bible well, and his sermons were straightforward, well-composed exercises in exegesis.

His orations for the baptism of the Holy Spirit were gentle reminders of the power of the Lord. He had a fine singing voice and played the guitar well. Yet quite often, his congregation consisted only of his mother and one or two of the original members. Hardly any of his congregation members had ever spoken in tongues; and there was not a single woman who had engaged in the behavior. Rather, the congregation's life was expressed almost exclusively by male activity, and the women participated only passively. Of the *secciones*—sections usually present in other Apostolic churches, that is, the men's, women's, and young peoples' (*Señores cristianos, Dorcas,* and *Juveniles*)—only the male adult group was represented. There was no separate service for the children, who were simply tolerated during the regular church services.

Even at this point, however, the members of the Utzpak congregation differed from the dominant society in a number of ways. The elements for this culture change were provided by the Pentecostal movement. *Evangelios,* as they were called, used *Paz de Cristo*—Peace in Christ —as their greeting. The men were no longer violent, and they did not drink or gamble. The women did not wear jewelry, and the girls attended no dances. The families did not watch any movies. When marrying, they insisted on a formal wedding instead of the consensual union widely practiced in Yucatán (and in Latin-America generally). And principally, a number of them, especially ministers, engaged in speaking in tongues. This type of trance behavior was not available aboriginally in Yucatán. There was some spiritism in the cities, but it was an importation from the Mexican heartland. Being possessed (by a spirit) was termed witchcraft by the larger society. Several forms of this were supposedly practiced and deeply feared, and the ostracism of the members of the congregation centered on this point.

Two other areas of culture change had also emerged. One concerned health, the other economic posture, and both evolved in stark opposition to the attitudes of the dominant society. Although the community at large gave increased credence to Western medical practices, the congregation emphasized the possibilities for supernatural healing and, oblivious to Western categories of illness, included among the ills that could be healed by praying not only physical ailments but also anxieties over jobs, fear of crop failure, rejection, and other sources of depression.

In the economic range the members professed to work only to provide the basic necessities and to use free time, not for finding additional employment for further gain, but for learning new hymns, for prayer, Bible reading, or instructing the wife and family in religious matters.

The Church

The church was located on a side street in the central section of the village. It was built by its members on a plot contributed by one of the original members. It was constructed of mud and wattle, with a footing of limestone rock. It was square, had wooden shutters for windows, a cement floor, and a high, pointed roof of corrugated tar paper over a tied wooden structure. There was a raised cement platform in the back of the church, serving as an altar, with a rostrum and a small table on it. The table was placed down in front of the rostrum when the person in charge of all or part of the service did not have the rank of minister and, thus, was not allowed on the platform. The table then served as the rostrum. Women (and children) were never permitted to ascend the altar. There were wooden chairs for the adult members and some small benches for the children. The church was decorated with paper streamers, some drawings of biblical scenes made by a member from a neighboring community, embroidered cloths on the table and hanging from the rostrum, two flower vases, and some plastic chandeliers. There was electricity, and the congregation had the use of a well.

The altar platform ended at a man-high wall, closing off the back part of the building and yielding a single small room with a dirt floor, designated as the *casa pastoral,* the pastor's house. The whole property had recently (1970) been surrounded by a wall piled from limestone rock, an *albarrada.*

The Service

The most important recurring event in the life of the congregation was the service. There were services lasting from two to three hours on Tuesday, Thursday, and Saturday evenings; on Sundays, there was a service of prayer for the Holy Spirit from six o'clock until eleven in the morning, Sunday School from then until one, and another service in the evening. On special occasions, such as birthdays, additional services were held in private homes. A typical evening service began with a hymn, then a prayer was spoken by all while the congregation was still standing, but had not gone to the altar. A *corito* was sung, which was a short hymn that everyone knew by heart. (*Coritos* have a rousing melody and a fast rhythm.) The singing of both hymns and *coritos* was accompanied by a guitar and *marimbol* music (a native instrument with a square wooden body as a resonator and metal strips fastened to it for plucking) and by rattles emphasizing the rhythm. The beat of the music was further underlined by clapping, which became very intense during the *coritos.*

During the subsequent period, testimonies were offered. Various parishioners recited a biblical text, gave praise for some recent blessing, or requested prayers for a personal concern. After another hymn, and a *corito* often explicitly asking for the Holy Spirit to manifest itself, the congregation went to the altar, and following the seating plan, the men knelt on the right side, the women on the left. The prayer during this altar call was loud, with each person speaking in his own words. Glossolalia usually occured during these altar calls, which might last up to twenty minutes (on Sundays, they extended to an hour or longer). The altar call ended with a bell signal from the pastor. There was another hymn, then various members of the congregation offered hymns in praise. In sequence, there was a reading from the Bible, a *corito*, a prayer for the offering, and then the sermon. After another hymn, there was a second altar call, a hymn, and then a prayer for the sick, who were asked to come to the altar to be prayed for by the congregation.

CASE HISTORY

Medium Onset: The Evolution
During the Summer of 1969

News about the arrival of a good preacher traveled fast, and previous members who had stayed away for years returned within weeks after the arrival of Lorenzo. This phase in the evolution of the events in the Utzpak congregation could, on the societal level, be called the *medium onset* in the terms of the wave model that I have proposed at the outset, because when Lorenzo started working in Utzpak, two of the original members, as well as Lorenzo and his helper, a young man he had brought with him from Campeche, had recently acquired the glossolalia behavior. The returning members brought along others of their kin, so that from near extinction the membership rose to 24 adult members by the end

197

of August, with many more sympathizers attending the services regularly.

Lorenzo introduced the missing sections (of the women and the young people), and instructed the members in the parliamentary procedures needed for running their organizations. He hammered away at the importance of tithing, and gradually, the income from the congregation began to increase from near nothing to perhaps 50 pesos (about $4.00 U.S.) a week, half of which the minister could keep according to the rules within the Apostolic organization. He introduced the *talento,* an institution also used in other areas of the Republic, where the church supplied the money or materials needed, the sections, the labor, and the profit realized in the sale, be it a hammock, prepared food, or other, accrued to the church.

The greatest significance of Lorenzo's work in Utzpak however, was his skill in inducing the altered state, and in teaching the person in trance to superimpose the glossolalia behavior. In a pattern I have not seen in any other Apostolic congregation, he instructed those who desired to acquire the baptism of the Holy Spirit to kneel close to the altar. He then had those who already were in command of glossolalia to kneel behind them. The entire congregation, but principally the knowledgeable members, were then asked to pray a single formula only and nothing else. This was "Séllalos, séllalos,"—"seal them, seal them," meaning "Come down, Holy Spirit, and seal these supplicants [the persons praying for the Holy Spirit to possess them] with your holy power." The supplicants themselves were to say, "Séllame, séllame,"—"seal me, seal me,"—and when they felt something "supernatural," that is, heat, pressure on their chest, the urge to shout or to cry, and especially, when their language changed from the formula to something else, they were not to stop but to continue, for this meant that the Holy Spirit was about to take possession of them.

198

Lorenzo himself, in addition, came and walked in between the supplicants, punctuating the rhythm of the formula with his fist, often going into glossolalia himself and shouting at them. I termed the whole process one of *driving*, in the sense that the complex manipulation to which the supplicant was being subjected was driving him into the altered state, not unlike the cheers of spectators driving an athlete to greater exertion. In psychological experiments, the term is used to describe an arrangement in which the subjects are exposed to rhythmical sounds or flashing lights that drive them into altered states of consciousness.

With his technique, by the end of August 1969, Lorenzo had 22 of his 24 adult members speaking in tongues, women as well as men. The increase in the number of glossolalia speakers was credited to the fact that the Second Coming was now much closer at hand than before.

The glossolalia of the parishioners at this point was quite loud, very fast, and in a significant number of cases indentical to that I recorded from recent speakers also in Mexico City and in Hammond, Indiana, namely a high ['u'u'u'u'u] or [bububububu] ([u] as in b*oo*b).

Gathering Momentum: Development in 1970

By the early summer of 1970, the congregation had changed in several ways. There had been another increase in membership, with twenty-four new candidates baptized from September 1969 to March 1970. The participation of the women, initiated in 1969, had gained in importance, in addition to the juvenile section headed by a girl. The prayer for the sick had become more formal, the sick kneeling at the altar, the congregation as a whole staying in their seats, and Emilio alone (instead of the entire congregation) praying for them. Other parts of the service were also more formalized. For the offering, the people

199

no longer came to the front in arbitrary sequence to deposit their money, but rather, select members passed from row to row collecting it, and then knelt on either side of the small table in front of the altar until the prayer for the offering was completed. Although these latter two changes represented elaborations, a curious breakdown seemed to have occurred in the area centering around the glossolalia. There was no longer the formal prayer for the Holy Spirit with its elaborate kneeling arrangement. Lorenzo, who during the previous summer had come down among the kneeling supplicants, bending over them to hear whether they were possessed by the Holy Spirit and thus spoke in tongues, now remained seated or kneeling on the altar podium. Instead of one, there were now two small tables, the second one for the record player received as a gift from a congregation in the United States. When not in use, Lorenzo would place these two tables on either side of the rostrum in such a way that they in fact separated him completely from the congregation.

There was a modification also in the glossolalia behavior of a number of the younger *hermanas* (female members) of the congregation. In August 1969 a young woman, Anita, spoke in tongues for the first time. She was still struggling with the problem of how to pick up the bell signal for awakening, that is, for the return to ordinary reality, when the pastor's wife, Cilia, came back from Campeche, where in her mother's house she had given birth to her second son. Cilia had learned to speak in tongues several months previously, but could not promptly awaken from her trance either, or perhaps had learned a "delayed return" in the Campeche congregation with which I am not familiar. Four *hermanas* between 14 and 16 years old, one of them married, learned to go into glossolalia shortly afterward (one on August 31, two on September 7, and one on October 5), and had acquired the same kind of delayed return from the altered state. Their comportment interfered with the structure of the service. Where before the various sections had been strictly separated, there was now a blurring of these demarcation lines between the various parts of the service, which had served psychologically to make a distinction between behavior within the confines of ordinary reality and that in the altered state. There were also a number of men who had recently acquired the glossolalia behavior, but for the time being they did not take over the pattern of delayed awakening.

Another group of men was in the attenuating phase of their glossolalia behavior. Their utterances were in part longer, though the episodes tended to become shorter. The overall intensity was considerably reduced. In some others, the drop was even further advanced, and they had only vestiges of the previous behavior still available to them, that is, brief glossolalia utterances on the substratum of a hyperarousal of the low intensity of the platform or plateau phase I outlined above. The majority of the men took this attenuation in their stride. Their conversion stories showed that they spoke in tongues because this was the proof that the community and they themselves expected of the fulfillment of the promise of the Holy Spirit and as confirmation of their membership; on the level of dogma, this was the precondition for entering into heaven. Nowhere was there a requirement that they should continue engaging in glossolalia. The experience brought them joy, hope, and a greater capacity for coping with a difficult cultural situation. But they were not desperate for the glossolalia behavior. It was certainty that they were seeking, and they found that.

However, there was a small group of men who had one aspect in common in their conversion stories: the trance experience and its concomitant, the glossolalia, brought them release from unbearable tension and anxiety. There were four of these:

1. Lorenzo, the minister, was the only native Spanish speaker in the congregation, city-born and bred. His religious history was one of relapses. He was born in Campeche and at fourteen he ran away from home. He came in contact with the Apostolics through a boy whose beautiful hymns he wanted to learn. He considered this contact his first conversion. After separating from this friend, he relapsed into "the ways of the world"— drinking, smoking, gambling, drugs, women. This relapse ended when he met an Apostolic minister who baptized him with water in December 1966. His conversion, he felt, also healed his severe sinusitis, but he soon returned to his former life ways and even engaged in illegal activities. He repented and in August 1968 had his first trance experience with glossolalia.

In the summer of 1969, his glossolalia was still very rapid, although not of the intensity usually seen at the inception of the behavior. Only a few utterances were slow enough that I was able to transcribe them.

By the summer of 1970, the utterances were longer and easier to transcribe. The episodes were shorter. His sermons revealed a man haunted by the fear of another relapse. All good humor had disappeared from his sermons, and references to the "filth of the world" and the torments of hellfire increased.

In addition, he experienced a clearly discernable culture shock, produced by this first intimate contact with the peasant world and by the fear that this group, which he considered socially inferior, might witness his defeat. He expressed this by barricading himself against the congregation. Also, as described above, he was openly rude to the men of the congregation. As to the women, he had been the one who had stimulated their participation in the activities of the congregation. This participation led to a male-female balance closely replicating the pattern existing in the Maya home. Being unfamiliar with peasant ways, however, he did not understand that the church was becoming identified with the home in the minds of the women and that other patterns, of which he was unaware, especially the independence of the Maya peasant women in money matters, would also assert themselves. Rather, he tried to push the *hermanas* into the dependency pattern that prevailed between men and women in the city. He asserted his male dominance by taking the money earned by the *Dorcas,* without accounting for its use, in the manner in which a city husband would dispose of his wife's money. The *Dorcas* answered by allegations of misuse of funds. His autocratic behavior with respect to property management also alienated some of the men; and in one instance, the dispute became so intense that he "read" an old and respected *hermano* out of the congregation by declaring his status as *hermano* void in an official declaration from the pulpit. These conflicts disturbed the equilibrium of the congregation at the societal level.

2. Emilio, a very gentle and retiring man, was a Maya peasant born in 1945. He used to be a heavy drinker. In his conversion story, he told of his *temor,* his anxiety, that seemed to have been with him for a long time. After he was baptized with water, in the Apostolic church, this apparently diffuse anxiety became focused on sin as interpreted by the congregation. Resolution of his anxiety did not come until a month later, in December 1968, when he began to speak in tongues.

His glossolalia episodes, in the summer of 1969, were quite long, accompanied by very little movement. A year later, little of the utterance was left intact. His performance when praying for the sick exhibited at every level his desparate attempt to regain the former level of the

203

experience: in a hyperarousal of low intensity, he pressed his arms against his rib cage apparently to duplicate the sensation of pressure so often reported in connection with the altered state, and he tried to impel himself by a tremendous kinetic (motion) pattern. His glossolalia was a mixture of meaningful fragments and unintelligible syllables, often he attempted in vain to break into vocalization at all. The explanation of his changed behavior he gave to the congregation was that he felt this tremendous urge to pray for the sick, and so his efforts were really on their behalf: he had been given the gift of faith healing. However, no cures by him were reported.

3. Anselmo, born in 1944 in a neighboring village, was a Maya peasant and also a barber. Before coming to the Apostolics, he passed successively through the Catholics, the Presbyterians, the Pentecostals, the Baptists, and the Jehovah's Witnesses; he was the only one of the *hermanos* to have such a varied history. His insecurity, expressed in his desperate search for the "right" church was heightened by his wife's being engaged in prostitution. It was probably for this reason that he moved from their home community to Utzpak. After joining the Apostolic congregation there, he spoke in tongues for the first time in July 1969. His wife continued in her previous activity, and perhaps in order to better compete for her favors, he opened up his own barber shop, which meant that he had to work mostly on Sundays, the prime working time for a village barber. Lorenzo warned him that such neglect of the services made people "cold" with respect to their relationship with the Lord. Perhaps this acted as a suggestion, for judging from the subsequent events, Anselmo may have felt the effects of attenuation as early as the spring of 1970. Possibly he attributed the perceived attenuation as a punishment for his neglect of church duties. This, added to his continued shame and frustration about his

wife's behavior, resulted in frantic attempts to regain the former levels of the altered state. In early May 1970, he did not feel well unless he prayed eight to ten times a day. This may have been the mechanism by which he pushed himself into heightened arousal.[8] Overshooting the mark, he had a series of visions, the most important of which were one in which he was attacked by demons, and another one in which he saw several candles in the process of being extinguished and heard a voice that told him that this was the condition of the Apostolic church and it was important for the *hermanos* to go out and evangelize, for Christ's Coming was close at hand.

4. Peregrino was born and raised in Utzpak and was from a family of some means. In the summer of 1969, he was in a different congregation, but often visited in Utzpak. His conversion story had in common with the others the factors of extreme anxiety and also the experimentation with other Protestant groups, in his case mainly the Baptists and the Latter-Day Saints, before coming to the Apostolics. After speaking in tongues for the first time early in 1969, he felt himself to be a different man, for previously he had often wanted to die; after this experience, he no longer thought of death. In 1969, his glossolalia was very rapid, and was accompanied by a strong kinetic pattern. In the summer of 1970, this motion pattern had almost entirely disappeared, and his glossolalia had slowed considerably.

The Peak: July 1970

When speaking of the glossolalia utterance, I called the highest point of the unit utterance a peak or discharge, because I perceived at that point a gathering of force, a dynamic cumulation of pressure that at the moment of highest concentration breaks or discharges. A very similar evolution now overtook the congregation on a societal level also, as reflected in the following (abbreviated) chronology of events.

July 11. Lorenzo returned from visiting several other congregations and reported that in one, four people had received the Holy Spirit, and in another, five. Also, a week before a bright light had appeared over the sky in Chetumal, and many people had seen it. Both the number of newly baptized and the mysterious light indicated that the Second Coming was close at hand.

July 24. The Devil was reported to have been seen the weekend before in the Utzpak jail. He had appeared to a prisoner there, asking him, *"Buenos días, caballero*—Good day, Sir,—would you like me to get you out of here?"* The man started shouting, and when the people got there, the Devil had vanished; they saw only his tail, which looked like that of a steer.

July 27. Lorenzo, and his wife Cilia, left on a visit to Campeche. Anselmo arrived with his wife, who was pregnant.

July 28. Lorenzo returned with the news, heard in Mérida, that Peregrino, while praying in the church at C., had had a vision. During the vision, the Holy Spirit had shown him many extremely dirty churches. There were many people inside, who, according to the Holy Spirit, were convinced that they were in well-ordered clean temples. The voice of the Holy Spirit then continued, "Why don't you enter these temples and make them clean? Christ will soon be here, and you people, what are you doing?" Peregrino had an attack of trembling, and he went to tell Gilberto, his pastor, about his vision. Gilberto then started on a journey, together with his brother Nicolas, pastor of the church in N., to notify the ministers of the various congregations that the Second Coming was imminent.

July 29, afternoon. The pastors Gilberto and Nicolas arrived in Utzpak and closeted themselves with Lorenzo in the church. The *hermanos* of the Utzpak congregation joined them, and occasionally there was very loud prayer and glossolalia audible from behind the closed doors.

July 29, evening. Service was held in the house of Valenciano. Only three men were present. The others were at the church, making plans with Gilberto and Nicolas in preparation for the Second Coming. Christ was trying to give them messages, using the bodies of the *hermanos*. The women were enjoined to hold vigil and pray through the night. In the church, they were told, the men were interpreting the messages contained in the tongues, a gift granted to them because of the imminence of the arrival of the Kingdom of Heaven. The men left to join those in the church.

July 30. While a number of women kept a prayful vigil in their homes, the men prayed and consulted in the church. Anselmo did most of the interpreting of the speaking in tongues. It had been decided that six of the *hermanos* would go to other villages to evangelize. Those men staying at home would contribute to the support of the women left without their husbands. These women would go to stay with the families where the fathers were still present. At one time during the night, Anselmo tried to hang himself, but was restrained by the other men. It was thought that the Devil had tried to destroy him because of his saintliness.

July 30, afternoon. All married couples were summoned to the church and were informed of the night's decisions. The two pastors, Gilberto and Nicolas, left for the next congregation.

July 30, evening. The service began with most of those

207

who had prayed through the night still in residual dissociation and others participating in the atmosphere of intense excitement. Initially, sixteen men and nineteen women with many children were present in the small church, with more and more people crowding in. A recent convert, Vicente, by spontaneously hyperventilating, pushed himself into such a high level of hyperarousal, that he exceeded the glossolalia level and had a vision of Christ standing on the altar beside the rostrum. Violeta went into an altered state with a very intense glossolalia, and could not be awakened again. Excitement mounted further as the evangelists ready "for the field" said good-bye. Most of those present were in and out of trance and very loud glossolalia, and when the group of young women mentioned earlier could not return to consciousness, Lorenzo lost control of the congregation entirely. Violeta, still in an altered state but with a somewhat lowered energy content, started sobbing out names of people resisting the call to total consecration, some of them members for years. Instead of a structured service, the congregation had broken up into groups, each absorbed with a different event. At one point, Anselmo was possessed by the Devil. Lorenzo and some other *hermanos* prayed over him in glossolalia. The Devil, they said, then escaped into the street, pursued by Anselmo and most of the men, and was driven off decisively by a tremendous burst of glossolalia. In other parts of the church, nonmembers suddenly began speaking in tongues. Lorenzo at the rostrum, also dissociated, shouted out additional names of nonconsecrated members, among them some who had criticized his financial behavior. Anselmo, with the stiff knees of hyperarousal, walked up and down the aisles cajoling those who had come to see the excitement and had not as yet made the commitment to be baptized. A number of them agreed to commit themselves. Lorenzo supported the drive for conversion, and was soon joined by others. The slogan traveled all around the room: this is the last opportunity; he who is not baptized will die eternally; Christ is coming soon. Violeta, still rigid and sobbing, in trance, was taken to the *casa pastoral* where she finally went to sleep.

July 31. Once more the *hermanos* stay all night in the church. Anselmo had a vision of a big wheel of many colors turning very fast, and then a person at a considerable distance from the wheel. Another *hermano* interpreted the vision for him, explaining that the figure was really Christ, standing in the middle of the wheel.

July 31, evening. The candidates for the baptism were instructed for the occasion. Several times, the Devil possessed one or the other of the *hermanos* who was then prayed over in the *casa pastoral*. When the wife of one of the recent converts declared her intention to become baptized, the Devil possessed Anselmo and said through his mouth that he desired this woman. The most prominent *hermanos,* under the leadership of Lorenzo, fought the Devil with a prayer spoken in tongues. He was finally defeated and left Anselmo. In a scene of high drama, Anselmo's wife Socorro, finally agreed to be baptized. Lorenzo hurled the most powerful supernatural sanctions at her to impress upon her that she could not return to her previous way of life. In the instructions given to the baptismal candidates, the principle of common property and the church's prior claim to the income of all the *hermanos* was enunciated.

August 1. Sixteen new converts were baptized in a nearby seaport.

The Platform Phase of Residual Dissociation: August 1970

With few exceptions, the members of the congregation were now caught in a state of residual trance, from which they were incapable of escaping.[9] The departure of nine men, not six as originally planned, for evangelizing in various villages, and their wives and children moving into the church, further emphasized the out-of-the-ordinary quality of the collective experience.

My analysis of the glossolalia utterances and observations of people in residual trance have shown that, under certain circumstances, the behavior can escalate into conditions of more intense hyperarousal. During the first week in August, this occurred many times over. Meetings were held every evening, but there were no regular services, for as soon as the parishioners knelt down, they began shouting, prophesying about Christ coming very soon. Unable to stop until exhausted, they then had to be taken, as if drunk, to the hammocks in the *casa pastoral*, where they continued screaming and sobbing, until they finally dropped off to sleep.

By the middle of the week, Nacho had returned from evangelizing. He had accompanied Floriano; watching the latter preach, he had suddenly become very angry, and had picked up a stone to hit him. He had not done it, but felt that he had committed a sin against the Holy Spirit and therefore was not worthy to stay any longer. After his return whenever he knelt to pray in the Utzpak church, he began crying, feeling severe pressure at the base of his skull, and he threw himself on the ground and remained insensate for extended periods. He even had these attacks while working in the *monte* (bush). Often, he was overcome by an urge to walk; he would leave the church, then lose his way (although Utzpak is his home), and an *hermana* would have to go after him to bring him back. Others were seized by similar restlessness, Emilio, also Lorenzo, and would then take the bus, going to N., then come back, again and again.

In the meantime, the church was getting dirty; the men had spit on the floor, the children had urinated, and no one had cleaned up after them.

The following week, Cilia came back from her trip, and was immediately caught up in the mental state of the congregation. The day after her return, Marta was in the *casa pastoral,* face flushed, eyes staring, breathing heavily. Another girl, Nina, suspected of being a skeptic, came in, and Marta ordered her to kneel down and pray. She knelt down, saying, " I will pray, but not to you, only to God." At this moment, Cilia came in, and Marta pointed to her, saying, "Satan has left Nina, and will now attack Cilia." Cilia, screaming, fell to the ground. Lorenzo, with four other *hermanos,* rushed in and started praying over her, but she struck out at them and kicked at them with superhuman force, so that they could not hold her down. Finally, they were able to put her into her hammock, where she eventually fell asleep and thus recovered.

By August 13, the prophesying took a new turn. Some of the young girls mentioned previously began accusing older members of lack of consecration, demanding that they leave the church. Eventually, a number of them actually did, saying that Satan had taken over the congregation.

On August 20, another new element entered. One of the same group of girls complained that the brightly colored dress of Nina disturbed her, and demanded that she take it off. Soon the demand escalated: everything red should be thrown out—the tables, the rostrum, the embroidered covers of the tables, even the Bibles with their red edges. Marta had a vision; she saw an eagle

211

flying overhead, screeching. It was Satan, she said, whereupon all doors and window shutters were locked, with people pressing against them, to prevent Satan from entering.

On August 22, Nicolas arrived from N., telling that an *hermana* there (a nineteen-year-old university student) said that everything in the church must be white. She also had everyone remove whatever was bright or shiny, such as buttons, glasses, ball-point pens. Only the suggestion about white was taken up in the Utzpak congregation, beginning with the instruction that all women should wear white dresses and white mantillas.

On August 23, Sunday, no Sunday school was held. Instead, the congregation was told to go home and burn everything in their homes that was not white. Many of them did—even such expensive possessions as clothes, blankets, and radios.

In the evening, many of the women came wearing white, and those who did not, were sent home to change. In addition, those who wore shoes were told to surrender them because they were not white. They were collected in a sack, and the sack was to be burned, but there was no gasoline; instead, the shoes were painted white the next day. On this same Monday, all the Bibles were collected from the dirt of the yard where they had been thrown and their edges painted black.

Decay: End of August and
Beginning of September

This activity, which on the symbolic level represented something of a compromise—painting white instead of burning and black instead of eliminating—may be regarded as outward indication that the platform phase of the hyperarousal was dissolving. Apparently, a parallel dissolution was also taking place in the congregation in N., where similar events had transpired. One of the original members of that group went to Villahermosa, Tabasco, to talk with the church authorities: and a week later an old, well-known, and highly respected *hermano* came from there to take part in the baptism in the seaport on September 10. He insisted there, and later in the sermon at the church, that what had possessed the congregation had been not the Holy Spirit but Satan. "And that I should have been one of those who thought that it was the Spirit of God," exclaimed Emilio at the seaport, as he wept bitterly.

The Congregation in January 1971

When I saw the congregation again there were few traces left of the events recounted here. The rostrum was still white, but the embroidered covers were back, and a few religious prints had replaced the drawings burned in August. A new *casa pastoral* had been constructed, and work had begun on pulling down the wall in the back of the altar in order to enlarge the church. This was needed, for the church now had about eighty baptized members. The men came to church dressed informally, and though the women had not thrown away their white dresses, colored ones were seen in equal numbers. Those wearing the 'ipil had taken out the tucks hiding the embroidery.

Of the principal actors in the drama, the teenagers had receded into the background. Anselmo had given up barbering, and no more prostitution was reported of his wife, who, incidentally, participated very little in the events of August. Emilio no longer prayed for the sick. Peregrino had a congregation of his own. Neither he nor Anselmo seemed to have had any more visions.

As for Lorenzo, the barricade between him and the

213

congregation was gone. Perhaps the fact that the new *casa pastoral,* though of mud-and-wattle construction, was square rather than oval like the traditional Maya home, represented, on the visible level, a compromise with which he could live, at least temporarily.

On weekdays, the attendance at the services was low. There was no prayer for the Holy Spirit on Sundays, and very few people spoke in tongues; only Lorenzo uttered a brief phrase occasionally. The children had their own service to keep them off the street.

No one mentioned communal property. When at the end of August the money saved by the sections had been spent, the women went home, instead of living in the church. Financial trouble also overtook the evangelists, and they drifted home in the latter part of August. Only one of them, a small cattle rancher, who had planned to go into the ministry before, was still away and had a congregation of his own. Instead, there was ritual sharing of food on a more generous level than before. In one of the families, a girl became fifteen at the end of January. Her mother showed me the pig they were going to slaughter for the occasion. "It is big," she said, "there will be enough for all the *hermanos.*" This celebration of the *de quince años,* very important in the city, had not hitherto been observed in the congregation.

As for the community at large, the *hermanos* were decried as crazed, as having had sex orgies—an interpretation of the girls screaming and being taken to the hammocks in the *casa pastoral* during the events in August. The Presbyterians said that Satan never attacked them because their religion was better than that of the Apostolics. This the Apostolics countered by pointing out that Satan need not attack the Presbyterians because he knows that he is already sure of them. He wanted to test the Apostolics because theirs was the true faith.

CONCLUSION

Our discussion has shown a group of people in the throes of a violent upheaval. In the same manner as the individual glossolalia utterance and the behavior of the individual in trance over time, it seems to me that this group experience also presents a wave from medium onset, via a peak or climax to attenuation and eventual fading out. This raises certain questions. Could it be that some of the violent discharges on the societal level reported elsewhere (for example, Worsely 1968) also arose in a similar fashion from a combination of factors, the most important of which is the sudden acquisition of the trance behavior by a group? This would bring with it a more or less simultaneous experience of the panic of attenuation, coupled with the inability of handling the residual dissociation. What might then happen on the level of the society at large would be that the latter may not be aware of the culture change in progress within a small group (in this case, the Utzpak congregation), but being very much informed of the sudden madness, visions, and so on, evidenced by the group, would then attribute the culture change observed in the group to the ecstatic upheaval. With the memory of the event fading, and a certain shame attaching to the details of the upheaval, even the group involved may accept this view.

Yet this is, in fact, not what actually took place. Rather, there seems to be in the case detailed above an evolution of several parallel processes. One is that of culture change. It proceeds slowly and inexorably, and it can neither be interrupted nor greatly modified by such cataclysmic events as those that overtook the Utzpak congregation. Even under the condition of lowered inhibition, characteristic of the platform phase of the residual trance, the present case shows neither reversion to purely Maya patterns nor the remaking of the group in the image of the city. The Maya women, who had previously given up the 'ipil, did not revert to it but sewed white dresses; and conversely, those who had not, did not suddenly assume city dress. Although the few available radios were burned, the public address system of the church was not destroyed, only put outside. The Maya language did not become the language of prayer, but neither was it outlawed within or without the church.

The changes that were instituted during the upheaval, such as praying in tongues in the *casa pastoral,* interpretation of the glossolalia, prophesying, extensive recourse to diabolic possession, all disappeared with the dissolution of the residual trance. It is the minute change that is continuing, principally on the social level—the evolution of an inner and an outer group of members, the more intensive training of the children, the gradual integration of the culture of the dominant society, such as the celebration within the congregation of the fifteenth birthday.

The other, separate process is the evolution of the altered state on the group level, its gathering momentum, its peaking and discharge, and its eventual attenuation. It had no effect on the culture change already in progress. Rather, its role remained restricted to what we might call the inner space of the people involved. As on the individual level, it also served on the societal one, that is, in the congregation, to confirm a supernatural premise. Fittingly, because of the disruptive effect of the experience that all participants eventually perceived, this was the evil principle: it transformed Satan from a formula into a living, a felt, an experienced reality.

Paradoxically, it also confirmed the belief in the Second Coming, perhaps because it had, for a brief instance, appeared so close.

1. The research for this paper was begun as a part of a larger study, which was supported in whole by Public Health Service Research Grant MH 07463 from the National Institute of Mental Health. The project, entitled Cross-Cultural Studies of Dissociatonal States, was under the direction of Dr. Erika Bourguignon, of the Department of Anthropology, the Ohio State University. The Denison University Research Foundation supported my field work in the form of a generous grant, and I received a Grant-in-Aid for Research from the Society of the Sigma Xi. The field work was carried out during the summer of 1968 in Mexico City and in the summers of 1969 and 1970, as well as in January 1971, in a Maya village near the northern coast of the Peninsula of Yucatán, Mexico. Unless otherwise stated, the observations and conclusions to follow are derived from this field work. Space does not permit extensive documentation of all the points advanced.

2. Ejido is a federally administered program for providing land for the rural population from large land holdings, *haciendas,* divided in the 1920s.

3. Learning *about* the glossolalia behavior takes place in the awake state, as the members of the congregation observe others speaking in tongues. The learning referred to here is the process by which the person acquires the capability of superimposing the vocalization on the dissociated mental state. For a detailed discussion and observational material see Goodman 1972, especially chapter 4.

4. The rate of utterance, that is, how fast the glossolalia is spoken, also varies over time in the same speaker, as I was able to show on the basis of an analysis of the utterances of the same speakers over several years, recorded by me in the field. See below and Goodman 1972.

5. An analysis I carried out on glossolalia utterances recorded in a Christian sect in Gunung Sitoli on the Island of Nias by Professor Wolfgang M. Pfeiffer of the University of Erlangen (Germany), and recently placed at my disposal (December 1971), strikingly confirmed this contention.

6. All names have been changed to protect the identity of the persons concerned.

7. The term *cluster* is used here to describe a situation where the first few members of the congregation represented several kin groups; subsequent members, however, were derived almost exclusively from the kin groups already represented, without involving the entire kin group membership. Thus, the membership of the congregation may be conceptualized as "clustering," rather than being an amorphous aggregate of unrelated individuals.

8. For arguments supporting my proposition that a hallucinatory experience is evidence of a higher arousal level than the glossolalia see Goodman 1972 *b.*

9. For the details of this phase, I am indebted to one of the young girls in the congregation, whom in this account I have called Nina. On her own initiative, and with only two years of formal school attendance as her educational background, she took notes during the entire upheaval, which she placed at my disposal in January 1971.

217

Religion, Altered States of Consciousness, and Social Change

REFERENCES

Blair, W., and Refugio Vermont-Salas. 1967. *Spoken (Yucatec) Maya.* Chicago: University of Chicago. Department of Anthropolgy.

Gaxiola, Maclovio L. 1964. *Historia de la Iglesia Apostólica de la fe en Cristo Jesús de México.* México D.F.: Librería Latinoamericana.

Goodman, Felicitas D. 1969a. Glossolalia: Speaking in tongues in four cultural settings. *Confinia Psychiatrica* 12:113–29.

————. 1969b. Phonetic analysis of glossolalia in four cultural settings. *Journal for the Scientific Study of Religion* 8:227–39.

————. 1971. The acquisition of glossolalia behavior. *Semiotica* 3:77–82.

————. 1972a. *Speaking in tongues: A cross-cultural study of glossolalia.* Chicago: University of Chicago Press.

————. 1972b. Glossolalia and hallucination in Pentecostal congregations. *Psychiatria Clinica,* forthcoming.

Hine, Virginia H. 1969. Pentecostal glossolalia: Toward a functional interpretation. *Journal for the Scientific Study of Religion* 8:211–26.

Hockett, Charles F. 1958. *A course in modern linguistics.* New York: Macmillan.

Lalive d'Epinay, Christian. 1968. *El refugio de las masas.* Santiago, Chile: Editorial del Pacífico.

Redfield, Robert. 1941. *The folk culture of Yucatán.* Chicago: University of Chicago Press.

Reed, Nelson. 1964. *The caste war of Yucatán.* Stanford, Cal.: Stanford University Press.

Wallace, Anthony F. C. 1966. *Religion: An anthropological view.* New York: Random House.

Wolf, Eric R. 1966. *Peasants.*Englewood Cliffs, N.J.: Prentice Hall.

Worsley, Peter. 1968. *The trumpet shall sound.* New York: Schocken.

6 : The Shakers of St. Vincent: A Stable Religion

Jeannette H. Henney

In 1966, and again in 1970, I visited the island of St. Vincent to study a fundamentalist Protestant church that incorporates states of altered consciousness into its system of beliefs and practices. The worshipers, popularly known as "Shakers," interpret these states in different ways depending upon the context in which they occur. During the church service, when an individual experiences temporary periods of dissociation, he is believed to be a receptacle for the Holy Spirit. But when dissociation occurs during periods of ritual retreat, it is interpreted as a "spiritual journey" for the worshiper. Shakerism has demonstrated its strength by its remarkable persistence throughout years of opposition and hostility—a strength that seems to stem, at least partially, from the refuge it offers its adherents from the reality of, and psychic injury from, socioeconomic deprivation.

THE ISLAND AND ITS PEOPLE

St. Vincent is one of the Windward Islands in the West Indies. It is approximately eleven miles wide and eighteen miles long, and is situated approximately 190 miles north of Trinidad and 100 miles west of Barbados. The island is very mountainous and boasts a volcano, Mt. Soufrière, that last erupted in 1902–3, causing extensive damage and loss of life. At the present time, Soufrière is considered semidormant. The soil is quite fertile, and unlike

Religion, Altered States of Consciousness, and Social Change

some Caribbean islands, St. Vincent has adequate rainfall. The average temperature is 80° F. (Duncan 1963; Great Britain Colonial Office, 1966).

The population of St. Vincent reached 91,326 by mid-1967, an increase of over 10,000 since 1960. Racial distribution reflects the history of the island, and according to the 1960 census was as follows:

Negro	56,207
White	1,840
East Indian	2,444
Mixed	17,444
Amerindian Carib	1,265
Other	748

(The Economic Planning Unit, n.d.)

St. Vincent was inhabited by Carib Indians in 1498 when Columbus discovered and named the island. The fierce, warlike Caribs were largely responsible for the late colonization of St. Vincent. After the African slave trade was established in the Caribbean, slaves escaping from plantations on Barbados and from shipwrecks in the vicinity sometimes found their way to St. Vincent, where they intermingled with the Caribs and eventually produced a people known as Black Caribs (Burns 1954).

The Europeans showed little interest in St. Vincent until the seventeenth century when the British and French periodically contested its possession. In 1783, the Treaty of Versailles awarded the island to the British, but lasting peace was not established on St. Vincent until 1796 when most of the Black Caribs, who had allied themselves with the French against the British, were deported to Honduras. The Amerindian Caribs had not been involved in the hostilities and were allowed to remain. The only remaining evidence of French occupation of the island

220

is some French place names. For more than a century and a half without interruption, St. Vincent was a British colony, and British influences, including language, predominate (Burns 1954; Duncan 1963). In 1969 St. Vincent became an Associated State of the United Kingdom, which gave the Vincentians control of their internal affairs.

An agricultural economy based on sugar as the dominant crop, a plantation system, and the institution of slavery developed in the Caribbean (Goveia 1965). In the peaceful years of the early nineteenth century, St. Vincent, as a participant in the general Caribbean economy, enjoyed periods of prosperity; but when slavery was abolished in the British islands in 1834, the whole economic balance was disrupted and never fully recovered (Ragatz 1928). The former slaves were reluctant to continue working as field hands and demanded wages that were unrealistic from the planters' point of view. Other sources of labor were tapped; between 1862 and 1880, 2,746 East Indian migrants arrived in St. Vincent to augment the labor supply (Garcia 1965).

A dismal economic outlook has continued to the present. Various crops have been introduced over the years in an effort to rejuvenate the economy, but each has met with some misfortune. Currently, the most important export crop is bananas. Tourism, which might afford some respite, has been developing more slowly in St. Vincent than in many of the other Caribbean islands, but it shows promise of becoming increasingly important. Existing facilities have been improved to make them more attractive to North American visitors: a luxurious resort hotel has been operating for several years, another is in the planning stage, and souvenir industries are being developed.[1]

Several demographic features of St. Vincent are relevant to a discussion of economy. First, the birth rate is one of the highest in the Caribbean.[2] Second, extreme mobility seems to be characteristic of West Indians. In 1963, 20,009 persons emigrated from St. Vincent, and 19,345 immigrants were admitted. Migration has been a popular means for handling individual as well as collective economic problems, particularly for lower-class males. Although, given the opportunity, women also emigrate, lower-class women are apt to follow an economic pattern that has been observed in other areas of the Caribbean and West Africa (Mintz 1960; 1964; Jahn 1968; Ottenberg 1959). A woman can raise a small crop and sell her surplus in the market, or, if she has sufficient capital, she can buy wholesale lots of a commodity and sell it in the market in retail lots. Long-standing custom seems to have reserved such marketing operations for women.

Before, during, and since the period of study, then, St. Vincent has been undergoing significant economic and political changes. Universal adult suffrage was not established until 1951 when a new constitution went into effect providing for the election of the majority of members in the Legislative Council. Election to public office has been one avenue to power and prestige for Vincentians, and the interest of the general public in political affairs has been intense. Indeed, for several years immediately prior to the acquisition of associated status with Britain, the political situation was so turbulent that action on the matter was postponed repeatedly(*Caribbean Monthly Bulletin,* February 1967).

SOCIAL STRATIFICATION

As in most other islands of the Caribbean, the stratification of St. Vincent society reflects to some extent the earlier presence of slavery. Hadley (1949:351) has defined the components of class structure with particular reference to St. Vincent. He identifies a "proletariat," composed of agricultural workers, fishermen, dock hands, and similar occupational groups whose members earn daily or weekly wages. Above the proletariat is the "unestablished, emergent or lower-middle class," whose members earn salaries by teaching in elementary schools, by working in lesser jobs in business and civil service, or by being landed proprietors. Hadley sees the "established upper-middle class," in which he places persons in the professions or in the more important business and civil service posts and whose families may have held the same status position for a generation or more, as the highest class represented on the island. He finds no true aristocracy in St. Vincent, only more or less wealthy people. By far the greatest number of people fall in the lower-class category; of those who are in the middle class, most are in the lower-middle stratum.

Although skin pigmentation and racial classification, as Lowenthal (1967:597) has observed, "do not *define* West Indian classes" (emphasis mine), they are unquestionably factors in class differentiation: "Generally the poorest people are black and those with the highest status are white or near-white" (Simpson 1962:30). The link with the slave era—when the slaves were almost without exception Negroes, the white minority constituted the dominant class, and an inevitable hybrid group arose to form a free, colored population—cannot be denied. However, with time, color has become more "a matter of culture"; education, occupation, and wealth have also influenced class ranking so that there is a tendency to consider a person, "colored," no matter what his physical characteristics might be, if he has achieved middle-class status, and "black," if he remains in the lower class (Lowenthal 1967:598).

RELIGION

With the beginning of English rule in St. Vincent, the Church of England became the established church. But it catered only to the free, white, upper class, to which the clergy themselves frequently belonged (Goveia 1965), and ignored the slaves, even denying them entrance to the church (Duncan 1963). Various sects worked among the slave populations in the Caribbean—the Quakers as early as the seventeenth century, the Moravians somewhat later. Some independent churches also developed. But the first direct religious influence intended for the slaves was brought to St. Vincent by a Methodist missionary in 1787. It is interesting that the demonstrations of intense religious excitement that distinguished Methodist congregations in Great Britain at that time were also apt to occur among New World Methodist congregations (Southey 1925). None of the other denominations were as successful in the West Indies as the Methodists, and Methodism became "the religion of the blacks" (Garcia 1965).

In 1960, most Vincentians belonged to either the Anglican (Church of England) or the Methodist church—37,671 and 26,537 members, respectively. The Roman Catholics had the next largest membership with 8,843. A number of other churches are on the island, but they are relatively insignificant.[3]

THE SHAKERS

The Shakers refer to themselves as "Spiritual Baptists"[4] or "converted people." The religion apparently developed in St. Vincent and has been functioning there at least since the early years of the present century. In 1912, an ordinance was passed "to render illegal the practices of 'Shakerism' as indulged in in the colony of St. Vincent." It further stated that "a certain ignorant sec-
224

tion of the inhabitants" was assembling and participating in practices "which tend to exercise a pernicious and demoralizing effect upon said inhabitants" (Rae 1926:1091). But in spite of the constant threat of discovery and prosecution, the Shakers continued to worship together. One of the "mothers" of the church recalled some of the difficulties that faced them. "The police used to persecute us like in the days of Saul. At meeting you couldn't shout. They would imprison you, take you under arrest, and make a case. One Sunday, there was a baptism, and from it they were in a meeting. Some police arrest and beat them. They had cattle carts. They handcuff them and throw them in the carts like beasts. Some got away and run hide. Some got 6 months, 9 months, 4 years, according."

A more tolerant attitude toward the Shakers began to prevail in the thirties, and they were permitted to hold their meetings without further interference. Their status was still questionable, however, until the ordinance was repealed in 1965. Today, a Shaker "pointer" has certain prerogatives commensurate with his position as head of a recognized church: he may christen infants, perform burial services, and, upon paying the fee for a license, perform legal marriage ceremonies.

Some of the clergy of the organized denominational churches in St. Vincent expressed resentment over the governmental action legalizing Shakerism. They interpreted the move as a political gesture to win Shaker votes, which they felt was unnecessary because the Shakers were essentially being given religious freedom before the ordinance was repealed. They admitted, however, that the Shakers seemed to be increasing in numbers and respectability since their status had been changed.

The attitudes of higher-class Vincentians toward Shakerism varied. An elderly gentleman, perhaps influenced by prejudices toward the religion that were prevalent when he was younger, was also disturbed by the government action. "People have left the organized churches and gone down morally. They are not uplifted. It is an African cult—a terrible thing for St. Vincent." Others regarded the Shakers more tolerantly, although they might mock them or apologize for them. Still other Vincentians, displaying pride in their African ancestry, pointed approvingly to aspects of Shakerism that they assumed were African contributions, mentioning particularly the emotion and spirit that characterized the services.

The Shaker congregation that was the principal concern of this study included about forty lower-class people, most of whom lived and worked in or near Kingstown, the capital and harbor city. The men were employed as dock hands, as delivery men, as members of road-building or construction crews, and so on. The women worked as domestics, seamstresses, or laundresses; or they loaded bananas when a boat was in the harbor. A few women who were married or who had formed a stable union with a man did not work. In several cases, their husbands had migrated to England or Canada, or were sailors, and they sent money back to their wives. Some women supplemented their resources in the traditional fashion by becoming entrepreneurs. One woman roasted peanuts to sell to the school children at recess. Another considered herself a "speculator." She bought produce in large quantities and resold it in small quantities, occasionally traveling to markets in nearby islands. Eventually, she bought a house with the profits from her various ventures.

The typical Shaker house was small (two or three rooms), with some land around it that provided space for a vegetable garden and a few fruit trees, and sometimes a pig or goat, and chickens. Almost every house had a radio, and some had electricity. None of the Shakers interviewed appeared to be desperately poor, nor did they regard themselves as such. According to them, the poor are those who cannot help themselves.

Most of the Shakers in the congregation had received some formal education. A few of them had more than a primary education, but most of them had considerably less.[5] During church services, most of the worshipers seemed to be able to read, although some required prompting when reading a Bible lesson to the congregation. A non-Shaker explained that illiterate Shakers may memorize long passages from the Bible and the multiple stanzas of hymns, and thus create the illusion of reading.

SHAKER CHURCHES

"Prayer houses," or "praise houses," are scattered throughout St. Vincent. Construction and furnishings may vary, but they conform to a general pattern. The simple, rectangular buildings accomodate 50 to 75 people. The altar at one end of the room may be elaborate with a raised platform, altar rail, satin or velvet altar cloths, wooden candelabra and cross, or it may be plain, with perhaps a kitchen table covered with a plastic tablecloth. Rough wooden benches, usually backless, provide seating. Some churches have electric lights, and others depend upon oil lamps and candles. The walls may be decorated with pictures of Christ or of Catholic saints. Some churches have a center pole, not necessarily of any structural function, with candles affixed to it and banners hung around it, that serves as a secondary focal point during rituals.[6] Certain altar equipment is ubiquitous: a glass of water with a flower, a candle, a brass handbell, a Bible, and a saucer.

Upon occasion, a church may be improvised. Meetings may be held in a village street, with a table for an altar and chairs borrowed from nearby houses; or meetings

227

may be held in someone's yard or house. If outdoors, a tarpaulin "borrowed from the Banana Association" may be arranged to form a tent. Outdoor services usually attract a crowd of curious spectators.

CHURCH STRUCTURE

Shaker churches are ordinarily autonomous. The congregation under study was unusual in that its "pointer" had five churches in various parts of the island under his direction. Visiting back and forth not only occurred frequently among the several churches directed by the same pointer but was a common practice with other Shaker churches.[7] Shaker congregations might also be invited to hold thanksgiving or memorial services in homes of individuals who were not themselves Shakers. Shaker visits were not limited to St. Vincent; a congregation might go to some of the small islands of the Grenadines to hold services.

Internally, each Shaker church has a hierarchical structure. According to informants, a positive emphasis is placed on obedience, "the first step to Christ." Each member owes obedience to those who hold higher ranking positions in the church and are thus "elder to him." Rank is supernaturally awarded to the deserving members during a period of retreat known as "mourning," and each position has its rights and obligations. A "nurse," for example, "cares for the candidates sitting on the mercy bench [a bench where candidates for baptism sit]; she can give them water, clean the lights, and take them outside if they want to go." She "takes care of the room, gets meals, and takes care of everything" for those who go to "mourn." And she is entitled to wear a distinctive uniform.

The apex position in the church hierarchy is held by

the "pointer," who should be a man—"a woman is not supposed to head a church, the leading instrument is supposed to be a man." Church leadership may be passed along in a family from father to son or brother to brother.

A "leader" seems to serve as an apprentice pointer. In the pointer's absence, a leader conducts the meeting. When the pointer is present, the leader assists him. After receiving the proper "spiritual gifts" from mourning, a leader may acquire a church of his own, or, under some circumstances, may become the pointer of the church he has served as leader.

Women greatly outnumber the men in the Shaker church. A congregation of fifty might include from ten to fifteen men. But all of the men have an office in the church, according to the pointer, whereas many women do not. This is interesting in view of the fact that some men had never "mourned."

In the congregation being analyzed, Pointer B. maintains strict control over the conduct of the members. "When you are in a meeting, you are supposed not to speak, but to listen attentively to the word of the Lord. You are supposed to say 'Amen' . . . and you also have to sing." Pointer B. is not above reproving a misbehaving worshiper publicly. He has a quick temper and a loud, raucous voice; and he carries a wide leather strap with which he pounds the altar to emphasize a point or to mark the rhythm of a hymn. But occasionally he uses the strap to lash out against a group of giggling or inattentive women.

Pointer B. may also punish transgressions of a more serious nature. During an outdoor meeting one evening, he questioned a woman at length about a wrong that she had presumably committed that had come to his attention through divine revelation—"the Spirit will reveal to me that something has been done wrong." The woman's crime had been to curse several other women. Pointer B. had the woman perform a ritual known as "taking a prove"[8] to validate his information and justify his subsequent action. Satisfied that he had rightly accused her, the pointer proceeded to strike her open palms several times with the strap. The situation was dramatic and emotion-ridden, and both the pointer and the woman on trial became more violently dissociated than was usual. The congregation strongly approved the pointer's handling of the case, and some of the bystanders expressed their approbation as well.

The possibility that the pointer might have been informed of the woman's misdeed by someone who had knowledge of it was flatly denied. However, it became evident from informal conversations and gossip that she was not well liked and was often criticized for her asocial behavior.

SHAKER MEETINGS

Shakers say that John and Charles Wesley were the originators of their religion, and, although some alterations have been made, a Methodist foundation can be readily recognized. Services are usually held on Wednesday, Friday, and Sunday nights beginning about eight o'clock. When a worshiper arrives, he kneels at the altar or center pole, crosses himself and prays, and perhaps drops a coin in the saucer on the altar before taking a seat. Everyone carries a candle, and many have Bibles and hymnals.

All of the women wear head ties because "it says in the Bible that women should have their heads covered in church." Most of the head ties are white; the colored ones indicate that their wearers have been to "mourn."

Men do not have to cover their heads, although some do. Shoes are supposed to be removed in church because "it is a holy place." The taboo against shoes seems to be less critical than the taboo against uncovered female heads; some individuals slip off their shoes, others do not.

Shakers who have been to "mourn" and who have received an office in the church may have the right to wear uniforms or insignia; and whenever one congregation visits another or when a church is having a special service such as baptism, everyone wears the full regalia to which he is entitled if he has it. In an ordinary meeting, however, most of the worshipers wear only part of the uniform—such as a rope belt—or none of it.

The early part of the Shaker service follows the Methodist Order for Morning Prayer fairly closely. There are no musical instruments used, so hymns are sung without accompaniment. Several rituals have been added to the Methodist service. In the first, the glass of water with the flower and the handbell that are part of Shaker altar equipment are used. Water is sprinkled from the flower three times, then the bell is rung three times in each of the four corners of the room, at the doorways and center pole, and at the four corners of the altar. The second ritual involves general participation. While singing a hymn, everyone walks around in follow-the-leader fashion and shakes hands with everyone else, each eventually returning to his own seat.

When the Order for Morning Prayer has been completed, the remainder of the meeting is devoted to preaching, long chanted prayers, "words of consolation," and hymns. In addition to the pointer and those who assist him, any member of the congregation may contribute to this part of the service. During this period, dissociation is most likely to occur. The service may continue an hour or more beyond midnight, and is brought to a close with a benediction and the Gloria Patri.

Depending upon the purpose of the meeting or the whim of the pointer conducting the service, other elements may be included, parts of the usual service may be omitted, or the usual order may be changed. A high degree of consistency in ritual seems to prevail, however, among Shaker churches, in spite of the absence of any supraorganization; and variations that can be noted between churches and between pointers seem to be of minor significance.

Meetings held at the homes of members for the purpose of blessing or christening the house, or a part of it, are popular. The altar-table for these "thanksgiving" meetings is scattered with fruit, corn, and farina. The usual Methodist Order for Morning Prayer is followed; but the preaching, "words of consolation," and prayers are concerned with the purpose of the meeting, and a special ritual is performed. In each corner and at the doorway of the room being blessed, a psalm is read, brandy is sprinkled three times, a piece of bread is left on a rafter, and the bell is rung three times. Chalk designs are also made on the wall and floor. After meetings held in homes, "beer and buns" are brought out, and a period of conviviality follows.

After a death has occurred, the family of the deceased, even if they are not Shakers, may invite a Shaker congregation to their home to conduct the traditional ceremonies that take place on the third night, the ninth night, and the fortieth night after the death. The memorial service follows the usual pattern. Food is scattered on the improvised altar as it is for a thanksgiving service; but the preaching, "words of consolation," prayers, and hymns deal with the central theme of death and the Christian expectations of the afterlife. Refreshments and a period of informality also follow memorial services.

DURING THE MEETING: POSSESSION TRANCE

States of dissociation that are a common occurrence during Shaker meetings are explained as possession by the Holy Spirit.[9] Such manifestations rarely appear during the early part of the service when the worshipers are occupied with responses, kneeling, shaking hands, and so on. If a worshiper does begin to slip into possession trance, as evidenced by a sob, a shout, or a shudder, perhaps, he quickly recovers.

As the service progresses beyond the conventional Methodist forms, there is opportunity for more improvisation and greater congregational participation. Any worshiper may play an important solo part at this time by offering "a few words" or a prayer. When a person sermonizes, he is apt to walk back and forth, often waving his arms about and appearing more and more excited as he warms to his subject and the situation. Meanwhile, the congregation maintains a steady, monotonous background of low singing or humming. Periodically, the speaker interrupts himself with a favorite device of the Shakers, saying "I t'ink I heard someone say . . . " or some other appropriate phrase to lead into a hymn that everyone then joins in singing. When a person offers a prayer, he kneels by the altar and chants the prayer while the rest of the worshipers chant a response at the end of each metered verse. During activities of this kind, dissociation is very likely to occur.

Through much of the service, the worshipers sit on the narrow, backless benches with their eyes closed, or half-closed, often holding up their heads and yawning. They give the impression that they are lost in their own inner concerns and paying little attention to what is happening around them. When they stand for a hymn, the worshipers keep time by swaying from side to side or by swinging about in a semicircle, pivoting first on one

233

foot and then on the other. They may also clap their hands or slap themselves lightly with a branch of sago or a book, or pound their Bibles with the end of a candle. When they are seated during a hymn, they mark the rhythm by rocking back and forth or twisting from side to side at the waist, by tapping their bare feet or clapping their hands, or by moving an arm and hand or their heads. Rhythm is a very important component of the possession trance phenomenon.

Possession trance occurs as the performance of a single individual, or as a performance in which several individuals are affected but each acts as a soloist, or as a group performance in which possession trance takes on choral aspects. When a person exhibits symptoms of developing possession trance, he may be the only one in the church to display such behavior at the time, or there may be several individuals scattered through the church in a similar state; he may be a member of the congregation, or he may be the person who has been performing, preaching, or praying.

The first outward indication of possession trance may be a convulsive jerk of an arm or arms, one or both shoulders, or the head. Or it may be a shiver, a shudder, or tremble; a sudden shout, sob, or hiss; a series of unintelligible sounds; or any combination of such movements or vocalizations. The affected person may suddenly stand up and dance in place. These external signs of inward lessening of control appear to be spontaneous; and for each possession trancer, they have a random quality lacking any rhythmic pattern. As far as the group is concerned, if several persons are affected at the same time, each displays a different set of symptoms. At this level of possession trance, symptoms viewed either for the individual or for the group are random and unpatterned; however, from one session to another, the movements and sounds of a particular individual can often be pre-

234

dicted and identified at this level, since each possession trancer seems to develop his own peculiar style. One "mother," for example, would let her head droop as though she were dozing, and then she would suddenly jerk it back, moving her arm with fist tightly clenched spasmodically forward and up and shouting, "Hi! Yi!" Another woman would shake her shoulders, jerk both arms forward and up, and sob.

If the affected person happens to be the performer, the first indication of developing possession trance may be a quaver in his voice. He may jerk or tremble or occasionally break into his own preaching or praying with a yell. He may become more and more restless and excited, and, if he is on his feet, he may pace to and fro more rapidly. But he maintains sufficient control to continue speaking and be understood. When one "mother" was addressing the congregation, her voice would tremble noticeably, she would become breathless and excited, and she would interrupt her sermonizing from time to time to utter a loud "Holy Ghost!"

The incipient possession trance may not proceed beyond this first level. The manifestations may subside more or less quickly; or they may persist, and possession trance may be maintained at this level; or there may be repeated returns to this level after periods of "normalcy." But the manifestations may develop further into the next level.

When possession trance continues into the second level, it frequently involves more than a single individual and becomes a group phenomenon. As more and more individuals become involved in the first-level type of random symptoms, a subtle shift, without a definite break and change, is made to behavior that is characteristic of the second level. Each individual, at this level, will have established an action pattern for himself that he repeats over and over quite rapidly. This may be only

235

an arms or head movement pattern, or it may involve more of the body. If the person is standing, his feet may be involved in the pattern of movements, but he never strays far from his own circumscribed area. Most possession trancers bend forward from the waist and, if standing, also bend their knees slightly. When one of the leaders was on his knees praying and had reached this level of possession trance, he would bend forward, putting his knuckles on the ground, gorilla-fashion, almost touch his head to the ground, and then jerk back up again with amazing speed. This movement was repeated over and over and was accompanied by gasps as he jerked back. Another leader, when he was seated, would bend his head almost to his knees and jerk his head up and back, bubbling his lips on the way down and audibly taking in gulps of air on the way up.

Whatever idiosyncratic movements or sounds or breathing peculiarities prevail, they become less conspicuous because of the concerted attention to the same rhythm pattern. Whether this level of possession trance has occurred as the outgrowth of a prayer, a sermon, or a hymn, there has been some singing, humming, or chanting to give the group a rhythmic beat to cling to. If the worshipers were singing a hymn, the words at the beginning would have been distinct and understandable. But when possession trance begins to appear as the singing continues, the words degenerate into repeated syllables; and these, in turn, with the achievement of the second level of possession trance, change into grunts and gasps emitted in unison, with each person maintaining the established beat.

In the first level of possession trance, the sounds of the various affected individuals can be singled out on a tape of the proceedings, and the person responsible for them can often be identified. But at the second level, the sounds are so well blended that it is impossible to

236

identify anyone from the sounds. There is neither shouting nor comprehensible speech produced at this level.

In crowded situations, not only are the sounds of breathing kept to a precise tempo but the motion patterns may be depersonalized and standardized so that all possession trancers, as if in a dance line, are producing the same movements. This was observed several times when the worshipers were standing huddled together. They were bent over at the waist with knees bent, and they bobbed up and down simultaneously keeping the rhythm.[10]

Eventually the patterned, rhythmic production is upset and slowly obliterated. If the possession trancers had formed a huddle, some of them now wander away from the group and undo the choral dance aspect of the phenomenon further by interjecting idiosyncratic movements that no longer maintain the established tempo. Breathing ceases to be a disciplined activity spaced at set intervals. Some individuals destroy the rhythm with irregularly timed yells and loud sighs. The second level may end as if by common, tacit consent of those involved, but at times there seems to be a signal—someone rings the bell or begins singing a hymn with a conflicting beat.

At the third level, movements and sounds are again without discernible pattern as they were at the first level. They become random and spasmodic, but, in contrast to the first level, the sounds produced are not spotty, occasional yells against a musical background. Possession trancers in the third level do not sing or hum, but gasp, groan, sigh, and shout. They are breathless and appear to be bewildered. The scene is one of confusion, but no special treatment is required to bring the affected persons back to normal, and the possession trances are terminated in a short time.

The possession trance period for a particular meeting may last only a short while, or it may last for hours.

An individual may spend from several minutes to an hour or more fluctuating between a near-normal state and the first level, and at any time then slip into the second level. A second-level possession trance for an individual may last from about five minutes to perhaps forty-five minutes, but the second level as described for a group usually lasts between five and ten minutes before some of the participants break away. The third level is short, a few minutes at most.

Most possession trances are not as simple as those outlined. Instead of returning to normal following the third level, possession trancers may again slip into second-level behavior, to return later to the third level, and so on. Or they may return to normal and, if the meeting is still in progress, return to a state of possession trance once more.

Certain worshipers can be depended upon to go into possession trance at almost every meeting, but others never seem to be affected. The Shakers explain that some people never "shake" overtly; the Holy Ghost enters them, but shakes them only within. On the other hand, they also say that "some people have a deeper zeal, they whip and shake more." The individuals who remain unaffected provide the background-rhythm pattern with their humming and singing for the possession trancers.

On several occasions a possession trancer, usually a woman who was more boisterous than the others or who had become so disoriented that she was in danger of falling was observed. Worshipers standing nearby helped her to her knees so she would not be injured. It is interesting that in one case the woman had just declared her intention to accept baptism and had been the focus of a long and impressive ritual. In another case, mentioned earlier, the woman had just been chastised by the pointer as a climax to an equally impressive and lengthy ritual. Several times the pointer was seen reeling, almost falling into a group of seated worshipers. This occurred on the evening described above, when he was taking the woman to task. More violent manifestations were also reported for persons being baptized. Ordinarily, possession trance behavior is extremely well controlled. without violence being done to the possession trancer himself or to others, and the experience is regarded as beneficent and welcomed. It would seem that the more violent behavior occurs as the aftermath of an emotionally charged situation and is atypical.[11]

Informants say that they know that the Spirit is going to come to them because they feel "a tremblin' within" before they begin to shake. When the Spirit comes, "it is very nice the way It take you and that Power have you and shake all your sins away." It feels "like a breeze passing through you—it makes you feel very light like you are going to faint, but you don't." When asked whether they experience amnesia for the possession trance period, informants replied that they remember shaking and shouting, but they remember only what happens between themselves and the Spirit. They would not remember if someone were to talk to them or touch them while the Spirit was shaking them. "When It comes, It really shakes you so you pay no attention to anything but the Spirit. When It leaves you, you feel relaxed and strong."

Shakers insist that they do nothing, aside from being "pure in heart," to attract or invite the Spirit to "manifest on" them. When it was suggested that they also might seek possession trance by devices such as the overbreathing reported for Jamaican revival cults (Moore 1965:64), they declared that such breathing was the result of the Spirit shaking them and not a preliminary to the Spirit's entry. And, indeed, as it was observed, the distinctive overbreathing phenomenon did not occur in the early moments of possession trance nor as an induction mechanism, but developed as possession trance proceeded into the second level, when the affected person appeared to be least aware of external happenings and farthest removed from reality and normalcy.

THE SIGNIFICANT RITUALS:
BAPTISM AND MOURNING

Baptism and mourning are the most important rituals for the individual Shaker.[12] The acceptance of baptism is a necessary step to becoming a Shaker, but no one seeks baptism unless he has had a dream or vision or some other experience that can be interpreted as a sign from the supernatural directing him to do so. Few members had heeded the first call promptly.

A frequent and important element in the dreams and visions was a "gentleman," white and dressed in white. Water and bodies of water were also important, and several informants mentioned stones falling from heaven but not hitting them. In some cases, a hymn, perhaps not previously known, was remembered as an outstanding feature.

One woman did not have a dream or vision. She had been in the habit of attending the meetings and "saw that they were good," and one evening, during the service, she felt something pushing her forward. Her legs felt very light, and she had to touch them to see if they were still there. She followed her impulse, went forward and knelt at the altar, and subsequently was baptized.

Ignoring a call to accept baptism may have physical consequences for the chosen person. One "mother," speaking of the eleven years between her initial vision and her final decision, said that she was "ill all that time. ... If I strong today, tomorrow I sick; and if tomorrow I strong, next day, I sick." But after baptism, "when you say your prayers and go to bed, you begin to see beautiful things, like in the Bible, and you realize there is a God alive."

Pointer B. does not baptize anyone younger than twelve. Children often accompany their mothers to the services, and they may be christened by sprinkling; but if they are to be Shakers, "they have to be baptized in the faith later." Since there is no provision for the specific religious instruction of children in the Shaker church, members' children go to other churches—usually the Anglican, Methodist, or Catholic—for their early religious education.

The person who decides to accept baptism becomes an important actor in a series of rituals. At the first ritual, known as "bowing," which takes place during a meeting, the person is officially recognized as a candidate for baptism. He is brought to the front of the church, to the "bench of repentance," which will be his reserved seat at every meeting he attends until he is finally baptized. With a lighted candle in one hand and the other hand held open with palm up, he is expected to sit and meditate constantly on his sins.

Between "bowing" and baptism, the candidate undergoes a period of training that may vary from several weeks to several months, depending upon when the pointer is finally satisfied with the preparedness of the candidate. It seems, however, that the pointer waits until he has a group of candidates that he feels is large enough to warrant holding a baptism ceremony, since it is obviously a matter of pride to be able to refer to an impressive number of "children."

The night before baptism, the "mothers" and leaders "give words of consolation so that they [the candidates] will be able to tread the way as us do." The culminating ceremony is held on Sunday about noon, but the candidates undergo an attenuated form of the "mourning" ritual in the praise house on Saturday night. Their feet

241

are ritually washed, and they are blindfolded. According to one member, "Three white bands are tied around your eyes. They lay you down as if you are going to mourn, and you does journey that one night." "Banding and lying down," stated the pointer, "is symbolic death before being born again in baptism." The night is spent in prayer and "askin' God's mercy on them."

Baptism requires immersion, so the Sunday ceremony is held at a nearby stream. The pointer, wearing a "long, white gown, like a minister," stands in the water—"he has to get wet"—and the cross bearer, holding a wooden cross about eight feet high, stands beside him. A "mother" described the procedure: "Two women, can be a mother or a nurse, take you to the pointer in the water. He holds you, dips you backward [under the cross] three times, in the name of the Father, the Son, and the Holy Ghost. After the first dip, some shake depending on how they are expecting to receive something. The pointer hands you to the mother. She takes you back and gets another to take to the pointer. When they come out of the water, they shake so you have to hold them up so they won't fall in the water again."

An "assistance mother," "nurse," or "matron" helps the newly baptized Shakers change their clothes; and "when you see them in white dresses and white veils with blue crosses on their foreheads and the men in white with white head ties, it is very beautiful." One member commented, however, that "it is a hard thing to take baptism."

"Mourning" opens the door for the ordinary Shaker to achieve a position of importance in the church. Used in the Shaker sense, mourning does not mean grieving for the dead. The person who "goes to mourn," mourns for his sins. Mourning is also referred to as "taking a spiritual journey" or a "pilgrim journey," or "going to

THE SHAKERS OF ST. VINCENT

the secret room." The spiritual journey is probably accomplished, in large part, by hallucinatory activity. Like baptism, mourning is undertaken in response to a sign from the Holy Ghost; but unlike baptism, it is not required of every Shaker. In view of the hierarchical structure of the church, it would not be desirable for all members to mourn, since the mourning experience determines a person's rank in the church, with those who have mourned enjoying a higher position than those who have not. Mourning can be repeated in the hope of deriving further benefits, or "gifts," from each experience.

When a Shaker decides to go to the secret room, he has to make some practical preparations. Mourning is a lengthy procedure, and there may be job responsibilities or family arrangements to be considered. Preparations for baptism and the final baptism ritual are handled in the evenings and over a weekend, but mourning involves continuous isolation and confinement for a period that may vary from six to fourteen days or more. When Sister W. and A., a woman and a man from one of Pointer B.'s churches, were making their plans for going to mourn, Sister W. said that they were going to have to "beg for jobs, a few days' work, because we have to have money to buy bands and food."

The night before Sister W. and A. were scheduled to enter the period of isolation, the usual Wednesday night meeting was held at the church; but the service centered on the pair going to mourn, and the fact that mourning is regarded as something of a feat was repeatedly expressed. "We do know it is not an easy task. . . . At the beginning it is rough and stony and some mortals faint by the way. As my sister and brother are about to renew the covenant, may they faint not."

Each pointer has a "mourning room," a special one-room shack, available for members of his church who go to mourn. On the following evening, many members of the congregation traveled to the country to Pointer B.'s mourning room to participate in the service before Sister W. and A. were "laid on the ground." The usual Shaker worship routine was observed first, while the mourners stood or knelt at one side of the room, clearly separated from the congregation and the ritual leaders by their position as well as by their air of detachment. Their eyes were closed, and their hands were held out with the palms up. A circular design made with chalk and with lighted candles balanced on it occupied a prominent place on the floor. It would serve the mourners as a "map" for their journey.

At the conclusion of the ordinary part of the worship service, the mourners became the focus of specific ritual procedures to prepare them for mourning. A basin of water was prepared "to wash the feet of the pilgrims." A "prove" was taken for each, and they were asked to confess their sins. With much accompanying ritual, several solid-colored "bands," resembling ascots, were tied over the eyes of each of the mourners, and a head tie was added that covered bands and head.

After the service was brought to a close, several women made the room ready for the mourners. They made pallets on the floor with burlap and put a pillow at one end of each, and they arranged pieces of cloth over a rope that was stretched across the room so that two compartments were formed to separate the sexes. The congregation departed, leaving the mourners to begin their period of retreat.

DURING MOURNING: TRANCE

A mourner's sight is restricted physically by the bands. His movements are restricted mentally by the Shaker

244

beliefs: a mourner must lie either on his right side or on his back, because "you can't get nothin' on the left." The mourner's diet is also restricted, but Shakers give every assurance that it is adequate.[13]

Three days elapse before the pilgrims talk to anyone, "except they have to go out or a mother talks to them—they pray all the time." Sister W. said that "on the third day they rise you from the ground. They have candles and the bell and the Bible set on the ground. You march around in a ring with the bell to your feet. You try to catch the song of the bell. Then you take off. Then you travel." During his travels, the mourner discovers what work he is to do in the church. "If you are to be a mother, you will see the dress you are to wear. You get gifts which have a symbol. A book means you have to go out and preach. A switch in hand means you are to be a leader."

Going to mourn is likened to going to school. Each time a Shaker returns, he learns more. The Holy Spirit "comes and teaches you all things," and the pointer gives the mourners "some charges" from the Bible and "teaches them how to live."

Some individuals are not fit subjects for mourning. According to Pointer B., "You, who have laid the pilgrim, will know. The Spirit reveals it to you. The nurse in the room may know. If the person went to the Spirit in malice against his fellows, they have to go back in humility and ask God's pardon and make things right with the person before they can have a frequent with the Spirit." If an aspirant mourner has perpetrated some evil, "the minute you take the band, the Holy Spirit will put you off. You will see those things you did in front of you, and you just can't get no place." Furthermore, "if you don't have faith, you run out. If you kill somebody, even throw away children, you can't get no place to try to mourn." It is the pointer's responsibility

245

to evaluate each subject's potential for mourning. An unsuited person "will go crazy if you don't release them. The pointer has to know what to do."

There is no prescribed length of time for a mourner to remain in the secret room. He stays "according to the limit of the Spirit." Sister W. had expressed the hope that if she were to "pray fast and pray hard" she would be able to leave in eight days, but she stayed ten. The pointer determines when a mourner may leave. "He knows when to dismiss you. He will ask you questions to see when you are ready to come out, if you've been any places."

When the period of mourning is over, a special meeting is held in the church so the pilgrims may "shout," or describe their spiritual journeys in detail to the congregation. In recounting their experiences, the mourners indicated that the content of the visions included much that was familiar, such as walking along the road to a nearby village. Some of the happenings described were of a somewhat less familiar nature to the Shakers generally, but were still within the range of possibility, such as having to sign something in an office situation. But much of what they told was extraordinary as, for example, hearing a voice that sent the angel Gabriel and Peter to visit the person.

Several Shakers who had mourned mentioned being "crowned." One woman said that on her journey she had seen the queen take her crown off her own head and put it on the woman's head. Such a vision entitles the mourner to the central role in the impressive and coveted bit of ritual when he shouts, "They put the Bible on your head and the mothers hold candles around your head." However, as with all gifts acquired on a spiritual journey, the pointer has to concur before any gifts are forthcoming, and "unless the pointer sees it too, you don't get crowned." Colors for head ties and instructions concerning other wearing apparel are also "given" to the pilgrim on his journey.

The restrictive conditions to which the mourners are subjected are so remarkably similar to those designed for certain formal investigations of the effects of sensory deprivation on the human organism that it would be reasonable to expect similar results. In fact, it might be suggested that, insofar as the results are the same, they are dependent on human biological reactions to the conditions of deprivation and that, to the extent that the results differ, they are influenced by the cultural makeup of the subjects.[14]

The pioneer work on sensory deprivation was begun in 1951 by Dr. D. O. Hebb and his associates at McGill University. Wearing translucent goggles to prevent patterned vision, gloves and carboard cuffs to lessen tactual perception, and with auditory perception minimized by a foam rubber pillow, soundproofing, and a masking noise, the subjects in the McGill studies were instructed to lie on a bed in a small room as long as they were willing, usually three or four days. An intercommunication system linked the subject with an experimenter who was always stationed outside the room. Subjects were taken to the toilet and given food on demand (Bexton et al. 1954; Heron et al. 1956; Heron 1961; Scott et al. 1959; Doane et al. 1959). Hallucinations ranging from imagery of a simple nature to full-blown scenes were reported (Bexton et al. 1954). Changing to opaque goggles decreased hallucinating, which was reestablished upon return to translucent goggles (Doane et al. 1959). One group of researchers (Bexton et al. 1954) found that their subjects had some control over hallucinatory content, but another study produced conflicting results (Heron 1961). The effect of propaganda presented to subjects during isolation was tested and compared with the effect on a control group. A change in attitude appeared in

247

both groups but was greater in the experimental subjects (Scott et al. 1959).

Later studies indicated that conditions of complete darkness, diffuse light or an unvaried visual environment, or visual monotony broken by intermittent stimulation were equally effective in producing reported visual sensations, although a monotonous visual environment was found to be more conducive than one that was unrestricted and patterned (Zuckerman 1969).

Freedman et al. (1961) found that hallucinations were reported in a study in which motility was restricted. But Zuckerman (1969) suggests that position is more important than activity. Lying on one's back seems to be more productive of reported visual sensations than other positions.

Jackson and his associates considered the effect of the subject's expectations on sensory deprivation studies and concluded that "prior knowledge of the expected or anticipated effects...motivation to experience and report, or not to experience and not to report, and the use of free-associative reporting" are important variables (Jackson and Kelley 1962; Jackson and Pollard 1962:340). In addition, Orne and Scheibe stressed the importance of "the matrix of social cues" or "demand characteristics" on experimental results (1964:3). They suggested that devices such as the panic button featured in Princeton sensory deprivation studies (Vernon 1963) serve as "eloquent instructions" for the subject.

Other experimental techniques have been used for restricting external stimulation (see, for example, Shurley 1962; Solomon and Mendelson 1962; Mendelson et al. 1961), but they differ radically from Shaker mourning room conditions and are less useful for comparison.

Some striking similarities can be seen between the sensory deprivation studies cited and the Shaker mourning experience. The physical conditions used in the McGill research and in the mourning room parallel one another to a remarkable extent. Both the mourner and the sensory deprivation subject remain lying down within a strictly circumscribed area. A monotonous visual environment is provided by the mourner's bands and the sensory deprivation subject's goggles. The mourner and the experimental subject are removed from their ordinary surroundings, deprived of their usual social contacts and routine activities, and placed in positions of regression, dependant upon the attendants in the mourning room or the observers in the test locale. Both are confronted with monotonous and reduced external stimuli, and neither is given prior information about the duration of confinement. Although the motility of the mourner is not restricted by any mechanical device such as was used in the McGill studies, the mourner is restrained by his beliefs and goals.

Like many sensory deprivation subjects, mourners report an assortment of visual and auditory phenomena. Zubek (1964) noted that increased precision in defining these phenomena was having an effect on research results. Zuckerman indicates that the problem of definition is as yet unsolved, however, and he uses " 'reported visual (or auditory) sensations' (RVS or RAS) as a generic term for all the phenomena" (1969:86). Wallace suggests that, for cross-cultural application, "hallucination" be defined broadly as "pseudoperception, without relevant stimulation of external or internal receptors, but with subjective vividness equal to that aroused by such stimulation" (1959:59). Since the mourners probably experience phenomena ranging from simple daydreams to complex hallucinations, it would seem appropriate to label them as "pseudoperceptions" or "reported visual, or auditory, sensations," both being conveniently inclusive.

Shaker mourners, like subjects in some studies, have prior knowledge of what constitutes "appropriate"

249

behavior in the mourning room. Many of them are repeating the rite and know what to expect and what is expected of them. All Shakers have the opportunity to hear returning mourners when they "shout in the temple" and share their travel experiences with the congregation, and past mourners are not reticent about discussing their journeys in ordinary conversation. In addition, all Shakers who are baptized are exposed to a shortened version of mourning the night before baptism.

Certain cues in the mourning room situation may further serve to communicate to the mourner what is expected of him. During the service before the mourners are "put on the ground," they are separated from the congregation and subjected to ritual treatment that emphasizes their sacredness and the solemn importance of their undertaking. The chalk design on the floor, referred to as a "map" for the mourners, provides "eloquent instructions" as to what they are supposed to do. The presence of their friends in the mourning room miles away from town indicates the importance attached to the ritual and those about to undergo it, and assures the mourners of moral support during the trying ordeal.

The "attitude of people toward their own hallucinations" as well as the "cultural response toward people who have hallucinations" are mentioned by Smythies (1956:338–39) as important factors in the production of perceptual phenomena. Since hallucinations are positively valued in the Shaker subculture, and since those who have visions are regarded as favored individuals, mourners are strongly motivated to "experience and report." An acceptable mourning experience not only evokes the pointer's approval, but also confers on the mourner a more prestigious position in the church and guarantees that he will be the center of attention at the post-mourning ritual. College students have been used as subjects in many sensory deprivation studies; and even

250

THE SHAKERS OF ST. VINCENT

if they did not regard hallucinations negatively, it is hardly likely that they looked upon them as a spiritual privilege. They may have been eager to cooperate with the investigators, but the rewards for experiencing and reporting perceptual phenomena would differ in kind and importance from the rewards awaiting the mourners. For a prestige-starved Shaker in a community offering few opportunities for the lesser-educated, lower-class individual to attain prestige (compare Mischel 1958), the benefits to be derived probably seem very worthwhile.

The experimental technique of continuous reporting that seems to facilitate the production of sensory deprivation phenomena (Jackson and Pollard 1962) also has its parallel in the mourning room. The pointer is kept informed of the progress of the mourner on his journey and offers suggestions and guidance along the way.

Anxiety and stress are characteristic of conditions of sensory deprivation and may contribute to the generation of perceptual disturbances (Zuckerman 1969). Although mourners are subjected to physical conditions similar to those experienced by research subjects, the Shakers probably find them less anxiety-producing because of their belief system, their personal goals, their greater prior knowledge, and their relationship to the pointer and the mourning room attendants. However, other sources of anxiety exist for mourners. The anticipated visions and gifts may not be forthcoming; or the pilgrim and the pointer may interpret the meaning and significance of the spiritual journey differently, and the pointer may refuse to acknowledge gifts claimed by the mourner. Uncertainty may stem from the knowledge that the pointer must reject unworthy aspirants and should release those without sufficient stamina for mourning; yet some pilgrims in the past have gone "mad" and required hospitalization. The constant presence of mourning room attendants, although a comfort, may also be a stress factor, emphasizing, as it does, the mourners' dependence and the possibility of something happening that might require their assistance.

Subjects under conditions of sensory deprivation were found to be more susceptible to suggestion than they would normally be, and the attitudes acquired under these conditions tended to linger. Shakers who had mourned were observed to be fairly dependable possession trancers, and were never seen as recipients of the pointer's anger or corrective measures. Mourning room indoctrination may have been partly responsible for their more serious approach and solemn demeanor and their facility in dissociation.

Several investigators have remarked on the ability or inability of subjects to control hallucinatory content. The content of Shaker visions seems to be restricted to culturally prescribed topics or to material that lends itself to culturally biased interpretations. Wallace has discussed differences that Slotkin found in "responses of clinically 'normal' White and [American] Indian subjects" to mescaline intoxication (1959:63). White hallucinations are "largely idiosyncratic in content," whereas Indian hallucinations are "often strongly patterned after doctrinal model." Wallace attributes these variations to "the setting in which the drug is taken" and the "psychological meaning" attached to its effects. The sensory deprivation subject's experience, like some White drug subject's experience, took place in a research setting. The Shakers, on the other hand, like the Indians, are engaging in an important religious ritual. Subjects in sensory deprivation experiments, like those in drug experiments, have little "commitment to or interest in" sensory deprivation. Many of them were paid to participate, which would give the experience a "job" flavor with no particular lasting personal benefits expected or any unusual satisfactions to be derived from it. For some experiments, unpaid volunteers, or even the researchers themselves, served as subjects. Their interest may have been greater than for the paid subjects, but was probably of a clinical or investigative nature; and the experiment was seen as a step to further knowledge but not as an end in itself. The mourners, however, like the Indians, are involved in an experience that has deep religious meaning for them, that gives them great spiritual satisfaction and permanent advantages. Mourning, for them, is an end in itself.

In addition to the effects of physical conditions acting on the human organism, psychological and cultural factors also appear to contribute quite significantly to the production of sensory deprivation phenomena.

SHAKERISM AND SOCIAL CHANGE

It has been observed repeatedly (Smith 1965; Ragatz 1928; Goveia 1965; Lowenthal 1967) that West Indian society is divided into separate and distinct sections. This seems to be a result of several factors, among which are: first, the early development of a "planter class," a slave population, and a hybrid group; second, the emancipation of the slaves without assimilation; and third, a general population whose members seem to be dedicated to a set of values that includes the maintenance of the existing social strata. Race and color, real or imputed, have been significant in the continuation of the divisions. Paradoxically, education, occupation, and wealth, and perhaps religion, have contributed to their maintenance. Persistent interclass attitudes have erected barriers that are difficult to surmount. "The elite and the middle class do not want to know anything about folk culture" (Lowenthal 1967:593), and many lower-class West Indians "retain much the same psychological attitude as did their forefathers under slavery" and have "repudiated middle class standards" (Hadley 1949:353,

253

356). Lowenthal has further observed, "What the sections of society do know about others they usually disapprove of" (1967:595). The lower-class Vincentian is in a frustrating position, hemmed in by the social climate and by the realization of his own inability to overcome the obstructions to his occupational, educational, and socioeconomic improvement.

Wallace has suggested that religious ritual may offer individuals a possible "avenue to identity renewal" (1966:140). Many avenues exist, all of them involving "some kind of identification with an admired model of the human personality, and differentiation from a despised model." Wallace and Fogelson define identity as "any image, or set of images, either conscious or unconscious, which an individual has of himself" (1965:380). They provide a minimal four-part division of a person's total identity that includes his real identity, claimed identity, feared identity, and ideal identity. For a typical Shaker, these identities might be described as follows. His feared identity seems to be an image of himself as a lazy, incompetent, inferior, and stupid individual. Pointer B., for example, was very much on the defensive when trying to explain why he could only find part-time work. He seemed quite anxious that he not appear unwilling to work or incapable. A Shaker's real identity is his image of himself in an occupational setting, as a dock hand, laborer, and so on; in the family situation, as a father, son, and so on; in the church context, as a pointer, nurse, and so on. His claimed identity might be an image of himself as a self-effacing child of God, as a hard worker, a good father, and so on. For his ideal image, he might picture himself as a person particularly chosen and favored by God, hence, superior; as a person eligible for supernatural rewards by reason of his righteousness and, consequently, a receiver of the Holy Spirit.

According to Wallace and Fogelson, an individual places a positive value on his ideal identity and attempts to minimize the differences between his real and his ideal identities while maximizing the differences between his real and his feared identities. Since an identity image depends upon internalization of the reactions and attitudes of others, a person's real, feared, and ideal identities "are built upon, and require, repeated validation in social communication" (1965:382).

For the lower-class Vincentian, validation of his ideal identity is not forthcoming in the social contexts in which it could be most convincing and meaningful to him; in these contexts, instead, it is his feared identity that receives frequent validation. The members of the upper classes express opinions that lower-class workers are indolent and undependable, and they may aggravate the injury to a lower-class individual's self-esteem by making such observations in his presence. If a person is a Shaker in addition to being a member of the lower class, he may be the butt of further disparagement: his belief system and his religious practices may be ridiculed.

But Shakerism does offer the lower-class Vincentian a means of soothing his injured identity image. Possession trance provides a most dramatic validation of his worthiness and reassures him that his feared identity and his ideal identity are not approaching congruence. Since the Spirit only shakes those who are pure, his righteousness is publicly demonstrated, and this is all the more significant because possession trance does not occur in the organized churches attended by the upper-class Vincentians.

In addition to possession trance, the worshiper can find other devices in the Shaker religion to bolster his identity image. Biblical texts, sermons, prayers, and hymns often stress that they are the chosen people of

God. Such texts as "He has gone to prepare a place for you" are repeated frequently, as are references to the coming of Christ and the Judgment Day, when the Shakers will receive their blessing. The worshipers are reminded that their sufferings are much easier to bear than the sufferings of Jesus were, and it is implied that they, being favored by God also, should expect and welcome suffering because it brings them into closer affiliation with the biblical heroes. The necessity of being baptized in order to be saved further underscores the gulf between the Shakers who, like Jesus, have been baptized and are therefore eligible for salvation, and the upper classes who have not.

The Bible provides the "admired models" with whom the Shakers can identify. "Despised models" from whom they can differentiate themselves are supplied by those who deviate from the Shaker concept of a Christian, and the upper class makes a convenient scapegoat. "With a few cents they find theirself in a high lifted way. They find they is too good to think about God. Those who have money don't think about Christ. They think about their furniture and money. That is their God." Being less endowed with worldly goods, the Shakers extol poverty and preach, "Empty-handed you go to Jesus. Do not put your faith in the material things of the world." Being excluded by the upper class, they exclude, indirectly but unequivocally: "Not everyone will be with Him, only those who do the will of the Father." Feeling rejected by the world, they reject in return, saying, "Think not of this world. This world has nothing to give you but shame and disgrace."

Although both men and women seem to be seeking restoration of a tolerable identity image through Shaker beliefs and activities, subtle differences in the objectives and satisfactions of the sexes seem to exist. Shaker men, on the whole, appear to derive less satisfaction from their lives in the larger society than the women do. Job opportunities seem to be fewer for them unless they emigrate, and the kinds of jobs that are available to them locally do not fulfill their aspirations. The women, on the other hand, seem to be more satisfied with the kinds of work they are doing. A greater number and a greater variety of work opportunities that can gratify some of their prestige cravings seem to be open to them. Shakerism compensates men for the lack of authority and prestige positions available to them by giving offices to all of them. It may, in fact, be necessary to offer men this additional feature in order to attract them to the church. Being more dissatisfied and apparently more eager for the monetary rewards of upward mobility than the women, the men may also be more sensitive to the ridicule aimed at the Shakers and more concerned about the effect that their affiliation with a disfavored church would have on their opportunities. The women, being more satisfied with their lives, may be less sensitive to public opinion and also less in need of the attraction of church status. Furthermore, those women who are heads of their own households may find some compensation in the church organization and the church discipline for the lack of a male figure in their home situations.

The Shaker means of identity renewal might also be regarded as a "ritual of rebellion," a ritual, according to Gluckman (1954:3), in which certain social tensions are able to be expressed. The Shakers exhibit their superiority over those to whom they are usually subservient by constructing an image of themselves as God's chosen people and demonstrating the validity of that image through possession trance. But, as Gluckman points out, such ritualized expressions of social tensions are made in a special context—one which does not disturb the system. Shakers are not revolting, they have no desire to overthrow the established system; but they are finding

fault with, and rebelling against, the "particular distribu-
tions of power" that prove to be so inequitable and disad-
vantageous to them. Their ritualized manner of rebelling
"allows for instituted protest" while it, simultaneously,
"renews the unity of the system" (Gluckman 1954:3).

Lewis has given some consideration to possession
trance phenomena and has observed that "women and
other depressed categories" frequently use a possession
trance to "exert mystical pressures upon their superiors
in circumstances of deprivation and frustration when few
other sanctions are available to them" (1966:318). Among
the Shakers, however, women do not seem to be any
more deprived than men, if as much; hence they do not
represent a "depressed category" by virtue of their sex.
Neither are the Shakers as a group exerting "mystical
pressures upon their superiors" in the same way in which
Lewis's examples are: possession trance among the
Shakers is not regarded as an illness; it does not require
exorcism; it is not an ailment that demands therapy and
attention from those who are being pressured. Rather,
it is a source of personal pleasure, an experience to be
sought and cherished. It might conceivably be argued
that pressure is being exerted on those who are superior
to the Shakers but that it is latent and covert. Neither
the Shakers nor their superiors recognize or perceive
any pressure.

Simpson (1965:127) has observed that the Shangoists
of Trinidad expend in religious activities their supply of
"time, thought, energy, and resources," that might otherwise be channeled into activities designed to implement
social, economic, and political change. Hence, Shango
helps to perpetuate the established order by consuming
the ingredients that could be used to bring about change.

Methodism, in its early days, also directed the
resources available to its followers into religious outlets
and focused their attention on the afterlife and away from

the injustices and inadequacies of the contemporary scene. It thereby helped to prevent disturbances to the prevailing system (Bowen 1937; Sargant 1959).

In similar ways, Shakerism monopolizes the time and energies of its devotees, drains away their pent-up frustrations in the release of dissociation and religious activities, and curtails resources that could be utilized for the initiation or promotion of change. However, there is a ritual complex in Shakerism that does function as a mechanism for adjustment to change, and might possibly operate as an agency for its initiation if the Shakers were to become more action-oriented. On the spiritual journey, a mourner may encounter features that are new and unusual for the Shakers. Later, when he shouts, the mourner shares these novelties with the entire congregation, which helps to prepare this less-advantaged portion of the population for innovations being introduced into the society. However, given the belief system surrounding the hallucinatory activity of the mourning room and the possibility of influencing the content of the visual and auditory phenomena experienced, in addition to the fact that the pointer guides the pilgrim on his journey, the mourning rite could conceivably serve as a device for the initiation of change. Another potential mechanism exists in the variation in possession trance for the pointer and for the ordinary Shaker. Although every Shaker is a possible host for the Holy Spirit, the pointer in a state of possession trance serves in a somewhat more elevated capacity as the agency through which the divine can work. Through the pointer, for example, the Holy Ghost can punish an erring worshiper. Supernatural messages issued through the pointer for the congregation could also be a potential force for change.

As the church functions presently, however, by permitting assertions of superiority and personal worth within a ritual context, by providing the worshipers with

259

an acceptable identity image, by helping them to become accustomed to innovations that may eventually reach them, and by discharging emotional tensions in possession trance activity and religious experiences, Shakerism serves to discourage any disturbance of the established system and contributes to the maintenance of the status quo.

1. Conspicuous changes occurred in the area of tourism between the time of my first visit in 1966 and my second in 1970.

2. A branch of Planned Parenthood has recently been established on the island and is reported to be making some progress, but thus far the effects have been insignificant.

3. Shakers are usually confirmed in one of the organized churches before they become Shakers and are counted as members of those ch. ches in the census.

4. Spiritual Baptists are also found in Trinidad, having spread there from St. Vincent in the early 1900s. In Trinidad, they are known as "Shouters."

5. In 1960, less than 4% of a total of 23,091 individuals between 5 and 14 years of age were illiterate, and less than 8% of the 40,643 persons 15 years of age or older were illiterate (The Economic Planning Unit n.d.).

6. M. J. and F. S. Herskovits (1947) described Spiritual Baptist churches in Trinidad, and they seemed to be very similar to Shaker churches in St. Vincent. However, the center pole in Trinidad churches received more attention. Simpson (1961), writing later, states that the center pole may be omitted from Trinidad churches even as in St. Vincent, which suggests that deemphasis of the center pole may be a trend in both islands.

7. Mischel (1958) described a similar visiting situation among the Shangoists of Trinidad.

8. "Taking a prove" is a divinatory method frequently used by Shakers. It consists of opening the Bible at random and noting the three verses indicated on each page by the thumbs. These passages are believed to carry a message for, or about. the performer.

9. For a more detailed version of this section, see Henney (1967).

10. This would appear to be similar to the "trumping and laboring" described for several Jamaican revival cults by Moore (1965:64).

11. Mischel and Mischel (1958) state that crises stimulate the induction of possession trance among Shangoists in Trinidad. Although Shakers did not seem to require any extraordinary stimulus for the usual possession trances, such stimulus seemed to be a factor in atypical manifestations.

12. Simpson (1966) has described these rituals for the Shouters of Trinidad.

13. This is not the consensus of non-Shakers, however. A Vincentian doctor, for example, stated, "They may keep mourners two or three weeks, and

starve them. They may not get enough fluids, and see all kinds of things. The teachers know full well that if you starve a person he becomes deluded and sees things. By suggestion, he is helped along.''

14. For a more detailed version of this section, see Henney (1968).

REFERENCES

Association of Caribbean Universities and Research Institute. 1967. *Caribbean Monthly Bulletin.* February.

Bexton, W. H., W. Heron, And T. H. Scott. 1954. Effects of decreased variation in the sensory environment. *Canadian Journal of Psychology 8:* 70–76.

Bowen, Marjorie. 1937. *Wrestling Jacob.* London: William Heinemann.

Burns, Alan. 1954. *History of the British West Indies.* London: George Allen & Unwin.

Doane, B. K. et al. 1959. Changes in perceptual function after isolation. *Canadian Journal of Psychology* 13:210–19.

Duncan, Ebenezer. 1963. *A brief history of Saint Vincent with studies in citizenship.* Kingstown, St. Vincent: Government Printing Office.

Economic Planning Unit. n.d. *Facts for investors on Saint Vincent.* Kingstown, St. Vincent, W.I.: Ministries Building.

Freedman, Sanford J., Henry U. Grunebaum, and Milton Greenblatt. 1961. "Perceptual and cognitive changes in sensory deprivation," in *Sensory deprivation* (editors P. Solomon, et al.). Cambridge, Mass.: Harvard University Press.

Garcia, A. 1965. *History of the West Indies.* London: George G. Harrap & Co.

Gluckman, Max. 1954. *Rituals of rebellion in South-east Africa.* Manchester: Manchester University Press.

Goveia, Elsa V. 1965. *Slave society in the British Leeward Islands at the end of the eighteenth century.* New Haven: Yale University Press.

Great Britain Colonial Office. 1966. *St. Vincent: Annual report for the years 1962 and 1963.* Colonial Office Colonial Annual Report Series. London: Her Majesty's Stationery Office.

Hadley, C. V. D. 1949. Personality patterns, social class, and aggression in the British West Indies. *Human Relations* 11:349–62.

Henney, Jeannette. 1967. "Trance behavior among the Shakers of St. Vincent." Working paper no. 8, Cross-Cultural Study of Dissociational States. Columbus: the Ohio State University, Department of Anthropology.

———. 1968. " 'Mourning,' a religious ritual among the Spiritual Baptists of St. Vincent: An experience in sensory deprivation." Working paper no. 21, Cross-Cultural Study of Dissociational States. Columbus: the Ohio State University, Department of Anthropology.

Religion, Altered States of Consciousness, and Social Change

Heron, Woodburn. 1961. "Cognitive and physiological effects of perceptual isolation," in *Sensory deprivation* (editors P. Solomon et al.). Cambridge, Mass.: Harvard University Press.

Heron, Woodburn, B. K. Doane, and T. H. Scott. 1956. Visual disturbances after prolonged perceptual isolation. *Canadian Journal of Psychology* 10: 13–18.

Herskovits, Melville J. and Frances S. Herskovits. 1947. *Trinidad village*. New York: Alfred A. Knopf.

Jackson, C. Wesley, Jr., and E. Lowell Kelly. 1962. Influence of suggestion and subjects' prior knowledge in research on sensory deprivation. *Science* 135:211–12.

Jackson, C. Wesley, Jr., and John C. Pollard. 1962. Sensory deprivation and suggestion: A theoretical approach. *Behavioral Science* 7:332–42.

Jahn, Janheinz. 1968. "A Yoruba market-woman's life," in *Every man his way* (editor Alan Dundes). Engelwood Cliffs, N. J.: Prentice-Hall.

Lewis, I. M. 1966. Spirit possession and deprivation cults. *Man*, n.s. 1:307–29.

Lowenthal, David. 1967. Race and color in the West Indies. *Daedalus* 96: 580–626.

Mendelson, Jack H. et al. 1961. "Physiological and psychological aspects of sensory deprivation—a case analysis," in *Sensory deprivation* (editors P. Solomon et al.). Cambridge, Mass.: Harvard University Press.

Mintz, Sidney. 1960. Peasant markets. *Scientific American* 203:112–18, 120, 122.

Mischel, Frances Osterman. 1958. "A Shango religious group and the problem of prestige in Trinidadian society," Ph.D. dissertation, the Ohio State University.

Mischel, Walter and Frances Mischel. 1958. Psychological aspects of spirit possession. *American Anthropologist* 60:249–60.

Moore, Joseph G. 1965. Religious syncretism in Jamaica. *Practical Anthropology* 12:63–70.

Orne, Martin T. and Karl E. Scheibe. 1964. The contribution of nondeprivation factors in the production of sensory deprivation effects: The psychology of the "panic button." *Journal of Abnormal and Social Psychology* 68:3–12.

Ottenberg, Phoebe V. 1959. "The changing economic position of women among the Afikpo Ibo," in *Continuity and change in African cultures* (editors William R. Bascom and Melville J. Herskovits). Chicago: University of Chicago Press.

Rae, James Stanley. 1927. *The laws of St. Vincent containing the ordinances of the colony in force on the 4th day of May, 1926*. Rev. ed. 2 vols. Millbank, S.W.I.: Crown Agents for the Colonies.

Ragatz, Lowell Joseph. 1928. *The fall of the planter class in the British Caribbean, 1763–1833*. New York: Century Co.

Sargant, William. 1959. *Battle for the mind*. London: Pan Books.

Scott, T. H. et al. 1959. Cognitive effects of perceptual isolation. *Canadian Journal of Psychology* 13:200–209.

Shurley, Jay T. 1962. "Mental imagery in profound experimental sensory isolation," in *Hallucinations* (editor Louis Jolyon West). New York: Grune & Stratton.

Simpson, George E. 1961. *Cult music of Trinidad*. Folkways Ethnic Album #FE 4478. New York: Folkways Records and Service Corp.

──────. 1962. Social stratification in the Caribbean. *Phylon* 23:29–46.

──────. 1965. *The Shango Cult in Trinidad*. Caribbean Monograph Series, no. 2. Institute of Caribbean Studies. Rio Piedras, P. R.: University of Puerto Rico.

──────. 1966. Baptismal, "mourning," and "building" ceremonies of the Shouters in Trinidad. *Journal of American Folklore* 79:537–50.

Smith, M. G. 1965. *The plural society in the British West Indies*. Berkeley: University of California Press.

Smythies, J. R. 1956. A logical and cultural analysis of hallucinatory sense-experience. *Journal of Mental Science* 102:336–42.

Solomon, Philip, and Jack Mendelson. 1962. "Hallucinations in sensory deprivation," in *Hallucinations* (editor Louis Jolyon West). New York: Grune & Stratton.

Southey, Robert. 1925. *The life of Wesley and the rise and progress of Methodism*. Edited by Maurice H. Fitzgerald. 2 vols. London: Oxford University Press.

Vernon, Jack A. 1963. *Inside the black room*. New York: Clarkson N. Potter.

Wallace, Anthony F. C. 1959. Cultural determinants of response to hallucinatory experience. *A.M.A. Archives of General Psychiatry* 1:58–69.

──────. 1966. *Religion: An anthropological view*. New York: Random House.

Wallace, Anthony F. C., and Raymond D. Fogelson. 1965. "The identity struggle," in *Intensive family therapy* (editors Ivan Boszormenyi-Nagy and James L. Framo). New York: Harper & Row.

Zubek, J. P. 1964. Effects of prolonged sensory and perceptual deprivation. *British Medical Bulletin* 20:38–42.

Zuckerman, Marvin. 1969. "Hallucinations, reported sensations, and images," in *Sensory deprivation: Fifteen years of research* (editor John P. Zubek). New York: Appleton-Century-Crofts.

7 : Umbanda in São Paulo: Religious Innovation in a Developing Society

Esther Pressel

Modern Brazil is a developing society in which technological change has brought a multitude of social innovations in the areas of economy, politics, family, and religion.[1] In most parts of Brazil, the traditional semifeudal rural agrarian economy has been or is in the process of being replaced by a technologically oriented, urban industrial economy. During the Vargas era in the 1930s, what had once been strong state and regional groupings became politically oriented toward the federal government. A new sense of national ideology and pride developed and remains quite strong in Brazil today. The federal government's emphasis upon modernization of agriculture and industrialization has led to the migration of large numbers of unemployed rural persons to urban centers where they hope to find jobs. City life has tended to weaken the large extended family system, and as a result a nuclear family orientation is becoming more prevalent. Sociocultural change is being accompanied by new life styles, modern role expectations, and changing values.

In this milieu of sociocultural transformation, social-psychological stress is manifested in the individual as he daily attempts to cope with new problems in his environment. Interestingly, many Brazilians turn to a spiritualist religion known as Umbanda for help in solving their personal difficulties. They may attend public spiritualist sessions held at Umbanda centers twice each week. There, they consult with spirits that are said to

264

possess the Umbanda mediums. Although Brazil has had a long history of spiritualist religions, it is interesting to note that Umbanda apparently emerged during the early period of modernization in the 1920s (McGregor 1967). Today, Umbanda diffuses to the smaller cities in the interior of Brazil as they become more connected with the modern socioeconomic structure. Umbanda, then, is a spiritualist religion that seems to be closely linked to changing life styles in a technologically based social structure. In describing Umbanda as a religious innovation in the developing society of Brazil, I shall first present background data on the Brazilian social structure and then data on Umbanda.

STRUCTURAL OUTLINE OF BRAZILIAN SOCIETY

Society

Brazil stretches 2,700 miles east to west and 2,500 miles north to south. In terms of land mass, it is the fifth largest country in the world and covers about one-half of the continent of South America. Brazil's population is approximately 85 million people, making it eighth in world population (Momsen 1968:7). Smith has characterized the tremendous diversity one finds in Brazil as a "cultural mosaic" (1963:12). The mosaic is, in part, related to the wide-ranging forms of natural environments—tropics, deserts, and temperate regions—that have helped to shape regional cultural differences in Brazil. From another point of view Brazil can be seen as a "melting pot" of races and cultures that occurred to a degree not found in the United States. In Brazil, the European Portuguese settled and interbred with indigenous Indian populations. Later, when African slaves were imported to labor on the sugar plantations in the northeastern part of the country, the Brazilian society came to include Afri-

265

Plate 1. A young woman from the audience is possessed and must be restrained by other mediums. (Photographs by Esther Pressel.)

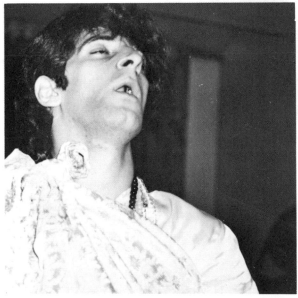

Plate 2. *Top*. Young man shows pre-possession concentration. *Bottom*. Same person is possessed by male *caboclo* spirit.

Plate 3. *Top left*. Normal facial expression of medium. *Top right*. Medium possessed, displaying hand gesture typical of *caboclo* spirits. *Bottom left*. Two *caboclo* spirits greet each other using stereotypic behavior. *Bottom right*. Female medium, 52 years old, possessed by male *criança* spirit about 5 years of age.

Plate 4. *Top*. Possession by *caboclo* spirit. *Bottom*. Cult leader possessed by *orixá* spirit, Iemanjá.

can physical types and cultural beliefs. In the past 100 years a new wave of immigrants from Germany, Italy, Japan, Poland, Portugal, and other countries has become a part of the population and national culture of Brazil. Although Brazil is composed primarily of African, European, and New World Indian races and cultures, Brazil's "major institutions, its language, and its basic ideal patterns of behavior are European ones, modified and developed in the New World environment" (Wagley 1963:24). Three things give modern Brazil unity: its "Great Tradition" of language and social institutions from Portugal; its particular development in the New World setting of races and cultures from the three continents; and its special nationalistic outlook since 1930. My study of Umbanda covered the short time period between December 1966, and November 1967. I did most of my research in the large metropolis of São Paulo. The study, however, is set within the larger time span of over four hundred years of blending of peoples and cultures. More specifically, this study of Umbanda should be thought of as a part of the industrialization and nationalism taking place in the past fifty years in Brazil.

Status of Society

Between 1500 and 1821, Brazil was a Portuguese colony. In 1822, Dom Pedro I declared Brazil an independent empire and set up a constitutional monarchy. Momsen (1968:29) tells us that in 1888, Isabel, the daughter of Dom Pedro II, decreed the emancipation of Brazilian slaves while acting as regent during one of her father's many trips abroad. The conservative plantation owners sided with the military and the liberal antimonarchists, who did not feel they wanted to deal with Isabel and her unpopular husband when Dom Pedro II died. The alliance forced the emperor to leave the country, and

Brazil became a republic on 15 November 1889. During the early years of the republic, Brazil had a formal democracy but was in fact ruled by a traditional oligarchy. Individual states had more power than the federal government. Then, in 1930, political power shifted from the plantation northeast to the industrial southern states. Getúlio Vargas assumed control of the federal government by military force. From the period of Vargas up to the present, Brazil has undergone a political and economic reorientation from traditional state oligarchies to a more tightly controlled central government that is forced to consider the ever increasing needs and aspirations and the opinions of the masses (Dulles 1966:4).

Class Structure

Formerly, Brazilian class structure was essentially a two-part system that included an elite class of European origin who held power and a lower class of peasants whose lives were directed by the elite. A very small middle class filled bureaucratic posts but it identified with the elite. Together, the elite and the middle class shared the written tradition inherited from Europe, or what Redfield has called the "Great Tradition." An upper-class person from the northeast had essentially the same cultural expectations and behavior as his counterpart several thousand miles away in the southern part of the country. On the other hand, the culture of the peasants varied greatly throughout the different regions of Brazil. Until recently, Brazil had a highly stable class structure in which upward mobility did not exist to any significant degree. Observers of the modern Brazilian scene agree that class structure today is in rapid flux and that social and economic mobility is definitely present. Wagley (1963:101–2) perceives four new classes emerging in Brazil today: (1) a new factory in the field proletariat;

267

(2) a rapidly expanding metropolitan lower class; (3) a new middle class; and (4) a metropolitan upper class. What follows is mostly a summary of Wagley's (1963: 111–31) observations on the emerging class structure.

In the rural areas a field proletariat has emerged as small family plantations and farms have been reorganized into the national marketing system. The companies give the field proletariat housing, and theoretically there is social legislation to protect the laborers. The traditional close personal ties between employer and worker are gone. As a result, the workers are turning more toward labor unions and politicians for help in improving their conditions and gaining their rights. The members of the field proletariat frequently are illiterate and vulnerable to charismatic leaders. Peasant leagues and other movements promise protection in an uncertain and impersonal world. As farming becomes big business and mechanization of agriculture occurs, increasing numbers of the traditional peasant class migrate to urban areas to seek employment. They form the rapidly expanding metropolitan lower class that also includes industrial workers. The migrants usually live in shacks located in the outlying *favelas,* or slums. Running water, sewage systems, and electricity are not always available in these areas. Women come to the city because they frequently can obtain work as domestics in middle- and upper-class homes. The first generation usually is rural in outlook and culture, but the second generation rapidly acquires new tastes for material possessions. Education in these areas is not good or is nonexistent. Though upward class mobility is possible, it is extremely difficult to achieve with an inadequate education and increasing competition as more migrants arrive on the scene. The industrial workers are usually better off than those living in the *favelas.* Their houses are better constructed and have more modern conveniences. It is not too unusual to find a television set in the homes of the factory workers. These people are in the upper part of the lower class, aspiring for upward mobility into the middle class. Many are hoping to achieve it through education and hard work.

Until recently, the middle class was not significant in either size or power. As industry and commerce have rapidly expanded, many new jobs have become available in offices and stores. One of the major criteria for being accepted into the middle class is an occupation that does not involve manual labor. In this respect, the middle class remains traditional in its outlook. But it differs from the old middle class in its increased expectations of material possessions that include a privately owned apartment or house, a car, and all the gadgets and conveniences one finds in a modern home. Whenever possible, middle-class people send their children to private schools, where they believe a better education can be obtained than in the overcrowded public schools. Spiraling inflation is the worst enemy of the new middle class. The traditional upper class in Brazil was a land-owning aristocracy. A new metropolitan upper class is taking the place of the old elite. People in this class are the owners of industries and commercial enterprises. Marriage, in many cases, welds together the traditional elite and the *arrivistas* from the middle class. The new upper class remains open, at least for the present, to those who can manipulate their way up through a combination of education, money, professional competence, and political influence.

Up to this point, I have been discussing class structure primarily in social, economic, and educational terms, and we have seen that Brazil has a form of complex stratification and an increasing amount of social mobility. There is another factor that is significant, and this is race. The traditional upper elite was, for all intents and purposes, white. The lower peasant class was composed of persons of African, American Indian, European, and mixed ancestry. Because much of the country's population is racially mixed, Brazil has often been looked to as something of a paradise of racial harmony. When the slaves were freed, nearly all records of slaving activities were intentionally destroyed by the government to ensure that all of its citizens were equal. However, the general rule of thumb, "the lower the class, the darker the color, and the higher the class, the lighter the color," is still present in Brazil. North Americans might fallaciously conclude that their own two-caste system of "black" and "white" is present in Brazil. This is not true, as evidenced by Harris's (1970:2) findings of 492 different categorizations of racial identity. Harris's subjects had a great deal of difficulty in agreeing among themselves as to just which specific category a particular person belonged. The Brazilian categories are not based on physical traits alone, but include other criteria such as education, wealth, and personal attributes. The individualistic interpretations of the various criteria of "racial categories" make it more difficult to practice the kind of discrimination found in the United States. Historically, both dark and light skin colors were present in the lower class. In the modern urban slums and in some middle-class areas, one finds a wide range of physical types. I would expect color to become a political issue in Brazil only if lower-class whites should begin to move into the middle class more rapidly and in larger numbers than Brazilians with African and Indian racial backgrounds.

Economy and Wealth

The most striking phenomena of the preindustrial economy of Brazil were its production of primary products, dependence upon world markets resulting in boom-and-bust cycles, and the importation of manufactured goods. In various periods, sugar, gold, rubber, cacao, and coffee have reached a peak and then have declined in importance. Brazilian industry began its slow growth in the southern part of the country in the early part of this century. By 1930, political power shifted to the south. During the Vargas era between 1930 and 1945, the central government began to control the selection of imports by heavily taxing luxury items and by providing incentives for the importation of machinery to make machines (Poppino 1968:243). During World War II and after, it was difficult to import goods from Europe and North America because of shortages in these areas. Brazilians found that they would have to produce their own goods or do without. In later years, industrialization became more a matter of economic nationalism. In the forty years between 1920 and 1960, the number of industrial plants expanded more than eight times, and the industrial labor force increased nearly seven times. During the same period, the population doubled (Poppino 1968:239). Industrialization has become more intensive in recent years, and imported industrial goods are being replaced by those produced in Brazil. Between 1948 and 1961, durable consumer goods imported fell from 9.8 to 1.2 percent of total imports. The domestic production of equipment rose from 29.9 to 46.8 percent between 1947 and 1959 while equipment imports fell from 24 to 15.6 percent (Gudin 1969: 3–4). From these statistics on industrial development, one can imagine the tremendous growth in the range of occupational statuses now available to Brazilians.

Power

According to Lopez, the real protagonists of the political system prior to the Vargas period were "oligarchical regional (state) groups, whose power was based, locally, on the economic, social and political power of the large land owners (the *coronéis*)" (1966:60). Lopez views the Brazilian political structure as having undergone a profound transformation since 1930. The focus of power is no longer on the governments of the states, but has shifted to the urban masses, who are playing a more crucial role. Lopez (1966:59–77) has analyzed some basic developments in Brazilian politics and society. The following is a summary of some of his material.

The real basis for the limited democracy Brazil has experienced lies in the concept of *populismo* (populism). Politicians appeal to the *povo*. This term refers primarily to the urban masses, specifically the industrial workers and the middle class. Although the old political structure to a great degree has broken up, no new formal structure has developed to mediate between the uprooted masses and the leaders on the top. Lopez believes that political parties can be disregarded as intermediary structures; therefore, national leaders must establish a charismatic relation with the urban masses. With urbanization and industrialization, a society that is more highly differentiated has developed. The national congress and the state legislatures reflect the heterogeneity of interest groups. In this modern sociopolitical milieu, Lopez sees the emergence of two new types of deputies—the economic group representative and the clientele politician. The economic group representative buys off, directly or indirectly, the *cabos eleitorais,* who act as "intermediaries between the large impersonal institutional framework of the city and the people of a neighborhood, a *favela* or a recreational club" (Lopez 1966:64). If their candidate wins a political seat, the *cabos eleitorais* can secure services for their clients, such as "obtaining a job, a place in a school or hospital, bringing water or electricity to a street, getting a public telephone installed, or having a bus route changed" (Lopez 1966:65). This system of electing a deputy involves smaller industrial concerns, or a small number of firms controlled by an economic group. It does not include a whole industry. Lopez (1966:66) does not see the Brazilian capitalists as being organized as a class to pursue political interests. The second type of deputy that has emerged is the clientele politician. According to Lopez, "He is really a bigger *cabo eleitoral* —one whose primary community (an ethnic group, the inmates of leprosy hospitals) is large enough to get him elected" (1966:66).

The role of the military in Brazilian politics cannot be ignored. Unrest and tensions, problems of food shortages and inflation, and the state of "semi-anarchy" (Busey 1969:82) of the Goulart regime brought General Humberto Castelo Branco to presidential power through a military coup in 1964. This was not an entirely new form of behavior for the army. In 1930, the military brought Vargas to power. Since an open democracy was restored in 1945, the army has intervened in political affairs on a number of occasions, the 1964 coup being its most overt maneuver. Observers agree that military intervention has always been relatively bloodless, for Brazilians do not like to kill other Brazilians. Technically, the constitution of 1945 provided for an orderly transfer of presidential power every five years. Between 1945 and 1964, two presidents survived their five-year terms (Dultra and Kubitschek); two presidents resigned under pressure (Vargas and Quadros) and were replaced by their vice-presidents (Filho and Goulart); and finally, Goulart was overthrown by the military in 1964.

Prestige

In the traditional political system of rule by the *coronéis,* wealth, power, and prestige resided in the same social status. Today, it is more difficult to always link these attributes in a single individual. Furthermore, the

273

problem is complicated by the fact that what is regarded as prestigious by one social class may not be acceptable to another. For example, the *arrivistas,* or nouveaux riches, often shock the old elite by "their ostentation, their manners, and their unscrupulous methods" (Wagley 1963:129). Their behavior, on the other hand, is accepted by some of the people in the emerging middle class because it represents a break with tradition. Another example of status inconsistency was the late, low-keyed President Castelo Branco. He lacked great charismatic appeal and therefore was not prestigious in the eyes of the *povo*; but he certainly wielded power. The "economic group" deputy, described in the preceding section, did not necessarily have great personal wealth, for he was financially supported by economic interests; however, he had some real voting power before the 1964 military coup. A general observation would seem to be that wealth, power, and prestige are no longer necessarily found together in the increasingly hetergeneous Brazilian society.

Change

From the preceding sections, one can conclude that a phenomenal amount of cultural change has been taking place prior to and during the period of this particular study of Umbanda. Since the time of Vargas, the national government has deliberately pushed for economic development in both private and public sectors of the economy. Large scale projects directly or indirectly backed by the federal government have included the Volta Redonda steel mill, the Brazilian cellulose and paper industry, the construction of Brazília, the Superintendência do Desenvolvimento do Nordeste (SUDENE), and the important currect project to open up and develop the Amazon region. The Brazilian attitude toward development perhaps can be best summarized in Kubitschek's statement of "fifty years of progress in five" (Dulles 1966:38). Both nationalist sentiment and currency inflation are part of Brazil's economic development. Development has, in part, been financed by printing currency. The amount of money in circulation at the end of 1955 was 69 billion cruzeiros. By the beginning of 1961, it had increased to 202 billion cruzeiros (Dulles 1966:38). During the Goulart regime that preceded the 1964 military coup, the cost of living went up 340 percent between 1961 and 1963. During the same period, the international monetary value of the cruzeiro decreased from 300 per dollar to 1,200 per dollar (Dulles 1966:48). National economic difficulties have been augmented by increasing population pressures in urban areas. Between 1950 and 1960, the urban population increased from 36 to 45 percent of the total Brazilian population. Urban growth accounted for 70 percent of the national population increase in the same decade (Chardon 1966:162). Most of the population growth has occurred in the industrial south and represents a rural-urban migration. The usual social problems associated with such migrations have been compounded by spiraling inflation. In this type of environment, economic nationalism comes to be seen as a national commitment to the betterment of living conditions for the *povo*. There exists an attitude that there can be no turning back, even in the face of the political upheaval that in 1964 put the military in power to somewhat stabilize economic conditions.

Umbanda in Brazilian Society

Umbanda seems to be primarily an urban phenomenon that diffuses to smaller Brazilian cities as they become linked to the developing national socioeconomic structure. Umbanda includes persons from every socioeco-

275

nomic class, but individuals from the upper-lower and middle classes make up the bulk of the membership. In the twelve Umbanda centers I visited in São Paulo, women accounted for 60 to 75 percent of the spirit mediums. Men, however, do participate in other ways. They act as drummers for Umbanda music and are important figures on the "boards of directors" of Umbanda centers. The majority of umbandists are in their twenties or thirties; a lesser number are forty years old or older.

No one knows with any certainty just how many umbandists there are in São Paulo or in the whole of Brazil. Unfortunately, the national census does not make a distinction between the spiritualists of Umbanda and of Kardecism, the latter being a more intellectually oriented spiritualist religion.[2] It does not make much difference, since many spiritualists still think of themselves as Catholics with regard to the official census. Umbandists tend to exaggerate their membership figures into "millions and millions of faithful." Camargo (1961:53–54) found that the Federação Espírita de Umbanda claimed 260 affiliated centers, followed by the União Espírita de Umbanda and the Igreja Cristã de Umbanda, which controlled 100 centers each. Other minor federations had 30 to 50 cult groups in them. According to Levy (1968:35), "The number of *centros* in the city has been calculated by the two inspectors as being about 4,000. I am confident that this is not an exaggeration."[3] The long lists of centers and meeting times found in Umbanda newspapers indicate that the figure of 4,000 centers may be fairly accurate. Some other indexes of the popularity of Umbanda are the elections in recent years of several state deputies who are umbandists in Guanabara (Rio de Janeiro) and Rio Grande do Sul. Attila Nunes campaigned by playing daily over the radio two hours of Umbanda music and chants interspersed with "news of what goes on in the world of Umbanda both here in the 'Aruanda' (the spiritual dwelling of Indian and Negro spirit guides)'' (McGregor 1967:179). The second Umbanda Congress in 1961 was held in Rio de Janeiro's Maracanazinho stadium (McGregor 1967:178), which suggests national strength. What is conspicuously absent is a national structure, nor are there any nationally recognized leaders. The authors of Umbanda books and the writers in Umbanda newspapers agree that the movement should be unified; but when one takes into account Brazilian individuality, nobody can agree on just how it should be done. Even in the city of São Paulo, there are at least fourteen very loosely federated bodies with which the centers may affiliate. About the only thing that each of the larger federations appear to manage is an annual meeting. The centers of a particular federation attend en masse in ritual garments to listen to the leaders of the federation extol the virtues and growth of Umbanda. Then, most of the several thousand mediums gathered there go simultaneously into trance, receiving spirits. The real functioning units of structure in Umbanda are the individaul centers. The observer can find centers in all parts of the city—rich and poor. Usually, they are located in middle-class and working-class districts. Some are above stores and in abandoned garages. Most either rent or own their own buildings near the main business districts as well as in ordinary residential neighborhoods of the city.

It is difficult to estimate the prestige of Umbanda. The size of the membership is one indicator. The election of umbandists to state legislatures is another. Popular magazines read by the middle and upper classes very frequently include articles and photographs of Umbanda activities. These reports are sometimes straightforward and at other times sensational in nature. The ideology of spirits is fairly common throughout Brazilian society, and I later discuss this matter in more depth. I would

277

say that, on the whole, Brazilians are very accepting of spiritualist religions. Some people, however, tend to think of Umbanda as being "lower class" and, therefore, less prestigious than some other spiritualist religions in Brazil. I found that the higher the class, the more reticence a person exhibited in disclosing the involvement he or his family has had with Umbanda.

UMBANDA AS A RELIGIOUS INNOVATION IN BRAZIL

The biological state of dissociation, or trance, and its cultural interpretation as possession by spirits represent extremely complex forms of behavior. Salman (1968: 198–200), summarizing the difficulties in studying such a complexity of behavior, has suggested that we try to understand the absolute necessity of analyzing trance and spirit possession on a variety of different levels. The five levels that he has recommended are: (1) the physiological level; (2) the level of the inner structures and functions of the personalities concerned; (3) the level of interpersonal relations; (4) the level of study that regards possession as a form of social behavior within a specific cultural environment; and (5) the level of possession behavior as religious behavior. These five levels would seem to represent the following aspects of man: (1) biological; (2)psychological as affected by the biological and social levels; (3) social; (4) sociocultural; and (5) cultural. In discussing the fifth level, Salman speaks of the need for a psychology of religion. However, the major portion of his discussion of possession as religious behavior seems to emphasize the study of religion as a set of cultural beliefs that a people have. To facilitate the presentation and analysis of data on Umbanda, I shall begin at the fifth, or cultural, level at which one views possession behavior as religious behavior. I shall then work my way through the data to the biological level of analysis.

278

Umbanda as a Religious Form of
Cultural Behavior

Umbanda centers represent an amazing variety of external forms, rituals, and beliefs, yet there are some features that seem to be basic. Everywhere one finds that the major ritual activity in these centers involves a state of dissociation that umbandists interpret as possession by spirits of the dead. The spiritual entities diagnose and treat illnesses and help to solve a myriad of personal problems of the believers who come to the two weekly public sessions in search of spiritual assistance. As I describe the centers and their activities in this section, the reader should be aware that each medium has his or her own highly individual interpretation of what is "right" and that a visit to any given Umbanda center is bound to yield some rituals and beliefs that are at variance with my descriptions.

Umbanda centers are divided into two major parts by a railing. Those who have come to ask for spiritual assistance sit in the rear half on wooden benches arranged in two rows. The two sexes, about equal in number, sit on opposite sides of the room. Usually, between 75 and 150 persons come for help. The front half of the center is devoted to ritual activities. Images of Catholic saints and of various spirits are placed on a white drape that covers the altar. Two or three drums that "call" the spirits to possess the mediums are at the one side of the altar. The cult leader and the mediums who practice in the Umbanda center stand in the front half of the building. Both men and women may assume the role of cult leader, although more often it is a woman. There are usually about forty mediums. About 8:30 P.M., the cult leader opens the *gira* (turn-around, that is, the session). As the drums are beaten, the mediums sway or dance to the rhythm. The audience joins in singing songs

279

for various spirits. An assistant brings a censer in which perfuming herbs burn. It is carried to the altar, to the drums, to each of the mediums, and finally to the members of the audience. A wave of the hand brings the fumes closer to purify the body and to offer protection against evil influences brought to the center. Each medium in turn prostrates himself before the altar as the cult leader blesses him and extends a hand to be kissed. In some Umbanda centers it is customary to sing a song for the benefit of any maleficient spirits that may be lurking around. This singing is supposed to indicate to these spirits that they are respected. However, the song also asks such spirits to leave, for they could possibly wreak havoc with the normal proceedings of the center, for example, mediums could experience a more hysterical type of possession. After more drumming and singing, an assistant takes up a collection from the audience. The cult leader may give a brief talk in which the faults in ritual behavior of the mediums are called to their attention. They are reminded of the virtues of love and charity and of the superiority of the works of Umbanda—small today, but grand tomorrow. Prayers are offered to the spirits for the sick and troubled, and then permission is asked of God to open the *trabalho* (work, that is, session of spirits who will "work" that night). Without drum accompaniment, the mediums and the audience together sing, "Eu abro a minha 'gira' / Com Deus e Nossa Senhora..." (I open my session/With God and Our Lady...). This song ended, the drums are once more beaten furiously, and as everyone sings, the mediums begin to call their spirits. As the heads and chests of the mediums jerk back and forth, the spirits *baixam*[4] (lower) themselves into their *cavalos* (horses, that is, mediums). Some spinning may also occur during the jerky movements. The facial expressions and mannerisms of the mediums are changed to those of their possessing

280

spirits. For the remaining two or three hours, the spirits are occupied with consultations with individual members of the audience in the front half of the center. Personal problems brought to the spirits include difficulties with love affairs, family disputes, getting and holding a job in a factory or office, studying for school exams, and business negotiations. Illnesses range from the physiological to the psychosomatic. Occasionally, a person who has come to a center for help unexpectedly goes into trance. The cult leader then tries to convince the individual that he should return as a cult member to develop his mediumistic abilities. Ritual activities in Umbanda centers revolve around two major sets of cultural beliefs. One set of beliefs has to do with five major types of spirits; the second involves a theory of spiritual "fluids," which has largely been borrowed from Kardecism.

Four of the five major spirit types are fairly ordinary and appear with regularity at Umbanda centers. First, the *caboclo* spirits possess the mediums once each week. They are said to be spirits of dead Brazilian Indians. While they are possessing the mediums, and therefore are believed to be utilizing the motor system of the mediums, the *caboclos'* faces display protruded lips, furrowed brows and eyes that slowly open and close, staring into space. A few may beat their chests and jump into the air, landing in a position ready to shoot an imaginary arrow. They like to puff on cigars while drinking beer. The *caboclos* are stern and aloof. If one should argue with an Indian spirit, the *caboclo* will quickly reprimand him. This particular type of spirit is appreciated for his advice in situations that require quick and decisive action, for example, getting and holding a job. The second type of spirit is the *prêto velho* that possesses the mediums at the second weekly session. These are spirits of dead Afro-Brazilian slaves. Stooped and bent over from many

281

years of hard labor, they tremble from old age. The *prêtos velhos* speak with slow and quivering voices as they smoke their pipes and sip red wine. Unlike the stern and aloof *caboclos,* the *prêtos velhos* are gentle and easy to approach. Seated on their low stools and conversing with someone who has come for help, they are almost grandfatherly in manner. These spirits, with their apparently infinite patience, are adept at handling long and drawn-out intricate personal problems such as familial difficulties or love affairs. Also, their extensive knowledge of herbal remedies is useful in treating illnesses. The third type of spirit is the *criança,* which is the spirit of a dead child, usually between 3 and 5 years of age. They usually appear once each month. The playful child spirit is more accessible than the other spirits. He skips, rolls, and tumbles throughout the entire Umbanda center, approaching members of the audience to ask for sweets and soft drinks. It is especially interesting to observe a 50-year-old medium possessed by a child spirit. Everyone present loves to tease these extroverted creatures. Unlike the *caboclo* and the *prêto velho,* the *criança* spirit is not so stringently defined by race and culture. If one asks for the child's ethnic origins, he will usually describe them; but ordinarily, the child is thought to be Brazilian, that is, without a specific ethnic identity. One can apparently ask the child spirit to help with any illness or personal problem; he does not seem to specialize as the other spirits do. The fourth type of spirit is the *exu* and his feminine counterpart, the *pomba-gira.* These are spirits of people who led especially wicked lives. Not infrequently, *exus* are foreigners. I encountered *exus* with such diverse backgrounds as French, Mexican, and Japanese. My informants indicated that there were also *exus* who were German, Italian, and Portuguese, although I did not encounter any with these ethnic backgrounds. I did, however, find some *exus* who were

Brazilian, but with special regional backgrounds. The *exus* are always antisocial characters and exhibit their base nature through cursing, off-color stories and songs, and bad manners in general. The more wicked *exus* may specialize in performing antisocial acts such as breaking up marriages and crushing business competitors. Other, "good" *exus*, said to be more evolved spiritually, may be used to counteract the more evil magic of the "bad" *exus*. *Exu* spirits are usually present in Umbanda centers one night each month.

The four spirit types described above can be either male or female. Both male and female mediums may be possessed by a spirit of either sex. I have outlined the general characteristics of each spirit type, but it should be noted that each individual spirit has its own particular personality. The more general role of each of the four spirit types is learned by every Umbanda medium. The more specific personality traits of each spirit seem to stem from the personality of the medium. Three of these four spirit types—the *caboclo*, the *prêto vehlo*, and the *criança*—are said to be "with light." This means that they had lived rather good lives and at death passed on into the *aruanda* (heaven). The *exus*, on the other hand, had led especially wicked lives. They failed to make it to heaven and are usually said to be "without light." Some umbandists claim that they do not "work" with *exus*. On closer inspection, however, I found this usually to be false. Other umbandists say that they practice only with "good" *exus* that are more evolved spiritually, that is, they have performed a number of good works that counteract the *magia negra* (black magic) performed by *exus* that are the less evolved spiritually. There are special centers known as Quimbanda that deal almost exclusively with black magic. The situation is not as simple as distinguishing between black and white magic. The matter is actually one of expediency and personal inclinations. In

283

reality, a continuum of sorts exists between Quimbanda and Umbanda. *Exus* differ from the other spirit types in one other important way. They usually demand some sort of payment, either in money or material goods, before a service will be performed for a client. None of the other spirits make this requirement. However, if a client is satisfied with the assistance he has received from the other spirits, it is quite proper to offer a small gift such as flowers, candles, tobacco, or any other ritual paraphernalia used by umbandists.

The fifth type of spirit, known as an *orixá*, differs markedly from the other four spirits and is therefore treated separately here. The cultural concept of the *orixá* spirits was brought to Brazil primarily by slaves from Yorubaland in Nigeria. In Brazil, the rapprochement between African religious traits and Catholicism was both structural and cultural (Bastide 1960). Structurally, both Catholic saints and the African deities—the *orixás*—were intermediaries between man on earth and a high, remote God, or Olorun. In addition to structural similarities, cultural beliefs about Catholic saints and the *orixás* were sometimes similar and could easily be syncretized. For example, the Yoruba deity Ogum, who was the patron of blacksmiths and protector of iron farm tools and iron weapons of war, became identified and equated in some regions of Brazil with Saint George. Saint George was usually depicted on a white charger, slaying the dragon with a long iron sword. The obvious material connection between African deity and Catholic saint was the iron weapon. Because the slaves no longer had their own farms and probably did not care about the use of iron tools for the production of their masters' crops, Ogum's role in warfare became more important in Brazil. Herskovits (1937) has pointed out that the slaves syncretized Ogum and other *orixás* with various saints of their masters until a distinctive cult known as Candomblé emerged. The slaves secretly held rituals on special days of the saints and openly practiced their religion after the emancipation of Brazilian slaves in 1888. Today in São Paulo, individuals of Italian and German descent say that the African *orixás* and the Catholic saints are one and the same. They point out that Africans and Europeans simply had different names for these spiritual entities. The rapprochement was made complete in Brazil, where cultures from two continents were merged in the sphere of religion.

There are, however, a few things about the *orixás* that have changed as the earlier Afro-Catholic cults evolved into Umbanda. First, the membership in Candomblé was primarily female (Landes 1947); in Umbanda, both men and women may be possessed by an *orixá*. Second, in Candomblé, the *orixás* possessing the women were regarded as deities. In Umbanda, although the *orixás* are still regarded as deities, they have become more remote from man on earth and send spiritual envoys to possess the Umbanda mediums. My informants believed that if an *orixá* itself were to possess a medium, he or she would explode from its great force. The spiritual envoys sent by the *orixás* are spirits of dead persons. Umbandists believe that they are more highly evolved spiritually than the other four spirit types. Unlike the other spirits, the *orixás,* or more accurately their disincarnate envoys, do not communicate with clients who come to Umbanda centers for assistance. In fact, the *orixás* rarely appear. They are important, however, as guardian spirits. Each Umbanda member is a *filho(a)* (son, daughter) of a particular *orixá*. An individual can learn who his *orixá* protector is after paying a fee to his cult leader for the necessary divination. However, divination does not always occur, and friends of the medium speculate on the matter. This is entirely possible because an *orixá* exercises a certain amount of influence over the everyday behavior of his *filho(a)*. For example, a medium (male or female) who is protected by the goddess Oxum behaves in a suave, very feminine manner.

Umbandists loosely organize their spirits into a hierarchy of *linhas, falanges,* and *legiões* (lines, phalanxes, and legions). There are seven *linhas,* each commanded by an *orixá.* Each *linha* is divided into seven *falanges* that, in turn, are subdivided into seven *legiões* of spirits. There is much disagreement over which spirits belong in the specific parts of the hierarchy. Even the seven major *orixás* that head the hierarchy vary from one Umbanda center to another. An arrangement of the *linhas* found to be common in São Paulo by Camargo (1961:38) follows:

1. Linha do Oxalá	–	Jesus Cristo
2. Linha de Iemanjá	–	Virgem Maria
3. Linha do Oriente	–	São João Batista
4. Linha de Oxóce	–	São Sebastião
5. Linha de Xangô	–	São Jerônimo
6. Linha de Ogum	–	São Jorge
7. Linha Africana	–	São Cipriano

One should note that in this particular arrangement, two of the major divisions—Linha do Oriente and Linha Africana—are not commanded by *orixás.* Many umbandists would argue against including the former. The latter, however, is very popular, and most of the *prêto velho* spirits are included in this subdivision. The *caboclo* spirits are found in various parts of the spiritual organization, but they are most frequently thought of as belonging to the hunter, Oxóce. Some umbandists believe that one of the seven major divisions is headed by Saints Cosmas and Damian, and they link the *criança* spirits to this *linha.* During the year, Umbanda centers hold special celebrations for the *orixás.* Members prepare special foods, and frequently alcoholic beverages are served.

Several centers may rent a bus to go to the ocean to honor Iemanjá, who is goddess of sea water. The Linha Africana is celebrated on May 13, which is the anniversary of the emancipation of Brazilian slaves. The special days of Oxalá (Jesus Christ) are Christmas and Easter. An Umbanda center may collect gifts for the needy at Christmas. Just as there is tremendous disagreement in beliefs concerning the *orixás,* there is a good deal of variation as to which *orixás* will be honored, and the nature of the celebration changes from one center to another.

It is now useful to turn to a discussion of the second important set of beliefs that direct much of the ritual activity in Umbanda centers. Umbandists place a great deal of emphasis on a theory of supernatural fluids. Supernatural fluids are spiritual emanations that surround one's body and affect one's well-being. These supernatural fluids are believed to come from three sources: (1) from one's own innate spirit; (2) from spirits of the dead, which are freely floating about; and (3) from incarnate spirits of persons who are close by. Both good and bad fluids exist. The latter are usually associated with the *exus.* An individual surrounded by bad fluids is sickly and trouble-ridden. A healthy individual free from anxiety is said to be surrounded by good fluids. Umbandists lump together illness and personal difficulties under the term "spiritual disorders." These are classified etiologically by umbandists. Camargo (1961:100–102) has drawn up a list of five commonly recognized causes of illnesses. I have taken a few examples from my field notes to illustrate these categories.

1. *Sickness as a consequence of religious negligence or ignorance.* This occurs when a medium has neglected to fulfill the *obrigações* (obligations) due his *orixá* or other lesser spirits divinely designated to protect him. These obligations vary, but usually include some food and drink

287

to be left for the spirit in an appropriate place or to be consumed by the spirit while it possesses its medium. A 25-year-old white male employed in the international accounting department of a major Brazilian airline constantly and inexplicably bumped into furniture at work and in his home, seriously bruising his arms and legs. He believed this was possibly caused by his failure to perform duties for his *exu*. It was highly probable that if his *exu* were to possess him, the spirit would demand the *obrigação* to be made in a cemetery at midnight— something that this young man greatly feared. To avoid learning more about the specific details of this duty, he attempted to restrain his *exu* from possessing him; however, throughout the year his personal control over the situation weakened considerably. At *exu* sessions it is customary to explode small amounts of gun powder as a means of driving away evil fluids. When this occurred, his *exu* would attempt to possess him, jerking his head up and back and drawing him backward from the waist until his face became contorted with pain. His knees would bend, causing his body to be drawn downward until his back was only a few inches from the floor. His hands stiffened into the hook-like forms of an *exu*. The shock was only momentary, and his rigid body would immediately collapse on the floor. He would get to his feet, a bit stunned and very sore. He reported neck and back aches the days following these sessions. Friends and spirits of his friends continued to remind him that the bruises resulting from apparently unexplained bumping into furniture were a sign given to him from his *exu* that an *obrigação* should be offered. Neck and back pains resulting from attempted possession by his *exu* would also continue. Sometime later in the year possession did occur. The heretofore restricted *exu* announced that his *cavalo* did not like him. He was assured that this was not true. He then stated that he would continue to make his *cavalo* ill until the necessary obligations were fulfilled. When the *exu* left, the young man became quite ill and rushed to the bathroom, where he vomited. As far as I am aware, the matter of the *obrigação* was not resolved during the period of fieldwork. However, the young man did begin to take the matter more seriously than he had up to that time.

2. *Magical etiology of illnesses*. A *coisa feita* literally means "thing done." Practically, it refers to an evil thing deliberately done through the black magic of the *exus* in Quimbanda. A service commonly performed is the blocking of the paths (*caminhos fechados*) of the client's competitors in business or love. Bringing illness is frequently one means of accomplishing this aim. A 40-year-old white male who was a solidly middle-class proprietor of a modern electrical appliance store and his wife were the supposed victims of a *coisa feita*. The wife underwent an operation on her internal organs. While she was in the hospital, a nurse incorrectly administered some medication and severely burned the abdomen and thighs of the patient, putting her on the critical list for a few days. Sometime later her husband was out driving his small bus when it skidded on the wet pavement. The door jarred open as the bus collided with another vehicle. He fell out, his head struck the pavement, and he was knocked unconscious. He suffered a broken nose and a gash on his head that required a number of stitches. Members of the Umbanda center where this man served as financial director held several sessions for him and his wife. The "good" *exus* of Umbanda "undid" the black magic of an evil *exu* of Quimbanda. Supposedly, it was the disappointed mulatto mistress of the husband in this case who had paid the evil *exu* to victimize her former lover and his wife. It is interesting to note here that in the cases of *coisa feita* involving male-female relations that I studied, all involved a female victimizing

a male. My informants were able to give me only one example of a male harming a female by means of an *exu* spirit. This man was regarded by observers as being somewhat "crazy."

3. *Perturbations provoked by spirits.* These are disturbances caused by spirits. An unhappy spirit of the dead may agitate the "fluids" in an individual, bringing illness or various kinds of personal problems. Such a spirit may come to disturb an individual to get revenge for things committed in a previous incarnation of the spirit. Sometimes the spirit is merely perverse and through its ignorance disturbs the life of an innocent victim. Such spirits need to be enlightened in a center as to their proper behavior. A young married man of European and possibly Indian origins, about 30 years old, was abnormally tense and nervous. One night he broke the furniture and dishes in his home and then ran out, not returning for several days. When he did return, he could not recall where he had been. His clothing and hair were covered with mud and leaves, suggesting that he had spent some time in a wooded area. His wife convinced him to go a center for spiritual assistance. At the first two or three sessions that he attended, when possessed by his spirit he rolled on the floor in a fetal position. At first, the spirit was apparently fearful of being touched by the cult leader. He thrashed about on the floor, striking and kicking anyone who came near. Considering some of his body movements during possession, some of the mediums secretly confided in each other that it was an *exu* that was troubling him. However, the cult leader worked with the young man on the assumption that it was only a wild *caboclo* spirit that was disturbing him and that needed to be enlightened through participation in the sessions. After several sessions with him, the cult leader was able to educate the spirit in the modes of behavior of a *caboclo*. The spirit began to dance in

UMBANDA IN SÃO PAULO

the normal manner, together with the other spirits in that center.

4. *Karmic illnesses.* A new incarnation of a spirit may bring trials in the forms of illnesses and other disorders to an individual. These may serve to redeem sins in a former life. An unmarried female of African, Indian, and possibly some European background felt that many of her problems and illnesses were trials sent as a result of her former wicked life as a French courtesan. At twenty-five, she was a well-developed medium with respected spirits in Umbanda. Despite this success, tiredness, nervousness, headaches, and social maladjustments persisted. Not able to attain the fame and wealth that she wanted as an actress, she was very discouraged with earning her living as a model for artists and photographers. It is interesting to note that this young woman, normally a very impatient individual, felt that she had learned from her *prêta velha* to control some of her impatience. The "old blacks" are spirits characterized by great calmness and infinite patience.

5. *Illnesses resulting from undeveloped mediumship.* This category is a general catchall. In a sense it overlaps any of the other categories in this list. Undeveloped mediumship is frequently cited when no other cause is easily discernible. One must learn how to interpret spiritual realities as well as defend oneself against these realities. Only through spiritual development may an individual retain sound general health by taking proper precautions.

6. To this list of etiological categories of spiritual disorders, I should like to add a sixth cause, which is *illnesses caused by "the evil eye."* The belief in *mau-olhado* is not limited in Brazil to spiritualist religions. As in other parts of the world where the evil eye exists, children are especially defenseless. Umbandists believe that adults with strong inborn mediumistic tendencies

291

are more receptive to the influences of the evil eye of others. They should develop their mediumship as a precautionary measure against bad fluids passed along through the mechanism of the evil eye.

In assigning one of these six categories, the manifestations of the illness are regarded as secondary. When assigning causes 1, 2, 3, and 6, what is taken into account is the behavior of the patient or of persons with whom the patient has social relations. When social-psychological signs are absent or unknown to the diagnostician, "undeveloped mediumship" is designated as the cause of illness or other misfortunes of the client. However, even after a course of successful development of the client's mediumistic capacity, illnesses and personal problems may remain. As in the case of the young woman who worked as a model, Karmic causes may be used to explain chronic states of poor health and difficulties.

The reliance on social-psychological signs rather than biological symptoms in the diagnosis of spiritual illness is due to three things. First, the same biological manifestation (for example, a headache or nervousness) may be due to any of the six causes listed above. Second, certain other difficulties arise from using biological symptoms in the diagnosis. Many illnesses caused by spirits appear to be exactly the same as those of purely biologically caused illnesses. Many claim that tuberculosis, chronic sores from burns, cancer, and liver problems may be manifestations due to spiritual causes. Some mediums cite numerous cases that spirits have cured after the patient had been given up by a medical doctor. The patients attest to the truth of the claim. Some centers specialize in spiritual "operations." Just as spiritual illnesses may appear to be the same as purely biological illnesses, umbandists admit that other manifestations may be the same as those of purely mental illnesses. Again, they like to cite cases in which a patient was temporarily released from a mental hospital to learn whether the illness could be cured spiritually. They believe that many psychiatric patients are not being cured simply because the etiology of the case is "spiritual" rather than "mental." The classification of the patient's disorder as a spiritual instead of a mental illness appears to be determined by whether a spiritual cause can be found and whether the patient can again become an adequately functioning member of his society.

A third reason for the reliance on social-psychological causes in diagnosis is the presence of effects other than illnesses. Inability to attain a desired level of wealth and status in an upwardly mobile society frequently appears with some illnesses. The insecurity involved in choosing unfamiliar roles in a rapidly developing society requires a certain modicum of assurance that one is doing the right thing in breaking with tradition. Failures occur, and explanations must be found. Psychosomatic illnesses are a natural result of a situation in which it becomes increasingly impossible to turn back to traditional ways. The relationship between a personal problem and illness, when explained by a common cause (bad fluids, perhaps) may be better understood by the patient and more effectively treated in a center.

To summarize this rather lengthy discussion, the major ritual activities in Umbanda focus on states of dissociation that are culturally interpreted as possession by spirits. The spiritual entities are said to diagnose and treat spiritual disorders that include both illnesses and personal problems. Two major sets of beliefs are important: (1) the belief in five major types of spirits, and (2) a theory of supernatural fluids that account for the well-being or spiritual disorders of an individual.

Spirit Possession as a Form of Social Behavior within the Brazilian Cultural Environment

Syncretic religions such as Umbanda are not at all unusual in Brazil, where Amerindian, African, and European have intermingled to a degree not found in the United States. During the colonial period in Brazil, religious beliefs and practices of the indigenous peoples were intermixed with Catholicism. Later, when slaves were imported from Africa to man the Brazilian sugar plantations, African religious traits and Catholicism were syncretized. Stemming from the Afro-Catholic point of origin are syncretic religions such as Candomblé, Batuque, Caboclo, Casa das Minas, Macumba, and Xangô. This list includes only the better-known possession-trance cults found throughout Brazil that have been studied by Bastide (1952, 1958, 1960), Carneiro (1940, 1964), Eduardo (1948), Herskovits (1943, 1955, 1959), Landes (1940, 1947), Leacock (1964 a, b, 1966), Ramos (1934, 1935), Ribeiro (1952, 1956), and Stainbrook (1952). These syncretic cults have borrowed varying elements from indigenous Indian religions and, in some instances, from the French spiritualism of Allan Kardec that is practiced by some middle- and upper-class Brazilians. In some cases, it appears that beliefs such as possession by dead ancestors may have been introduced from the Congo and Angolan areas of Africa. The cultural concept of possession by spirits has historically been present and widespread in Brazil. A spiritualist religion such as Umbanda is nothing new to the Brazilian scene. However, the earlier religious cults were tied to a traditional social structure, and membership was predominately lower-class Afro-Brazilian. What makes Umbanda so unusual is its ties to the modern milieu of urbanization and industrialization. The majority of umbandists are part of the emerging middle class or a part of the upwardly mobile part of the lower class. In São Paulo, 50 percent of the Umbanda membership is entirely of European origin. In some instances, orientals participate. Umbanda includes a wide spectrum of economic and educational statuses. Some individuals with university degrees actively participate as mediums for spirits. Why should a spiritualist religion like Umbanda emerge with such popularity in a cultural setting of expanding technology and rational economic principles? Obviously, the historical presence of the cultural concept of possession by spirits is a partial answer, but not a sufficient one.

Some other answers may lie in the nature of the Catholic church and in the availability of health services in Brazil. The hierarchy of the church tends to be oriented toward the traditional upper elites in Brazil. It has a great deal of difficulty in recruiting priests in Brazil, and many of its present priests are missionaries from other countries (Wagley 1963:237–38). In short, the church does not seem to be equipping itself to deal with the personal needs of the masses in Brazil. It is interesting to note that Umbanda is not the only spiritualist religion that is developing to fill this religious vacuum. The protestant Pentecostal sect is also growing, as well as a religion known as Kardecism (Willems 1966). Both involve spirit possession—the former, possession by the Holy Spirit; the latter, possession by spirits of the dead. Umbandists also deal with problems of health. Though there are private physicians, they are usually too expensive for many Brazilians to afford. The government has public medical services, but one must wait in line. In both cases, the patient does not get the personal attention—so important psychologically to well-being—that he can obtain during "spiritual consultations" at an Umbanda center.

Another reason for the popularity of spiritualist religions in Brazil may be related to the cultural premise, "Man has a spiritual self." The concept of a spiritual self is frequently discussed within the narrow confines of religion. However, in Brazil, as in much of Latin America, the spiritual self is something that has a scope considerably wider than its religious meaning. The concept of the spiritual self is perhaps best understood by examining what constitutes the self-image of an individual. According to Goodenough (1963:178) the self-image is divided into personal identity and social identity. Social identity is defined in terms of social rights and duties. On the other hand, personal identity refers to how one conducts himself in an individual manner within the boundaries of his social status. It also includes any other features of the individual to which no social rights and duties are attached (Goodenough 1963:178). It seems to me that personal identity is symbolized in Brazilian culture as the spiritual self. For Brazilians, the spiritual self represents an individual's inner worth, dignity and integrity. These qualities of a person are sharply distinguished from his social value. For Brazilians, it is quite possible for a highly valued person to be poor in monetary means, but rich in terms of a spiritual self. I believe it is somewhat difficult for many North Americans to understand the great importance that Brazilians attach to the concept of the spiritual self. In our culture, we tend to emphasize social identity and social worth to the near exclusion of personal identity, or spiritual self. If one can mentally grasp the significance of the spiritual self in Brazilian culture, then perhaps it is easier to understand why Brazilians do not find it difficult to accept the related cultural concept of spirits that can possess.

There is something else that is related to the premise, "Man has a spiritual self." This is the idea that it is difficult for one to know and understand the spiritual self of another unless there is a very close personal relationship between the two. Family and a small circle of friends are the only people who can come to know the spiritual self of an individual. This fact sets people into two very distinct categories for Brazilians. Santos (1966:240) refers to these categories as the "I-you, we-they" attitude of Brazilians. An individual has as little to do with "them" as is possible, for "they" do not understand one's spiritual self. There are practically no sets of reciprocal rights and duties associated between "us" and "them." The North American notion of casual friendship, as a type of "in-between" relationship, is not commonly found in Brazil. I believe an understanding of these Brazilian attitudes helps explain why Umbanda spirits are so popular. An individual may have personal problems with someone in his family or circle of close friends. However, he may not feel able to discuss his difficulties either with family or friends or with outsiders, ("them"). It seems to me that the concept of spirits is a very convenient way for resolving this dilemma. A person who comes to Umbanda is speaking with a *spirit* and not to the *medium,* who just may happen to be his sister, his close friend, or even one of "them."

In this section, I have been discussing several aspects of Brazilian culture that help explain the acceptance of spirit possession as a form of social behavior within the context of the religious institution of Umbanda. The historical background, the inadequacies of the tradition-oriented Catholic church and of medical facilities, and the important concept of the spiritual self are all a part of the cultural environment of Umbanda. It is now useful to turn from this more broad sociocultural view to the more specific social level of interpersonal relations where we can begin to understand the actual functioning of spirit possession.

Spirit Possession in Interpersonal Relations

Two major types of interpersonal relations seem to emerge from the data on Umbanda. One of these has to do with the relation between a spirit and a client who comes to public or private Umbanda sessions for help.[5] If the client is reasonably stable psychologically,[6] the spirit will make suggestions that are geared toward reestablishing the social norms dictated by Brazilian culture. For example, a spirit may tell a client how he should handle a difficult son or daughter or a wayward spouse. Some other personal difficulties that appear in my field notes include the following: problems of getting or holding a job; reducing the rent of a building that housed a small spaghetti factory; division of a small estate; increasing the number of retail buyers in a restaurant and in a beauty salon; increasing the number of retail sellers for a man who produced straw hats and purses; and determining who had stolen some musical instruments from someone's home. Usually there are the headaches, nervousness, and feelings of depression that go along with such difficulties. The spirits may or may not single out a specific spiritual cause for such difficulties, but in all cases they offer advice. Special rituals are performed by either the spirit or by the client at the direction of the spirit. He may tell the individual who has come for help to light a candle, to pray to a specific *orixá* or saint, or perhaps to fill a glass with water that will draw bad spiritual fluids away from the client. In the cases just mentioned, the client was fairly stable psychologically. On the other hand, if a client appears to be somewhat unstable and is not functioning very well, or perhaps needs the social support of an Umbanda center, the spirit may single out one of the six causes of spiritual disorders. The cult leader may suggest that the individual begin to develop his mediumship. That is, the client will learn to become a medium for the spirits at the center.

The second major type of interpersonal relation that I found in Umbanda was the relation between a spirit and an individual who was not acting in the role of client. In this type of situation, the spirit seemed to be used by the medium to represent his normally hidden or inner desires vis-à-vis other individuals. It might be helpful to give several examples of the interaction of spirits with their mediums' friends and families. In one case, a woman who displayed a great deal of aggressiveness and initiative told me that the spirits had driven away her husband, who had always had financial difficulties. Normally, a Brazilian woman should submit to her spouse, but in this instance, her spirits had said that she must develop her mediumship and that she could not do this while the familial altercations were so bad. After 15 years of separation from her husband, she was a successful cult leader. Her spirits then announced that her husband would return—which he did.

Another interesting case involved a man whom I shall João.[7] He had a female *exu* spirit by the name of Margarida. One night, as some of us prepared to leave a restaurant, João ran into the street, where Margarida possessed him. The female *exu* announced that she sexually wanted two men who were passing by. After Margarida left, three of us climbed into a taxi. A few minutes later the car had stopped, and João began to pull out his wallet to pay for the fare. Suddenly, Margarida possessed him again, and the billfold went back into João's pocket. After all, women do not pay for car fares! A more interesting incident involving this young man occurred several months later. We had gone to the home of one of João's friends. The host was wearing extremely brief shorts that João kept commenting on. João's gestures and speech were obviously feminine, and we all recognized that he was somewhat under the influence of Margarida. At one point, the female *exu* attempted to possess João, but he was able to restrain her with some difficulty. A few minutes later, João's *prêto velho* spirit possessed him. The spirit calmly told the host to change from his brief shorts into long trousers. After this was done, João became more relaxed.

In another case, two men—Juvenir, who was 25 years old, and Renato, who was about ten years older—shared an apartment. Renato was a more mature individual who had agreed to the request of Juvenir's sister to look after her brother. Juvenir often chafed under Renato's admonitions on proper behavior for a 25-year old man. At private spirit sessions, when Juvenir was possessed by his *criança* spirit, he would stick out his tongue and make other childish faces at Renato. Since it was a spirit, Renato generally ignored the gestures, but under other circumstances he would have become angry with Juvenir.

These examples illustrate the interaction of a medium and his spirit with others. All the cases seem to indicate that spirits may represent alternate roles that a medium may use in his interpersonal relations (Bourguignon 1965:57). The case of João is especially interesting in that we observe that he was first under the influence of Margarida, but somehow it was an inappropriate alternate role in the specific social situation. The problem was solved when a second type of spirit, the *prêto velho*, came to the rescue as an alternate role that allowed João to tell his host to put on some less sexually stimulating clothing. The spirit roles are usually accepted as valid by the medium's friends and family. However, people do sometimes question the validity of spirit roles. Two cases involved a spirit directly asking for money on behalf of his medium. In another case, a cult leader's spirit announced to the entire Umbanda center that his medium no longer had sexual relations with her husband. Somehow, these forms of behavior were not socially acceptable, even for spirits. In a fourth case, someone had pinched a medium to find out whether she were possessed. The medium responded, and the "tester" decided it was a fake possession.

Inner Structures and Functions of a Spirit Medium's Personality

The three aspects of a spirit medium's personality I shall discuss in this section are: (1) the cultural structuring of spirit possession into the personality of an individual; (2) the fact that possession states in the novice are usually due to some inability of his personality to adequately function in its sociocultural environment; and (3) the rewards that reinforce a person's decision to continue practicing as a medium in Umbanda over a long period of years.

Possession behavior, like all other forms of cultural behavior, is learned. I observed children between the ages of three and five imitating, in a playful manner, the body movements for inducing and terminating possession states—a back and forth jerking of the head and chest. They had visited Umbanda centers and were repeating at home for their own amusement what they had seen. Their behavior was not discouraged, and it provided entertainment for their elders, who were mediums. However, their fun-making was not recognized as spirit possession, for it lacked the accompanying spiritual disorders or the intent to be possessed for the purpose of helping others with their problems. In addition to learning about body movements, the children had also learned the accompanying cultural concept of possessing spirits from their family. Usually, it is not until an individual reaches adulthood that he begins to find the

301

concept of spirits significant to his personal life. It is then that he encounters difficulties such as obtaining employment or has problems with his family. At this time, his family and friends may urge him to secure spiritual aid at an Umbanda center.

Individuals who are beginning to develop their mediumship undergo some special training. Various techniques may be used to help a person learn to dissociate himself from his surroundings. The trance state that is induced seems to aid a novice in learning the proper roles of his spirits. The techniques used are similar to those used in hypnosis, such as having a novice focus his attention on a lighted candle. Another technique is to turn an individual around about five times in front of a cult leader, who then induces a trance state by passing his hand across the face of the novice and snapping his fingers. Another way of inducing trance involves a cult leader holding the two hands of a novice, relaxing him, and rocking him back and forth on his heels. This can easily lead into the head-chest jerks that signal possession by a spirit. Perhaps the most frequently used means for inducing trance is to have a novice turn himself around dozens of times until he loses some mental contact with his surroundings. The person may easily fall because he feels dizzy, and people gather in a circle about him to prevent any serious accidents. After a novice goes through this sort of activity over a period of several sessions, he usually begins to pivot on one foot, which prevents falling. Also, when he stops turning, he will not fall if he simply puts his body weight on one foot and balances himself with the opposite foot and leg. I never heard a cult leader explain the pivot maneuver or the body-balancing technique to a novice; they seem to be unconsciously learned by the individual himself. The head-chest jerks are then added. Once a novice is experiencing a state of dissociation, a cult leader will often tell or show the "spirit" how it should behave. The cultural structuring of spirit possession into the personality of an individual is both an imitative process and a process of more directed learning of trance and spirit roles.

A second factor of personality that can be taken into account is that possession states in a novice are usually due to some inability of an individual to function successfully in his specific sociocultural environment. To illustrate this point, I present some data on one of my major informants, a fifty-two year old mulatto. Cecília was born in a rural area outside of São Paulo where her father worked as a cook on a farm and her mother was a seamstress. When Cecília was about ten years old, her mother attempted suicide. Cecília learned about special spiritual forces from a Syrian who was called in to bless her mother. She first came into contact with Umbanda while visiting relatives in Rio de Janeiro when she was fourteen. When she was seventeen, Cecília moved to São Paulo, where she worked as a cook in a wealthy home. Three years later, she married a man who had a pushcart from which he sold ice cream. He gradually worked his way up until he operated a bar. They had three children—a girl when Cecília was twenty-five and set of mixed twins the following year. Then a series of events began to occur to upset their secure family life. Her husband fought with and fired his employees, and soon lost his bar. The oldest girl died when Cecília was twenty-eight, and the boy twin was killed by an automobile the following year. A friend suggested that Cecília should go to an Umbanda center for spiritual help. There, a spirit advised Cecília that she needed to think seriously about her mediumship, for her dead mother had a mission to fulfill through her. She felt sad upon learning this news because she had never wanted to become involved with spiritualism. Cecília left temporarily for the nearby port city of Santos, where

303

she bathed in the ocean waters. She believed this helped prepare her spiritually. When she returned, she attended a session that was a mixture of Kardecism and Umbanda. At the table of mediums, she was possessed by her mother's spirit. Cecília learned that her mother's suffering in life had been due to undeveloped mediumship. The disincarnate spirit could evolve, however, through Cecília's own spiritual development. The group of mediums then passed to another room, where they received Umbanda spirits. A *caboclo* possessed Cecília whose name was Sete Forquilha (Seven Fork). At a later session, she was possessed by Pai Augostinho, a *prêto velho*.

There were never any doubts in Cecília's mind that spirits existed, but she was reluctant to become a medium. Still, strange things occurred that seemed to push her in this direction. One night she dreamed that she and her husband were fleeing through a wooded area. Pursuing them was her Indian spirit, who was carrying a spear. The *caboclo* caught up with them and attempted to seize her from her husband for the purpose of sexual relations. Some other unusual events occurred during this period of about a year. One day while alone in her kitchen, she saw and talked with a cowboy spirit. Several days later, she became violently ill and rushed out to see an Umbanda cult leader. While there, Cecília was possessed by four spirits. The following is her account of what happened:

> As the cult leader started talking with me, I received a Japanese[8] spirit. He said that every time I didn't want to go to the center, he was going to come and strike me with these things. And then he told the story of his life. That he had been a prisoner of war. He had hid children in a tunnel so they wouldn't get killed. He was discovered and put into solitary confinement. A room so small he could only stand up in it. They threw hot water on his head until he was forced to tell what he knew at times.

He then said that all of the symptoms I felt were his. And that he was going to stay by my side. That he was one more light which would be at my side while I practiced spiritualism. He bid the cult leader goodbye and left. And then I received the *boiadeiro* (cowboy).[9] When he left I received an old boyfriend who had died in an accident.

He said that he wanted to possess me, because he also needed to evolve spiritually. But that he wasn't going to stay with me. He had come only this one time. He said that while he was still alive he had wanted me very much, but now he was staying only to protect me; that he was going to open the road for me so I would have some luck; that I had found someone who would care for me just as he would have done if alive; that he had come only to ask for a pardon for certain things. He had courted me but had liked another girl. He did wrong by the other girl. I knew it and separated myself from him. He didn't want me to leave. Thought that I should marry him, even with things as they were. But I said to him, "Why should I make the other girl unhappy? I don't have to. I'm free. I'm still young. Marry the other girl." I didn't want him anymore. Then he tried to attack me, but even at this I still told him that I didn't want him anymore. I *really* didn't want him. Even now I like him less because he wanted to come against me. He followed me around to all the places I went. Where I'd go he'd follow. So, his spirit had come this time to ask for pardon. That he was wrong. And after he left, my uncle's spirit came. All of this in one day!

In addition to these rather strange spiritual events occurring in Cecília's life at about age thirty, her husband was believed to be experiencing the effects of a bad *exu* spirit. He had had a mistress who had become dissatisfied with him and had supposedly paid an *exu* spirit to bring harm to him. Cecília claimed that as a result he had gone berserk, selling his possessions and smashing his car with his bare fists. (He was by this time a taxi driver.) Her neighbors told her that she should urge him to go to a center for help. When he refused to go for a spiritual consultation, Cecília went herself. The cult leader told her that she would have to develop her mediumistic abilities to help her husband overcome his spiritual problems. Cecília had been reluctant to develop her mediumship, but the fate of several disincarnate spirits and of her family seemed to rest upon her willingness to become a medium. She believed that it was the will of God and that she no longer could ignore her destiny.

These data on Cecília suggest that possession states in the novice can be linked to the inability of the personality to function adequately in its sociocultural environment. In the span of two or three years, a number of events had occurred in Cecília's life that might have led her to seriously question the security of her roles as wife and mother. Her husband had behaved in a peculiar way, ruining the business he had built up. Sometime later, he was involved with another woman. Two of her children died. If we regard spirits and dreams as projections of the inner personality, it is evident that Cecília was troubled by events in her daily life. The Japanese spirit seemed to be a projection of Cecília's personal warfare. He was a prisoner concerned with saving children from being killed. He was in solitary confinement and was forced to tell what he knew when hot water was thrown over him. These are perhaps projections of Cecília's concern with the death of her children, with her aloneness, and with her inability to hold back her feelings and her unconscious desire to express them under stress. It is also interesting to note that at a time when her husband had a girl friend, her old boy friend possessed her as a spirit and that she had a dream about her *caboclo* spirit pursuing her for the purpose of sexual relations. The short time she spent at the seashore at Santos probably gave Cecília time to think more about developing her mediumship. When she returned to São Paulo, she was not yet willing to admit that she would like to assume the role of spirit medium, but three spirits that possessed her spoke her inner desires and needs. Her dead mother's spirit could evolve only through Cecília's own spiritual development. The Japanese spirit said that if she did not develop her mediumship, he would bring her more spiritual problems; he added that he would be a light by her side if she did practice spiritualism. The spirit of her dead boy friend came to her because he needed to evolve spiritually and said that he would help her by bringing some luck. It appears that Cecília was unable to openly accept her personal need to develop her mediumship. Instead, she made her decision on the basis of the spiritual needs of the spirits of her mother, her boy friend, and her husband, who refused to go to a center for spiritual help. Cecília impressed one as a person who thought of herself as independent and capable of handling her own problems. She was not able to see in herself a special need to get out of the house and away from her husband several nights a week as an Umbanda medium role would require. Therefore, her spirits seemed to speak her inner desires and personal needs. It is interesting to note that of the six spirits that possessed her at this time, five of them were male. I believe this was an expression of her personality that included more aggressiveness and independence than one normally expects a Brazilian woman to have. Today, she says that her participation in Umbanda has given her personal freedom that other Brazilian women do not have.

The third item relating to personality that I wish to discuss are the rewards that reinforce a person's decision to continue practicing as a medium in Umbanda over a long period of years. For a very few individuals—specifically, cult leaders—being a medium can be a financially rewarding role. Cult leaders usually do not become wealthy, but they can manage to support themselves. But for most Umbanda mediums, the rewards are more personal. In Cecília's case, being a medium meant that she could spend a great deal of time outside of her house and in the presence of other men with her husband's approval. Furthermore, a medium such as Cecília who has developed his or her spiritual capacities and uses them in unselfish ways to help others is awarded a great amount of respect by others. I believe that a large number of mediums also attend Umbanda centers, in part, for the social life it offers. In addition to regular sessions, there are *festas* (parties, celebrations) for the *orixás* with special food and drink; there are outings to the seashore to celebrate the goddess Iemanjá and to the forests to pay respects to the *caboclo* spirits; there are group visits that the members of one Umbanda center make to another. When an individual decides to practice in a particular center, there is always the possibility of making new friends among the mediums. Then, there are the more theatrical and aesthetic aspects of Umbanda that bring personal satisfaction to a medium. The special ritual garb, the public dancing and singing, and the attention one gets while possessed cannot be overlooked. Whereas the character of most spirits in public Umbanda sessions is somewhat formal, the spirits at private sessions can become extremely entertaining to both their intimate audience as well as to themselves.

Some Biological Aspects of Dissociation in Umbanda Mediums

Dissociation, or trance, is a biological phenomenon that Bourguignon (1968:332) has defined as "a state in which we observe a certain alteration of consciousness, an alteration which may bring about changes, in varying degree, of certain functions: changes in concepts of identity, in memory functions, in sensory modalities, etc." (translated from the French by Bourguignon). Salman

308

(1968:198) has pointed out several physiological features of importance to a biological study of trance: the central nervous system, the ascending reticular system, the Papez-McLean circuit of limbic lobe, thalamus, and hypothamus. My field study of a few biological aspects of trance was considerably more modest in scope and depth. I relied on observation of objective external aspects of trance behavior and subjective reports given by my informants. This section includes my findings on seven items: the types of trance recognized by umbandists, preparation for trance, induction of trance, means for sustaining trance, termination of trance, feelings after trance, and the relation of trance states to emotional states.

First, it is interesting to note that umbandists categorize trance, or more accurately mediums, into three types—conscious, semiconscious and unconscious. Informants estimated that only 15 to 35 percent of Umbanda mediums are unconscious during possession. I estimate that no more than about 5 percent of the mediums experience a deep unconscious trance with the following criteria: glazed eyes for two or three hours; profuse perspiring for two or three hours, even when not physically active; production of more saliva than normal, but no frothing; some difficulty with motor coordination, that is, jerky movements and some difficulty with speech; unconsciousness; and the need to be supported for approximately 30 seconds after trance. One of my informants, who said that he was a semiconscious medium alternating between conscious and unconscious states, while possessed rolled his eyes upward so that only the whites of his eyes were displayed. This seemed to occur only while he was in deep trance. When possessed by a child spirit, he was in a lighter state of trance and conscious, and the extreme upward movement of his eyes did not occur. Conscious mediums exhibited fewer external physiological changes, but they did report changes in body image. They felt their body growing larger and more powerful when possessed by a *caboclo* spirit. When possessed by a child spirit, they felt lighter and smaller, and a few mediums reported that the lightness in weight enabled them to spring upward like a child. One conscious medium reported that when she was possessed, people and objects in the room appeared to her to be small and far away.

Second, umbandists prepare themselves for trance states by avoiding heavy meals and alcohol on the day they go to a public session. This practice is fairly routine, but not universal. Total abstinence from food is not common at all. Third, the induction of trance usually is accompanied by polyrhythmic drumming and handclapping, singing, and ringing of a bell. Mediums are often dancing and spinning up to the point of the head-chest jerk that signals possession by a spirit. At a few of the more subdued Umbanda centers and at most private sessions, a medium may rely more on quietly concentrating on the arrival of his spirit. Only the head-chest movement occurs in these cases. Fourth, the trance state is difficult to sustain over a period of two or three hours unless the medium is in a deep unconscious state of dissociation. Facial expressions, voice, and gestures are modified by all mediums, and glazed eyes appear in nearly all mediums. However, after about twenty minutes of possession, facial expressions, voice, gestures, and eyes return to normal in the conscious mediums, although they are said to be possessed over a period of two or three hours. I observed mediums drinking alcoholic beverages in private sessions. This practice may aid in sustaining trance when drumming is not present as it is in public sessions. Fifth, trance is terminated when the cult leader announces that it is time for the spirits to return to their heavenly dwelling places. There may be some spinning on the part of the mediums, followed by head-chest jerks. The medium frequently drops back into the arms of someone who is waiting to break the fall. Sixth, mediums report that they feel very relaxed after trance. Tensions they may have had before trance are no longer present.

The final item of importance in this section is the relation of trance states to emotional states. It appears to me that trance states may frequently be related to what Festinger (1957) calls cognitive dissonance, or conflict, at the cerebral level. Festinger (1957:18) states that cognitive dissonance acts in the same way as a state of drive or need or tension. Just as the presence of hunger leads to action to reduce hunger, the presence of dissonance leads to action to reduce it. As such, it seems to me, cognitive dissonance represents an internal force that provokes a state of stress in the body. The cognitive conflict an individual experiences and the resulting physiological stress are often manifested as depression or aggression in umbandists. It seems that the more common conscious trance state and possession are an attempt on the part of the individual to deal with conflict and other emotional feelings exemplified in some of the preceding sections of this paper. To some extent I regard the acting out of a spirit role as a type of ego defense mechanism. A novice in Umbanda has not yet learned to play or to utilize spirit roles. Therefore, if his other ego defense mechanisms are weakly developed, additional cognitive dissonance and physiological stress may build up, for depression and aggression are not always acceptable either to the person himself or to the people he interacts with. The added dissonance and stress may be the reason that it is fairly easy to induce a brief state of unconscious trance in the novice. Also, cognitive dissonance and stress may occasionally build up in a developed medium who is normally conscious during possession, causing him to shift into a state of unconsciousness. This occurred one night in a private session to Cecília, whom I discussed earlier. Her spirit said a number of things that would have been quite unacceptable to Cecília; for example, he was going to make her urinate in the middle of a public session at a center and that he would cut each year of her life in half for every year she was not a cult leader. As this was happening, Cecília went into a deeper unconscious trance. After the spirit had sent a glass filled with beer crashing to the floor, Cecília fell backward into a catatonic-like state for about three minutes before the others present were able to revive her. The data in this section indicate that trance is an extremely complex form of behavior that obviously needs more laboratory and field study.

CONCLUSIONS

My intention in this paper has been to demonstrate that Umbanda is a religious innovation in the developing society of Brazil. The first part of this study was a discussion of major transformations, or macrochanges, in Brazilian economy, social structure, and politics. The data presented in the second part suggest that trance and spirit possession represent microchanges at the level of the individual. Possession trance allows the individual an enlarged field of action—that is, freedom to modify his own situation, and perhaps that of others—that is not available to his "normal" self (Bourguignon 1965). Cognitive dissonance and stress may lead into possession trance states. In the Brazilian milieu of urbanization and industrialization, cognitive dissonance and stress in both medium and client are linked, in part, to personal difficulties in playing new economic and social roles and to conflict between traditional and modern social mores and roles. Umbanda's great significance in modern Brazil lies in its role of mediating macrochanges in the larger society and microchanges at the level of the individual.

To anyone who has studied the historical background of folk religions in Brazil, one of the most interesting questions has to do with the particular cultural form Umbanda assumed in the sociocultural environment of change. The *orixa* spirits that were so important in the ritual activities of earlier cult forms in Brazil were promoted to higher oblivion in Umbanda. Instead of possessing individuals, as they had in Candomblé, it is now believed that the *orixás* send spiritual envoys, that is, highly evolved spirits of the dead, to possess Umbanda mediums. It seems to me that the retention of the *orixás* signifies the great importance umbandists attach to the African heritage in their religion. However, umbandists see themselves as Brazilian, not as Afro-Brazilians. This would help explain why the *orixás* have been "moved upstairs," so to speak. It is similar to what occurred in Christianity. The Old Testament of Jewish life and belief is viewed as a significant part of the Christian religion, but the major everyday doctrine of Christians is found in the New Testament. Umbanda, like Christianity, is accepted by a broader population than the earlier ethnic-oriented religions of Candomblé and Judaism. In addition to this change in the nature of the *orixá* spirits, two non-*orixá* spirits in Candomblé, namely, the *criança* and the *exu,* were retained but somewhat modified in Umbanda. Two other spirits, namely, the *prêto velho* and the *caboclo,* were present in other earlier Brazilian spiritualists religions, and were added as important everyday spirits to Umbanda. In the past, there were many other types of spirits. Even today, umbandists are possessed by other spirit types, but why do they not assume the central importance that the *caboclo, prêto velho, criança,* and *exu* spirits have in Umbanda? It seems to me that the answer to the question of the particular cultural form Umbanda has emerged with can be related to the fact that the four major spirit types in Umbanda are cultural symbols that have multiple referents, and all are linked to change.

First, three of the four spirit types apparently symbolize the major ethnic heritages in Brazil. The *prêto velho* and the *caboclo* represent the African and Amerindian contributions to modern Brazilian culture. The *exu* seems to represent the other foreign elements, frequently European.[10] Some umbandists have noted that the child spirit is "just like us," that is, the *criança* has the outgoing personality of Brazilians, and he lacks a specific racial identity. The emergence of these four symbols in Umbanda coincided with vast social and economic changes since the late 1920s that reoriented Brazilian perspectives from regional groupings to one that was more national. According to Wagley (1963:270), Brazilian writers at this time began to recognize the importance of African and Indian cultures in their national life styles. Umbanda, then, is something of a "national folk religion." Each medium, so to speak, "incorporates" his national heritage as four spiritual symbols. As noted earlier, Umbanda diffuses to the smaller cities in the interior of Brazil as they become integrated into the national socioeconomic structure and begin to accept the culture of the modern Brazilian "masses."

Second, I believe the spirit types represent points along the evolutionary stream of Brazilian spiritualist religion from which Umbanda emerged. The African origins in Umbanda are the oldest. Indian and European cultural elements were later added to the earlier African religions. This is symbolized in the relative ages of the four spirit types. The *prêto velho* is the oldest, the *caboclo* and the *exu* are middle-aged, and the child spirit, which symbolizes the new Brazilian, is the youngest.

Third, some of my informants expressed the idea that the spirits were like a family: "The indulgent *prêto velho* is like a grandfather; the stern *caboclo* is more like a father; and the child spirit is like a brother or sister." In contrast, the antisocial *exu* is like a stranger. The functional importance of this set of symbols cannot be overestimated in the life of an individual who has left his family to migrate to the city.

Fourth, it seems to me that when the four spirit types are considered as a combined unit they represent a well-balanced personality. There are the calm and indulgent *prêto velhos,* the stern and aloof *caboclos,* the playful and innocent *crianças,* and the aggressive and base *exus.* Each medium must learn to successfully play the roles of each of the four spirits. One of these personality traits may be weakly developed in an individual. In the social context of Umbanda, such a mode of behavior is learned and is carried over into the individual's life outside of the religious context; for example, an impatient individual learns to relate the calmness of his *prêto velho* to his everyday life. All of these traits are useful in a milieu of rapid culture change in which one must adapt to new social and economic roles. Most of my informants were either upper-lower or middle class, and all were upwardly mobile.

To summarize, it seems that these four spirits emerged in Umbanda because they have at least four different sets of referents that relate to cultural change. The first set of referents represents change at the level of national identity. The second set has to do with change within the evolutionary stream of Brazilian folk religions. The third set of referents deals with changes in the social structural unit closest to an individual, that is, his family. The fourth set of referents is the most individualized or personal. These four sets of referents of four major Umbanda spirit types form a continuum from mac-

315

rochanges to microchanges found in Brazil and help to explain Umbanda as a religious innovation in the developing society of Brazil.

1. The work reported in this chapter is part of a larger study that was supported by Public Health Service Research Grant MH 07463 from the National Institute of Mental Health. The project, entitled Cross-Cultural Studies of Dissociational States, was under the direction of Dr. Erika Bourguignon, of the Department of Anthropology, the Ohio State University.

2. Kardecism was brought to Brazil from France in the nineteenth century. Kardecists tend to be in the middle and upper classes in Brazil. Members are possessed by spirits of dead doctors, lawyers, teachers and even kings. Followers of Kardecism usually view themselves as being more intellectual than umbandists.

3. Levy is referring to men of the *delegacia de costumes*, or special police, who deal with "moral" affairs. In the case of Umbanda centers, they look into complaints stemming from loud drumming into the night.

4. I use the Portuguese orthography throughout this paper. The *x* is equivalent to the English *sh*. An *m* at the end of a word indicates that the preceding vowel is nasalized, e.g., *-am, -em, -im, -um*. It is not a bilabial *m*.

5. I hope that sociologists will forgive my use of the term inter*personal* relations to refer to the interaction between a spirit and a person. The term seems to be quite appropriate for describing this particular Brazilian phenomenon.

6. I should point out that the use of the terms "psychologically stable" and "psychologically unstable" are mine. Umbandists, themselves, talk instead about "spiritual disorders" that must be controlled by supernatural means. Umbandists also discuss "psychological problems," but confine the use of this term to behavior that an individual can control without supernatural aid. What umbandists consider "psychological" and what they regard as "spiritual" seems to be a matter of personal inclination.

7. This name and all other personal names used in this paper are fictitious.

8. This possession occurred sometime during World War II.

9. The spirit she had seen in her kitchen several days earlier.

10. As noted earlier, *exus* sometimes represent special regional characters in Brazil. This aspect of *exus* might be related to the second set of referents in which the *exu* plays the part of the "outsider." More fieldwork in areas outside of São Paulo is needed to help clarify this problem of the *exus* and their "ethnicity."

REFERENCES

Bastide, Roger. 1952. "Le batuque de Pôrto Alegre," in *Acculturation in the Americas* (editor Sol Tax), pp. 195–206, vol. 2. *Proceedings and Selected*

Papers of the 29th International Congress of Americanists. Chicago: University of Chicago Press.

———. 1958. *Le candomblé de Bahia* (rite Nagô). Paris: Mouton and Company.

———. 1960. *Les religions africaines au Brésil*. Paris: Presses Universitaires de France.

Bourguignon, Erika. 1965. "The theory of spirit possession," in *Context and meaning in cultural anthropology* (editor Melford E. Spiro). New York: Free Press.

———. 1968. "Divination, transe et possession en Afrique transsaharienne," in *La divination* (editors A. Caquot and Marcel Leibovici). Paris: Presses Universitaires de France.

Busey, James L. 1969. "The old and the new in the politics of modern Brazil," in *The shaping of modern Brazil* (editor Eric N. Baklanoff). Baton Rouge: Louisiana State University Press.

Camargo, Candido Procópio Ferreira de. 1961. *Kardecismo e umbanda: Uma interpretação sociológica*. São Paulo: Livraria Pioneira Editôra.

Carneiro, Edison. 1940. The structure of African cults in Bahia. *Journal of American Folklore* 53:271–78.

———. 1964. *Ladinos e crioulos: Estudos sôbre o negro no Brasil*. Rio de Janeiro: Editôra Civilização Brasileira S. A.

Chardon, Roland E. 1966. "Changes in the geographic distribution of population in Brazil, 1950–1960," in *New perspectives of Brazil* (Editor Eric N. Baklanoff). Nashville, Tenn.: Vanderbilt University Press.

Dulles, John W. F. 1966. "Post-dictatorship Brazil, 1945–1965," in *New perspectives of Brazil* (editor Eric N. Baklanoff). Nashville, Tenn.: Vanderbilt University Press.

Eduardo, Octavio da Costa. 1948. *The negro in northern Brazil*. Seattle: University of Washington Press.

Festinger, Leon. 1957. *A theory of cognitive dissonance*. Evanston, Ill.: Row, Peterson and Company.

Goodenough, Ward. 1963. *Cooperation in change*. New York: Russell Sage Foundation.

Gudin, Eugenio. 1969. "The chief characteristics of the postwar economic development of Brazil," in *The economy of Brazil* (editor Howard S. Ellis). Berkeley and Los Angeles: University of California Press.

Harris, Marvin. 1970. Referential ambiguity in the calculus of Brazilian racial identity. *Southwestern Journal of Anthropology* 26:1–14.

Herskovits, M. J. 1937. African gods and Catholic saints in New World negro belief. *American Anthropologist* 39:635–43.

———. 1943. The southernmost outposts of New World Africanisms. *American Anthropologist* 45:495–510.

———. 1955. The social organization of the candomblé. *Congr. Internacional de Americanistas* 1:505–32.

———. 1959. The panan: An Afrobahian religious rite of transition. *Caribbean Quarterly* 5:276–83.

317

Landes, Ruth. 1940. Fetish worship in Brazil. *Journal of American Folklore* 53:261–70.

———. 1947. *The city of women.* New York: Macmillan Company.

Leacock, Seth. 1964a. Ceremonial drinking in an Afro-Brazilian cult. *American Anthropologist* 66:334–54.

———. 1964b. Fun-loving deities in an Afro-Brazilian cult. *Anthropological Quarterly* 37:94–109.

———. 1966. Spirit possession as role-enactment in the batuque. Paper presented to the 65th Annual Meeting of the American Anthropological Association, Pittsburgh, Pa., November 17–20.

Levy, Maria Stella. 1968. "The umbanda is for all of us." Masters thesis. University of Wisconsin, Madison, Wisconsin.

Lopez, Juarez R. B. 1966. "Some basic developments in Brazilian politics and society," in *New perspectives of Brazil* (editor Eric N. Baklanoff). Nashville, Tenn.: Vanderbilt University Press.

McGregor, Pedro. 1967. *Jesus of the spirits.* New York: Stein and Day.

Momsen, Richard P. 1968. *Brazil: A giant stirs.* Princeton, N.J.: D. Van Nostrand Co.

Poppino, Rollie E. 1968. *Brazil: The land and people.* New York: Oxford University Press.

Ramos, A. 1934. *O negro brasileiro.* Rio de Janeiro: Editôra Civilização Brasileira S. A.

———. 1935. *O folklore negro do Brasil.* Rio de Janeiro: Editôra Civilização Brasileira S. A.

Ribeiro, René. 1952. O teste de Rorschach no estudo da "aculturação" e da "possessão fetechista" dos negros do Brasil. *Boletim do Instituto Joaquim Nebuco* 1:44–50.

———. 1956. Possessão—problema de etnopsicologia. *Boletim do Instituto Joaquim Nebuco* 5:5–44.

Salman, D. H. 1968. "Concluding remarks," in *Trance and possession states* (editor Raymond Prince). Montreal: R. M. Bucke Memorial Society.

Santos, John F. 1966. "A psychologist reflects on Brazil and Brazilians," in *New perspectives of Brazil* (editor Eric N. Baklanoff). Nashville, Tenn.: University of Vanderbilt Press.

Smith T. Lynn. 1963. *Brazil: People and institutions.* Baton Rouge: Louisiana State University Press.

Stainbrook, Edward. 1952. Some characteristics of the psychopathology of schizophrenic behavior in Bahian society. *American Journal of Psychiatry* 109:330–34.

Wagley, Charles. 1963. *An introduction to Brazil.* New York: Columbia University Press.

Willems, Emilio. 1966. "Religious mass movements and social change in Brazil," in *New perspectives of Brazil* (editor Eric N. Baklanoff). Nashville, Tenn.: Vanderbilt University Press.

III

Some Conclusions

8 : An Assessment of Some Comparisons and Implications

Erika Bourguignon

We began by setting out a framework for investigations into altered states of consciousness, with emphasis on institutionalized, sacred states. We may now consider what we have discovered in the analysis of a series of specific bodies of data as well as the implications and conclusions we may draw from these data and from our varying approaches to them, particularly as they apply to the subject of social change.

In our introduction, a large amount of statistical material was summarized, an approach pursued in more detail in Greenbaum's first chapter as it applied to data on a specific region, Sub-Saharan Africa. Can the conclusions of this research be applied to the societies studied in depth in this volume? The data for our statistical studies, it will be recalled, were drawn primarily from tribal societies (see appendix for listing of societies). How are the societies presented here to be characterized? The Nguni, discussed by Gussler, and the Palauans, studied by Leonard, may be considered tribal peoples, whose way of life has been modified over time, and these modifications are an essential part of the subject matter analyzed. The remaining field studies, however, deal not with total societies but with segments of highly differentiated societies. St. Vincent, being the smallest, may in some respects be considered the simplest. Yet this is a developing nation, with international ties, dependent on the world market. The segment from which the

Shakers are drawn represents the proletariat. They are largely literate; their identification is with Christianity.

The subjects of Pressel's study, the membership of Umbanda, live in a large metropolis, the city of São Paulo, and may be taken as representative of urban Brazil. They include a broad spectrum of the population, both with respect to class and to race or ethnicity. The appeal of the cult is to an even broader segment of the population, who utilize it as occasional clients rather than as members. The beliefs of the cult are highly syncretic, including Catholic and spiritualist elements, but interestingly, a great and explicit African contribution. Indeed, the Vincentian Shakers, who are for the most part clearly of African descent, show much less African influence in their beliefs and rituals than the Brazilians of Umbanda, many of whom are entirely of European extraction.

The Apostolics of Yucatán, studied by Goodman, draw their members from the Maya peasantry of this relatively undeveloped region of Mexico. Indeed, Goodman stresses the peasant character of the movement she observed. As in St. Vincent, the focus is on Christianity, and the Maya population here gives little evidence of retention of, or syncretism with, their ancestral religious practices or beliefs.

Thus, our Caribbean, Brazilian, and Mexican studies deal with groups appealing to a portion of a complex, diversified, stratified developing society, not with the society as a whole, except as that society represents the context for the groups and events studied. This is a major difference from the tribal and modified tribal groups, such as the Nguni or the Palauans; however, as the ways of these tribal peoples are modified by their contacts with the modern state systems, into which they are integrated—or forced—they, too, become segments of larger societal wholes.

The Nguni (Zulu), the Palauans, the Vincentian

Shakers, the Brazilian Umbandists, and the Maya Apostolics all have some forms of possession trance. What do they have in common? Both the Nguni and the Palauans traditionally had stratified societies, and neither had slavery. Both were differentiated by wealth and divided into hereditary clans; and in both, there was some room for the striving, achieving individual. These tribal societies correspond well enough to the picture of a possession trance society we developed from our statistical studies because they have the requisite degree of complexity. The three other societies are more complex, having not only class stratification but a highly differentiated division of labor and a complex state system. In each of these three cases, we are dealing only with one group within a particular segment of the population. Indeed, the Maya Apostolics are quite atypical of Maya peasants in their beliefs and practices, although their type of religion is spreading in the area, as it is throughout Latin America.

Greenbaum, in her second chapter, as we have seen, hypothesizes that possession trance is more likely to be present in more rigid societies than in more flexible ones. In testing this hypothesis, she redefines "presence of possession trance" to mean the existence of a person through whom the spirits are believed to speak, and who thus offers a socially acceptable source of decision-making to whom the individual can turn. Other types of possession trance are not considered relevant to the hypothesis.

The Zulu with their strong political hierarchy, and warfare and religious complexity as well as other types of complexity are rated "rigid" by Greenbaum. She sees a similar pattern of "autocracy-hierarchy-central authority-fixed rites" in Leonard's data on Palau, and also rates this society as "rigid." One difference between these societies, similar in many respects, should however

323

be noted: the patrilineal, polygynous Zulu expose women to particular stresses absent among the matrilineal, primarily monogamous Palauans.

Mediums, fitting Greenbaum's narrower definition of possession trance, existed in traditional Palauan society, as they did among the Zulu (Nguni). Among the Palauans, the traditional mediums were official oracles, tied to the power of the chiefs, by whom their office was ratified. The mediums offered individual and collective advice, and thus fulfilled the hypothesized role. There is little evidence that possession trance gave them great personal satisfaction or served to solve their individual problems. As noted by Leonard, the majority of surviving traditional mediums are old men.

Among the Nguni, as described by Gussler, the function of acting as oracles of the spirits—in this case, the ancestors—and thus serving as decision-makers, is supplied by the diviners. Indeed, the power inherent in this role, which included the identification of witches, was so great in earlier times that the autocratic Shaka attempted to eliminate the diviners (Ritter 1957). Thus, although the mediums among the Palauans were apparently identified with the centers of power, the hereditary chiefs, among the Zulu, the diviners represented a potential opposition to the king in his effort to consolidate his power. However, in addition to the public, societal function of possession trance for the Nguni, this behavior also has personal functions for the individual diviner.

Of the segments of three complex societies that we have studied, only the Brazilian Umbanda cult, with its advice-giving mediums, satisfies Greenbaum's redefined category of possession trance; the Vincentian Shakers and the Maya Apostolics do not do so, or do so only marginally. How are the societies in which these groups exist to be viewed with respect to rigidity? There appears to be at present much greater individual mobility among

Brazilians than among either the Vincentians or the Maya. Indeed, for both of these latter groups, mobility for the young is almost entirely dependent on education and emigration; but education is, to a considerable extent, contingent on emigration. Possession trance does not provide a decision-making authority for individuals in these societies. However, it does provide the individual with the certitude of having been "saved" and the evidence of this for his peers. Membership in these groups provides some possibility of acquiring a new and positive status *within that group*, although not within the larger society. Indeed, in the larger society, membership in the group may be despised. Among the Maya, particularly, it may lead to ostracism even within the family. Yet group membership offers its own rewards and provides new ties, and, among the Maya, an extended social and cultural horizon. Young men may be sent to Bible schools and may become missionaries elsewhere; ties are established with other churches, even as far away as Mexico City and the United States. There is a degree of self-manipulation that, through the avoidance of "sin"—expensive and possibly addictive habits—leads to savings in money and energy, which are invested, however, in the church and not in potential individual economic advancement. Both among the Maya and the Vincentians, through emphasis on Bible study, the churches encourage literacy and, importantly among the Maya, knowledge of Spanish. For the Maya, then, more than for the Vincentians, church membership has the latent function of providing a cultural and social reorientation, which potentially may be relevant to social mobility in a traditionally rigid society. The ecstatic experience of possession trance appears to provide much of the motivation for church membership, and, as Goodman points out, the intensity of that experience is highly valued. The major reorienting factor, then, appears to be church membership, not the

325

existence of a decision-making instance. For the Vincentians, the larger societal implications appear to be of less significance, and the status attainments are limited to prestige within the group.

Brazil, on the other hand, is a highly mobile developing society. Pressel places much emphasis on the stresses experienced by individuals as a result of this move from a very rigid, primarily agrarian society to a modern industrial one. The need for assistance in the decision-making that the clients of mediums seek—clients who may not themselves be members of Umbanda—appears to derive from the fact that they live not in a rigid society but rather in a society that is becoming less rigid. Perhaps to a generation brought up in a flexible society, attuned to dealing with the decision-making involved in such a setting, mediums would not be necessary. In the Brazilian situation, it appears to be the transition from rigid to more flexible circumstances that provides the greatest stresses. It might also be noted that though the Umbanda cult is relatively new, the existence of mediums in the context of Afro-Brazilian cults is not. Indeed, these cults appear to have flourished since the arrival of African slaves in Brazil. Another mediumistic group is found in Kardecism. Perhaps what has changed most in recent years is the group in the population that makes use of mediums for the solution of its problems.

Because of the presence of many groups in such complex societies—subcultures and ethnic groups as well as ranked status groups, diverse religious affiliations, and political ideologies—it is difficult to apply the flexibility-rigidity criteria developed for tribal societies; thus, such a crude application as that attempted here does not represent a true test of the hypothesis, nor does a sample of three societies. Nonetheless, as we have seen, the attempt at applying the criteria has proved to be heuristic.

We noted earlier that among the Nguni possession

trance plays two roles: a public one, serving the society in the form of the diviner's clients, and a private one, serving the diviner's personal needs. Consequently, as we consider the several societies under discussion, we may compare them precisely with respect to the relative importance they give to these two functions of possession trance, the public, hypothesized by Greenbaum, and the private, demonstrated by Gussler. In Palau, as we have already noted, the public, societal function appears to predominate, whereas both are in evidence among the Nguni, although there may have been different emphases at different historical periods. Again, both are strongly in evidence in the Brazilian Umbanda cult. On the other hand, among the Vincentian Shakers and the Maya Apostolics, the societal public decision-making function—indeed, a mediumistic function of possession trance altogether—is but vaguely adumbrated at best. For the most part, the primary, if not the only, function of possession trance is its importance for the individual, who believes himself "saved" as a result of the experience and who derives euphoria and personal strength from it. Thus, Palau represents one pole of a continuum and the enthusiastic Christian churches the other: in the first instance, the emphasis is almost exclusively on the societal function of possession trance; in the second instance, it is on the personal function. The Nguni and the Brazilian Umbanda cult fall between these two extremes, exhibiting both functions of the possession trance phenomenon.

We may now turn to the consideration of another hypothesis concerning possession trance. For Gussler, as we have seen, the importance of possession belief and possession trance among the Nguni lies in the observation that it provides compensation for those hardest pressed—women and weak men. It possibly may also provide compensation for those nutritionally as well as

327

structurally afflicted, providing change in wealth and diet as well as in status and influence. Thus, we may differentiate here between two kinds of compensation: subjective expressive compensation provided by the emotional satisfactions derived from the experience of possession trance itself, and objective instrumental compensation provided through a change in status resulting from the social recognition accorded to possession trance, and, in the case of the Nguni, possession illness. Subjective expressive compensation for personal and socially induced stresses may be seen to be present not only among the Nguni diviner-candidates but also among Umbanda mediums and among the faithful of the Shaker and Apostolic churches in St. Vincent and in Yucatán, respectively. There seems to be little evidence of such a cathartic or self-enhancing experience in Palau. As far as objective instrumental compensation is concerned, we found it among the Nguni in the status transformation that results from becoming a diviner. It is present also for the leaders in Umbanda and among the Shakers; there appears to be somewhat less evidence of this among the Maya Apostolics. Such status transformation exists also among Palauan mediums, but here it is not clear whether any kind of compensation is involved.

The existence of both types of compensation, the subjective expressive and the objective instrumental, suggests that, as Lewis (1966; 1971) has argued, some spirit cults may indeed represent responses to deprivation. However, as noted, two different although sometimes overlapping types of deprivation appear to be involved: deprivation in personal satisfaction and deprivation resulting from low social status or lack of power. However, there is no evidence in any of our societies that possession trance itself or membership in cult groups did in fact involve the utilization of supernatural sanctions against those responsible for the deprivation, which

Lewis (1966; 1971) posits. Also, we have noted earlier the difficulty of applying Lewis's category of "amoral peripheral spirit cult" (Lewis n.d.) to any of our examples.

Gussler's discussion of the Nguni raises the issue of pathology, emotional illness as well as perhaps nutritionally induced illness. Interestingly, it is the only one of our several studies to do so. Among the Nguni, illness, interpreted as possession, may last for as long as several years. Only for short periods during this time is the patient likely be dissociated. However, dissociation, viewed as possession trance, is induced during the therapeutic initiation ritual. Once a diviner, the individual may only occasionally use possession trance in her (or his) professional activity. Thus, illness in this case is a prior condition for which possession trance is utilized as a cure. Wallace (1961:281–83) has analyzed the Zulu data presented by Callaway and argues that initiation involves a therapeutic personality transformation. Gussler, as we have seen, interprets it as a therapeutic status transformation. Both of these views, which are complementary, see the illness as present prior to possession trance, which itself is not pathological but therapeutic.

In our other societies, frank pathology may exist in some individuals seeking possession trance, but this is not a necessary precondition for the development of the behavior. Indeed, much evidence is presented in our studies to show the importance of learning in the acquisition of the behavior in the several societies. In none of the societies in our series of field studies is the behavior considered pathological by the people themselves, but, on the contrary, it is both encouraged and rewarded within the group in which it occurs. Neither have we any evidence of its leading to pathological disability. On the contrary, where personal compensations are involved, resolution of personal stresses seems to be evident. With

329

the possible exception of the Palauan case, in which the activity of the traditional mediums was apparently almost exclusively a societal matter, we may apply to our materials the conclusions drawn by the Brazilian psychiatrist René Ribeiro (1956). Working with members of the Afro-American Xangô cult of Recife, he found that the psychological significance of the possession trance experience varied from individual to individual, being cathartic or therapeutic for some and pathological for others as viewed from a psychiatric perspective. Such evaluations can be arrived at only from the psychodynamic study of specific individuals, not from the analysis of cultural forms. Two psychiatrists, Field (1960) and Pfeiffer (1971), have strongly stated, on the basis of field data collected in different parts of the world, that dissociational states need not necessarily be pathological phenomena but must be considered in a cultural framework. We have attempted to do so.

Gussler's Nguni materials also suggest that certain preconditions may provide a motivation to seek possession trance and facilitate its induction. This matter of a culturally defined precondition and of individual motivation may usefully enlarge the scope of Ludwig's (1968) discussion of factors leading to the induction of altered states of consciousness.

Yet another issue in the study of possession trance is raised by Leonard's Palauan materials: the possibility that such states may be induced by means of drugs, in this instance, specifically, betel. It is interesting to note, first of all, that this is the only society in which this question arises. There is no evidence of the use of trance-inducing drugs in any of our other societies. The material on betel that Leonard is able to assemble suggests that it may best be considered a secondary factor in producing the altered state. Alcohol may also be considered in the category of mood-changing substances. It is used in some contexts in the Umbanda cult, we are told, but it appears that persons first go into possession trance and then, acting as certain spirits, drink and smoke. Alcohol may thus help to sustain the state in this group; it does not induce it or cause it, as a rule.

A recurrent behavior pattern in possession trance is the existence of ecstatic vocalizations, termed glossolalia. This phenomenon is particularly striking among the Maya of Yucatán and, to a lesser degree, among the Vincentian Shakers. Among the Nguni, we are told, foreign spirits may speak in foreign languages; but here it is not certain whether we are dealing with fragments of the actual languages of neighboring groups, which may be known to the possession trancer, or with glossolalia proper. Similarly, in one instance we are told of a contemporary Palauan medium producing the English speech of a spirit. Goodman (1972) has studied the glossolalia phenomenon intensively. She sees it as a learned behavior and describes this learning process in some detail. Glossolalia is learned in an altered state, is produced during such a state, and, indeed, is expressive of the state. As such it reveals features that can be accounted for in terms of hyperarousal of the central nervous system and that are therefore constant among subjects regardless of the language they speak (that is, whether English, as among the Vincentians, or Spanish or Maya, as in Mexico). Furthermore, the detailed phonological analysis of glossolalia utterances, recorded on tape, permits inferences concerning the neurophysiological state of the individual: his breathing, the constriction of his throat, his energy level, and so on. The analysis of recordings of such utterances, therefore, provides a useful tool for the physiological study of altered states.

It is interesting that in spite of the constant aspects of glossolalia, and the fact that this behavior is typically used in our two enthusiastic Christian churches, it does play a somewhat different role among the Vincentian Shakers and among the Maya Apostolics. Among the Shakers, speaking in tongues is only one part of the possession trance. The kinetic aspects of the experience of "being shaken by the spirit" appear to be primary. There is no formal attempt to teach people to speak in tongues, and no great reward is attached to it. The possession trance has a strong collective aspect in its performance; the rewards, however, are subjective. For the Shakers, furthermore, possession trance, including glossolalia, is only one type of religious experience; they also foster another type of altered state in their "mourning" ritual. For the Maya Apostolics, glossolalia is the central aspect of "baptism by the spirit," and every effort is made to induce this behavior in individuals. It is a public demonstration of being saved and is recognized by the group, in the person of the minister, as a key event, a veritable rite of initiation. Goodman stresses the phenomenon of attenuation, over a period of time, of the intensity of the trance-glossolalia experience among the Maya and relates this to the similar curve of peak and attenuation of the socioreligious upheaval she observed among them. The analogy in the pattern of the individual glossolalia utterance, the pattern of possession trance behavior over time, and the evolution and eventual attenuation of the upheaval are indeed provocative and raise the question of whether this represents a model of a particular kind of socioreligious movement. Rarely does an observer have the opportunity to study the entire history of such a movement in such a brief span of time. The hypothesis presented is bold and clearly calls for testing on other comparable bodies of data.

Because of the peculiarities of the Maya Apostolic church, a comparison with the Vincentian Shakers is of special interest. No attenuation in the intensity of the possession trance experience is reported by Henney for the Shakers, neither in her observations nor as reported to her by her informants. However, perhaps a longer period of observation of specific individual's would be required to test Goodman's hypotheses concerning attenuation among the Vincentians. The Shakers are known to have existed as a separate church since the beginning of this century, perhaps longer. There is no evidence of any kind of upheaval or crisis having taken place among them during this period of time. Also, where Goodman stresses the peasant character of the Maya Apostolics, the Shakers are proletarians. The role of glossolalia in the two groups also differs notably. Perhaps the very great stress on glossolalia among the Maya Apostolics—the fact of making it the central religious experience, the test of worthiness—leads, on the one hand, to the great intensity with which this behavior is sought and experienced. On the other hand, this very desire for the behavior seems to lead to an inability to sustain such a high level of arousal over time. That is, as habituation sets in, the intensity of the experience is reduced as is the satisfaction derived from it. Indeed, in some respects the behavior described by Goodman resembles a form of addiction.

The attenuation phenomenon, which appears so important to Goodman on the basis of her own data, does not appear in any of our other accounts. This may be the result of differences in methods of research employed. Several additional factors may also be relevant to this. The Apostolics and the Shakers exhibit a different form of possession trance than our other groups: it is not mediumistic and yields primarily private subjective expressive satisfactions. The other groups under discussion here, the Nguni, Palauans, and Brazilians of Umbanda, enact the roles of spirits and engage in sometimes complexly individualized forms of impersonation. Our two Christian churches do not impersonate or

333

individualize; all of the possession trancers are filled with the Holy Spirit, and the scope for individualization of the behavior is highly limited. Where the societal role of medium is being fulfilled, the private satisfactions of the possession trance experience are not in the foreground of the activity; it is therefore not sought with the same motivation and also probably not with the same intensity. As attentuation occurs, if it does, this is not a matter of major importance: the medium or impersonator can play his largely histrionic part with minimal dissociation, perhaps, at times if necessary, consciously playing the role as the occasion demands. The Apostolic, to whom the personal satisfaction is primary, would gain nothing by so doing, and attentuation may then well represent a crisis of faith, a sign of a loss of grace, and so on.

As noted, the Vincentian Shakers are less concerned with glossolalia as such, and value the kinetic and often collective experience of the possession trance. In this context, the individual is not singled out for performance. His personal distinction is emphasized in his decision to undergo baptism and the further rite of "mourning." Both in the preparation of the baptism and in the "mourning" ritual, another altered state, visionary trance, is sought. In none of our other societies do we find such a patterned form of non-possession trance. Although visionary trance is a patterned, formally induced part of Shaker ritual, it appears to have erupted spontaneously among the Maya Apostolics during their eschatological crisis. It took hold of them, as it were; they did not control it through ritual forms. In comparison with the Maya Apostolics, the Shakers have in the existence of this further ritual an addition to their array of religious experiences. However, there is a feedback between the various types of experiences, for visionary trance appears to reinforce the ability of individuals to go into possession trance at appropriate times.

Henney points to the many impressive similarities between the manner in which visionary trance is produced among the Shakers and the production of hallucinations in experiments with sensory deprivation. As in the case of Goodman's analysis of glossolalia, we have here evidence of a psychophysiological substrate of religious experience. The Shakers, furthermore, are not unique in the application of practices of sensory deprivation to their preparations for visionary experiences. This type of trance is indeed widespread among the peoples of the world, and sensory deprivation is probably as important as hallucinogens in the production of visions. In our group of case studies, however, the Shakers are the only ones who exhibit visionary trance as well as possession trance.

We have noted the brief and cataclysmic character of the upheaval, the eschatological crisis among the Maya Apostolics, who are peasants, and the stable character of Shaker religion among the Vincentians, who are proletarians. The Brazilian metropolitan middle-class or upwardly mobile lower-class individuals who flock to Umbanda face rather different problems. Whereas the Maya and the Vincentians are poor and live in societies where few opportunities exist for them, the urban Brazilians, who make up the membership and the clientele of Umbanda, live in a rapidly changing, economically expanding society. Here we have neither the stability of the Shakers nor the hope for the end of the world of the Apostolics. The problems faced are problems of daily living, matters of economic or career success, family and love life, health, and interpersonal conflicts. The Umbandists seek from their religion not solutions to the problems of the world, or personal salvation, but the resolution of problems of day-to-day living. For the mediums themselves, there is also the opportunity for expressive venting of various aspects of their personalities through the complex language of role-playing,

335

as they impersonate a series of highly individualized spirit entities. On the societal level, however, Umbanda seems to me particularly fascinating as a symbolic and dramatic blending of the cultural contributions of a series of historic and ethnic streams that make up modern Brazil, and as the symbolic expression, furthermore, of that blending. Where the Maya Apostolics, in their upheaval, consciously attempted to prepare for the Second Coming, this process of symbolic expression of cultural unity among the Brazilians does not appear essentially to be a planned, intentional, conscious process. Rather, it appears to be an emergent of the actual blending that is taking place in the society. The multi-ethnic and multiracial membership of the cult centers reveals this as clearly as the varied provenience of the spirits.

We may now attempt to sum up what we have discovered with respect to the relationships that may exist between social change and possession trance. Our five case studies reveal a great deal of variety. This variety is, in part, due to the fact that our cases include several levels of social integration: tribal societies in various states of transitions, peasants, proletarians, and urban lower- and middle-class individuals. In each of these societies, one or more forms of possession trance exist. We have distinguished several such forms: the mediumistic and the personal, and among the personal we have distinguished between the instrumental and the expressive forms. In addition, we have found ritualized visionary trance in one group (St. Vincent Shakers) and possession illness in another (Nguni). Our examples have clearly demonstrated the influence of belief on behavior and the important role that learning plays in the acquisition of possession trance behavior. Furthermore, in our statistical studies, both with respect to complexity and to rigidity, we have been able to show the relationship between the belief-behavior complex on the one hand and social structure, on the other. Specifically, the discussion of rigidity has suggested that microchange—that is, change on the level of individual decision-making—is facilitated by possession trance in rigid societies.

The existence of possession trance in a society may itself represent an innovation, as is the case among the Maya. Here, change introduced from outside the society brought the church, with its practice of possession trance, into the area. In addition to whatever function this may have in producing further changes, its very existence represents an innovation. The other extreme is represented by the Palauans, among whom the practice existed in the traditional society but is being lost with acculturation. Among the Nguni, the Vincentians, and the Brazilians, it is a retention, although often a highly modified retention, of earlier cultural patterns. The form possession trance takes in a given situation is itself, then, a response to cultural change, the behavior being modified as the belief system and the social structure change.

On the other hand, possession trance, as we have seen, may channel cultural change in various ways. It may inhibit it, as it appears to have done in St. Vincent, or stimulate excitement approaching a crisis, as appears to have been the case among the Maya Apostolics. Yet again, it may serve as a facilitating factor for social change, as in Umbanda.

Possession trance, as a form of culturally patterned and sacred altered state of consciousness, is a multifaceted phenomenon. Because of its psychobiological substrate, it reveals constants wherever we find it. Yet it is subject to learning and by this means, it is amenable to cultural patterning. As such, it takes on a striking variety of forms. Indeed, we might consider additional refinements of classification in pursuing our principal theme, the relationship between possession trance, as a particular form of altered state, and social change. Thus,

337

we may ask, how variable or standardized is possession trance in a given society or in a particular social group? I should like to suggest that there may well be a relationship between the stereotypy of the behavior and the conservatism of the institutions it serves. The more the individual possession trancer is obligated to play an invariant role of limited range, as among the Shakers, the less the possession trance can be utilized for innovation. Conversely, the more the possession trancer is given the opportunity to respond to questions and to vary his behavior, as in Umbanda, the greater the potential both for the expression of a strong personality and for innovation. A second type of altered state, visionary trance, may serve to reinforce the social and personal effects of possession trance. The key to a stable religion and a stable situation is the ability to utilize altered states under controlled, ritualized conditions. When these states get out of hand, when they appear to burst forth outside of ritual constraints, crisis results, both for the individual and for the group.[1] This is clearly seen in the contrasting use of visionary trance among the Shakers and the Maya Apostolics. Because, as Ludwig (1968) has pointed out, altered states increase suggestibility, they heighten the common faith of those who experience them jointly. This is seen in the greater devotion of those Shakers who have been to mourn, and it is seen even more dramatically in the upheaval described by Goodman.

These observations cannot hope to exhaust the rich materials presented by our various authors; they can only hope to highlight, through comparisons, some points of interest and significance. What appears to emerge clearly from our discussions, however, is that altered states in general and, perhaps, possession trance in particular represent potentially important and dramatic instruments of social power and, thus, of social change. As such, they deserve our attention.

1. This may well have important implication for the present situation in the United States, with respect to the so-called Jesus Freaks and other Pentecostalists as well as various aspects of the drug scene.

REFERENCES

Field, M. J. 1960. *Search for security: An ethno-psychiatric study of rural Ghana.* Evanston, Ill.: Northwestern University Press.

Goodman, F. D. 1972. *Speaking in tongues: A cross-cultural study of glossolalia.* Chicago: University of Chicago Press.

Lewis, I. M. 1966. Spirit possession and deprivation cults. *Man* 1:307–29.

———. n.d. Possession cults and public morality. *Proceedings of the Colloque:* Cultes de Possession [Paris], forthcoming.

Ludwig, Arnold. 1968. "Altered states of consciousness," in *Trance and possession states* (editor Raymond Prince). Montreal: R. M. Bucke Memorial Society.

Pfeiffer, W. M. 1971. *Transkulturelle Psychiatrie: Ergebnisse und Probleme.* Stuttgart: Georg Thieme Verlag.

Ribeiro, René. 1956. Possessão: Problema de etnopsicologia. *Boletim do Instituto Joaquim Nabuco de Pesquisas Sociais* 5:2–44.

Ritter, E. A. 1957. *Shaka Zulu.* New York: G. P. Putnam's Sons.

Wallace, A. F. C. 1961 "Mental illness, biology and culture," in *Psychological Anthropology* (editor F. L. K. Hsu). Homewood, Ill.: Dorsey Press.

Epilogue : Some Notes on Contemporary Americans and the Irrational[1]

Erika Bourguignon

America presents itself to itself and to the world as a land of freedom, democracy, and equality. Yet in recent years, we have had to face a "counter-image" of a society of violence, inequality, and oppression. Similarly, America projects an image of a secular society, epitomized in rational management and production and symbolized by a technology of superhighways and trips to the moon. Indeed, to one living in a middle-sized city of the Middle West, the selective, and thus distorted, picture of this industrial, rational, and efficient technological society, as it emerges from a reading of, for example, accounts in the French press, is frequently startling. The rational image, it would seem, might well need to be tempered by a counter-image considering some of the irrational aspects of contemporary American society. For example, efficiency is largely built into machines, not into people; rational production techniques appear to require a sales approach that appeals to the irrational in the potential customer. And space flights, the ultimate in technological achievements, raise the suspicion in some minds that such meddling with the moon, which it is said is "God's country," accounts for disturbances in the weather. Such a counter-image of an irrational society arises from an analysis of advertisements, as well as from the materials presented at a recent "Conference on Marginal Religious Movements in America Today" (Zaretsky and Leone, ed., in press). Although we cannot undertake

340

here a full-scale analysis of the irrational in American life, a consideration of the place of enthusiastic forms of religion in this country and the involvement of the young with such religions appears appropriate at the conclusion of this volume. Just what is the place of sacred altered states of consciousness in contemporary America and what have we learned from the several sets of data and analyses presented in this volume that may help us to interpret these phenomena?

Sects, cults, and movements of varying numerical strength and duration abound on the American scene in a bewildering variety of forms, offering alternate solutions to the problems of living, alternatives to the technological world, and to the formalism of the major denominations. Much attention has been given to a portion of this marginal religious scene by the press and the mass media, whether in the form of more or less serious reporting or in a dramatized and fictional form. Yet religious innovation and deviancy are not a new phenomenon in this country, where such groups have sprung up continuously since the founding of the colonies. The Puritans, after all, were a deviant minority religion in England. Other minorities have come to these shores over and over again: Anabaptists (Mennonites, Amish), Shakers, Quakers, and Methodists are among the best known. Others had their origins here: Mormons, Spiritualists, Seventh-Day Adventists, Christian Scientists, Jehovah's Witnesses, and the large variety of Pentecostal, Apostolic, and Holiness churches. Some, like the Shakers, have virtually died out. Others, like the Quakers and the Methodists, who, in their beginnings, included altered states in their ecstatic forms of worship or in their patterns of conversion, have abandoned these practices and have become "respectable." "Respectability" is rather an important concept here, with two major meanings. On the one hand, these groups have shown great

341

social and economic success and have become pillars of the society. However, on the other hand, the very idea of ecstatic religious practices is also associated with lack of "respectability": within the norms of proper behavior, such abandonment of self-control appears indecent at best and mad, at worst. Religious movements and upheavals of considerable violence have swept this country, too, among which the Great Awakening and the Kentucky Revival of the eighteenth century are the best known. On a much larger scale, they present a striking series of resemblances with the upheaval among the Maya Apostolics described by Goodman. Such upheavals appear to justify the fear of loss of control, for in the upheavals not only does the individual relinquish, as in altered states of consciousness generally, partial or complete ego control over his actions but social control as well is distorted. Thus, it is necessary to distinguish such wild-fire, short-lived, trance upheavals not only from stable religious groups that make use of institutionalized altered states within a ritual framework but also from those movements—revitalization movements, millennial movements, and so on—that reach a degree of organizational structure and gain control over the religious and ecstatic experiences of their members. It can surely be said with confidence that all human societies require, in order to survive, a degree of rational control over their technological, economic, and social processes. They vary, however, to the degree to which the irrational—the daemonic, in the Greek view—is allowed to make itself felt. Weber's Protestant Ethic—not as a unique historical phenomenon, but as a recurrent cultural type[2]—is, perhaps, the type of value structure that allows least expression for, and has least sympathy with, the ecstatic experience. The nineteenth-century view of progress, not only from simple to complex but from a primitive mentality to a civilized one, is associated with an evaluation of the ecstatic as savage and childlike.[3]

The so-called marginal religions existing in the United States today include millions of people and have touched a great many more, yet no estimate of their numbers is readily available.[4] The marginality of these religious groups rests on a number of aspects: they may be geographically marginal to the major population centers, like the black and white Holiness and Pentecostal churches of Appalachia and the Deep South; they may be intellectually marginal to the scientific "establishment" in their biblical fundamentalism, their rejection of the teachings of evolution, and their practices of faith healing; or, like some of the flying saucer cultists, they may be concerned with visitors, actual or potential, from outer space. They may be culturally marginal, like those who reject major aspects of Western tradition and accept a variety of exotic cultural forms, whether these be pop-culture figures or middle-class college students—or drop-outs—who turn to various forms of Hinduism, as in the Krishna Consciousness movement. Other rejections of Western, Judeo-Christian culture are found among some groups of Blacks who turn to West African, Afro-Cuban, or Afro-Haitian forms of religion or reconstruct their own version of Islam, as the Black Muslims have done. A feature shared by many of these groups, and a further aspect of their marginality, is their experience—as a part of conversion, or as a part of regular and frequent ritual practice—of altered states of consciousness. For the Christian groups in particular, this is linked to beliefs is spirit possession. It is this typical form of ecstatic experience that brings this major segment of the American religious scene rightfully within the purview of this book.

Yet, if such movements and such groups have a long history in this country, as we have seen, why is it that the press has recently turned to some of them with such interest? Holiness religions, tent revivals, spiritual preaching, speaking in tongues, faith healing, and other works of the spirit have, curiously, long been virtually unknown to much of the urban middle class, from whom they are geographically as well as socially isolated. Indeed, to the extent that the urban middle class consists of the descendants of nineteenth- and twentieth-century European immigrants, they represent culturally and ethnically alien life styles as well. Yet, in the 1960s glossolalia appeared in the Episcopal church and a type of Pentecostalism now exists among Catholics. Neo-Pentecostal "Jesus Freaks" are appealing to white middle-class college students, even to some who were not reared in a Protestant tradition. However, the greatest attention has been attracted by the so-called drug movement, by the attempt to link hallucinogenic drugs (LSD, peyote, psyilocybin, and so on) to religious, predominantly Hindu-derived thought systems. The drugs, it was argued, particularly by Leary and his associates, assisted in the "expansion of consciousness," a concept that has since been widely extended by Reich's view of the emergence of a "Consciousness III" (Reich 1970; Nobile 1971), "consciousness raising" sessions of women's libbers, encounter groups, and others.

Although deviant religious movements of various sorts have frequently appeared on the American scene, as we have said, they have had marginal impact or have transformed themselves, becoming less deviant and moving into the mainstream. At times, they have led to a major exodus, as in the case of the Mormons, or to social encapsulation or isolation, as in the case of the Mennonites, or again, to what La Barre (1970) has termed "failed Messiahs," as among the leaders of snake-handling cults of Appalachia. The current novelty in the growth of new religions is their appeal to, and their development among,

344

<p/>
the relatively prosperous, well-educated young—the very people whom commencement speakers are forever telling that they are the future leaders of America. It is thus part of the larger picture of the youth culture, the generation gap, the crisis of the university, of dropping out, and of the so-called counterculture. It has struck home among groups generally relatively immune to such aberrant manisfestations. This, one might venture to guess, has been its appeal to the press. Its larger significance lies in the social, economic, cultural, and political context within which it occurs. It is difficult to comment on these developments with any confidence because of their highly ephemeral nature—the rapid changes as well as the great diversity of local manifestations. In the universities, and particularly in the major centers of the East and West Coasts, the drug cults appear to be passé, at the same time that marijuana appears to have become a way of life and the nation faces a major heroin epidemic. The Krishna movement, other oriental-derived religions, and the Neo-Pentecostals appear to offer a halfway house, a resocialization agency for some of the drug users. The current economic retrenchment in this country may well affect the picture in the immediate future in major ways.

As we have noted, the ritual utilization of altered states of consciousness is a significant feature of many of the "marginal" religions. Such utilization, together with belief in several types of spirit possession and supernatural inspiration, are an integral part of Western religion, being rooted in both the Greek and the biblical tradition. Several of the major denominations recognize the possibility of spirit possessions of a demonic nature and maintain a ritual of exorcism, although they now rarely make use of it. The Holiness and Pentecostal churches, however, are more likely to make use of such rituals in faith healing. There is a rich folklore of demonic possession, and novels, plays, films, and television dramas have drawn on this lore extensively.[5] Visionary trances, ecstatic trances, speaking in tongues, and so on, attained as a result of mystic excercises, fervent prayer, or even dance, similarly have a lengthy and complex history in the Christian churches and in Judaism as well (Oesterreich 1922; Scholem 1961). We have seen some derivatives of such Christian churches in Goodman's study of Maya Apostolics and Henney's study of the Shakers (Spiritual Baptists) of St. Vincent,[6] who say their religion was founded by Wesley. We have seen other such derivatives of Christianity in the South African Separatist churches, as discussed by Gussler. In many instances, the use of speaking in tongues, of faith healing, of belief in demonic possession, even of snake-handling as in Appalachia (La Barre 1962), derives directly from a somewhat literal reading of New Testament texts. Consequently, these features are not unique to the American scene, but may appear where such literal readings recur anew among diverse groups.

American "marginal" religious groups employ a variety of means to induce altered states of consciousness. For example, Whitehead (n.d.: 53–54) speaks of the phenomenon termed "exteriorization" by Scientologists ("the sense of being outside one's body") and relates it to stimulus deprivation; she suggests the similarity of this state to the hallucinations produced in sensory deprivation experiments. The Scientologists, thus, are seen to resemble the Vincentian Shakers, described by Henney, in their technique of inducing an altered state. Whitehead adds that this experience of "exteriorization" is what "makes Scientology so attractive to those experienced in drugs and meditation." The introduction of drugs as a means of attaining altered states, as practiced in the drug cults among the American young, constitutes a major innovation on the American scene. It is an innovation derived, interestingly enough, from American Indian sources. Indeed, the psychedelic movement has combined American Indian drug usage with a Hindu-Buddhist ideology in the context of an apparently secular, rational, technological twentieth-century American society (Bourguignon n.d.). Thus, like American Indians, and in some instances borrowing the substances from them, they use drugs. Like some oriental religions, they may employ techniques of meditation. Leary and some of his associates combined the two by adapting texts from the Tibetan Book of the Dead for meditations to structure the drug experience.

Although these practices fostered the development of a "drug movement" in the United States, such a movement must be seen in a worldwide context. Among the spiritual ancestors of this movement may be counted such figures as Aldous Huxley and the Belgian surrealist writer and artist Henri Michaux. Thus, on the one hand, the American youth counterculture is part of the American scene with its particular problems and characteristics and its particular history. On the other hand, it must also be seen, in the context of a broader contemporary field, as the convergence of several historical and cultural streams. These include a European literary and artistic tradition and experimentation with drugs as well as the influence on Europeans and Americans of Hindu religious traditions at several points in recent history. One historical precursor of the present scene has been identified by several authors (for example, Bell n.d.; Adler n.d.; Bersani 1971) as surrealism. The surrealists, particuarly in the 1920s, also sought new forms of consciousness and the destruction of the existing social order. Paul-Henri Bourguignon (1946), writing shortly after the end of World War II, noted on the occasion of a surrealist exhibition, how curiously outmoded it all looked. Twenty years earlier, they had wanted to blow up the world; and when it did explode in war, they had in no way

347

been responsible. And now, their antics had become meaningless. As Bersani has put it: "The vision of revolutionary transformations of consciousness is perhaps a fantasy of escape from history rather than a viable inspiration for programs of historical change" (1971:16). Surrealism had been a symptom of its time of crisis, a "fantasy of escape from history," not a cause of social change.

As part of the worldwide picture in the context of which the ecstatic trends in American youth culture or counter-culture must be considered, we may cite yet one more specific example of considerable interest. This is the "Liverpool Mass," the work of the French composer Pierre Henry, commissioned for the inauguration of Christ King Cathedral in Liverpool. This electro-acoustical composition involves a systematic "pul-verisation" of the liturgical text, breaking up, compress-ing, and restructuring syllabic units, destroying intelligi-bility, distorting the sounds of the text by electronic means, by throat constriction, by the modification of breath patterns, and so on. The disorienting destruction of the liturgical text, the lack of intelligibility, the frequent repetitions, and the heightened emotional intensity of the delivery make one think of glossolalia—or rather, a kind of glossolalia in reverse, as it were. That is to say, where the ecstatic vocalizations of glossolalia are the product of an altered state, this "pulverisation" of language in a sacred context may well aid in the bringing about of an ecstatic altered state. There is no stated intention here of reproducing glossolalia. Yet the product suggests a reversal of the glossolalia process, whereby the simula-tion of certain aspects of the ecstatic state may bring about that state, perhaps by serving as a guide to medita-tion. It is perhaps no accident that Pierre Henry based an earlier composition, titled *Le Voyage,* on the Tibetan Book of the Dead. Parenthetically, it should be noted that there are other examples of the use of the simulated symptoms of altered states as means of inducing such states. For example, Henney found hyperventilation to be an expression of possession trance in St. Vincent among the Shakers. A kinetic movement associated with hyperventilation, similar to that reported by Henney as an expression of possession trance in St. Vincent is reported from Jamaica where this behavior and the hyperventilation are used to induce trance.

We may thus attempt to place the religious movements that appeal to the educated young into a historical context. There are, perhaps, few truly new ideas to be found among them. However, one of the most striking features of these movements appears to be their voraciously syncretic character, the apparently indiscriminate incorporation, into a loose scheme, of found symbols, ideas, and practices. Thus, the Children of God,[7] fundamentalist, glossolalist Christians, have adopted not only a communal form of organization but also the collective child-rearing practices of the kibbutz, even to the detail of calling the children's nurse by the Hebrew term *matapelet*. They hope to emigrate to Israel to await the imminent Second Coming. However, not only are the far corners of the world made to contribute to the resulting melange, but the attic of history is scoured for its potential contributions as well. Thus, we also observe the springing up of various types of witchcraft and satanism (Zaretsky and Leone, eds., n.d.), Tarot cards, astrology, and other forms of occultism.

The question that confronts us is whether this current wave of marginal religious movements in the youth counterculture, seeking altered states of consciousness, represents, like surrealism in Bersani's words, merely a "fantasy of escape from history" or a harbinger of a new social order?

In discussing the relationship between altered

states—specifically possession trance—and social change, we suggested that those who suffer greatest inability to modify their own lives in a given society under existing circumstances will be most likely to make use of altered states. In the United States, traditional enthusiastic churches have provided their members in possession trance a way of dealing with two major problems: illness, by offering faith healing, and self-respect, by offering salvation. This represents, in our terminology, microchange, change on the level of the individual, thus helping society to go on without major changes. This offers a safety valve. For the youth counterculture, whether in the drug cult, Krishna movement, or even the Neo-Pentecostal "Jesus Freaks," the situation appears somewhat different: here, the institutional framework in which altered states may be experienced had to be created first, thus shaping for a segment of the society, however small, a variety of new institutions. These are both ritual groups (cult groups, "churches") and domestic institutions, in the form of various types of communes. The crisis identified by the presence of altered states is not one of illness or self-respect or other relatively specific problems. The crisis is one of life styles, of seeking and developing alternate ways of living and of experiencing life.

A useful approach to an anlysis of the current scene may be found in a comparison between the so-called counterculture in the United States, with its drugs, its mysticism, its rejection of the Establishment, and its communes, on the one hand, and the Umbanda movement, on the other. As we have seen, Umbanda, too, is a reaction to stress, to personal and social disorganization. Brazil, like the United States, is a complex society, and Umbanda appears in its most urban, industrialized sectors. It is a society made up of a heterogeneous population of diverse ethnic and racial sources. São Paulo has not without reason been called the Chicago of Brazil. The comparison, then, is not unreasonable or arbitrary.

As we have seen, Umbanda has little organizational structure and consists of many shifting, loosely linked small groups, each centered about a strong leader. Similarly, there is much individual and group variation in the specific contents of beliefs and rituals. Yet, over all, in spite of its syncretisms and innovations, Umbanda represents a religious point of view coherent with what many other Brazilians believe. Many, if not most, Umbandists consider themselves Catholics; and the Christian God, Jesus, the Virgin Mary, and many of the saints are found in its pantheon, both by name and in statuary and other forms of representation. Most strongly, however, Umbanda resembles the various Afro-Brazilian cults, with their syncretisms of West African and Catholic elements. Yet the cult is adapted to an urban, middle-class setting. Furthermore, the major transformation of Umbanda lies in its concern for possession trance involving not African or Afro-Catholic spirits but recently deceased humans, who, though linked to Afro-Catholic spirits, have their particular identities and individualities. Thus, there is a similarity to Kardecist spiritism. Umbanda provides cathartic experience for the mediums and advice and healing both for the mediums and their clients. It provides an ideology that makes the world understandable and provides tools for dealing with problems. The Umbandist is not an odd individual who has isolated himself from major portions of his society by adherence to ecstatic practices. He shares major forms of belief and world views with, one would venture to guess, most Brazilians, recognizing that variation in particular interpretations are expected and readily tolerated. By cutting across race, ethnic, class, and age groups in its composition and by providing multilayered symbols, Umbanda is an emergent expression of Brazilian society.

It provides a transition for individuals from a patriarchal, familistic traditional society to an urban, individualistic society.

What now of the American youth culture? It, too, involves no large-scale organization, but many small groups. For example, it has been estimated that there are about 3,000 "hippie" drug-based communes, about a third of them rural (Zablocki, cited by Adler, n.d.). These and other communes vary widely in their social and religious forms, but generally there is a rejection of the "establishment" way of life, a search for a new life and a new consciousness. There is little ideological sharing among them, for commues may be fundamentalist or Krishna in orientation or may represent a variety of other points of view.

Thus, a whole series of features that set off the American situation from the Brazilian are already clearly stated: the opposition to the larger society; the lack of ideological sharing among the aspects of the "movement" on the one hand and the ideological isolation from the larger society; the isolation of a segment of an age group that largely represents a particular educational and economic stratum of the society; and the search for a new way of life, not for solutions to problems of daily living in the existing society. There is a wish to find alternative ways of living; and thus not only to modify the society but to modify the self. All of these features contrast the United States youth counterculture with Umbanda. Both involve the experience of altered states of consciousness. But, whereas the Umbandist seeks to become a medium because, he is told, he has mediumistic abilities that he must develop in order, in part, to solve his own problems, this kind of preoccupation appears to be alien to the Americans. Rather, altered states are not gradually learned and framed within a religious tradition that has long made use of them. On the contrary, altered states are induced by drugs to result in "instant mysticism" or by dramatic conversion experiences, as among the Neo-Pentecostals. Most strikingly, where Umbanda's shared and unifying symbols have emerged, have grown out of, the psychological and social experience of a people, no such shared symbols appear to be emerging on the American scene. There is some attempt at inventing religions, but no unification and shared identification appears to be forthcoming. It is as if the long history of American secularism, of the "institutionalization of rationality," which Moore (1963:104) tells us is associated with industrialization, has somehow blocked the sources of symbol formation.

La Barre (1970:44) has noted that "religions are always tailormade, projectively, to fit current individual anxieties . . . religion [is an adaptation] to the inner world of man, his unsolved problems and unmet needs"; and again, it is "the response of society to problems the contemporary culture failed to solve" (1970:44). If we are to accept this view, it is clear that the anxieties, the unsolved problems of Brazilian and United States society are different in many ways. The Brazilian is learning to adapt to a new, industrial society, and he attempts to do so by reworking the symbolic tools of his adaptation to an earlier, familistic and traditional society. The young American finds himself in a society that is in advanced stages of industrialization, in which few traces of a familistic traditional background exist for him. He reacts to discontinuity and isolation. He seeks a place in a group, in communes and absolute authority in Neo-Pentecostalism or in the Krishna movement; he seeks the verification of intense experience through ecstatic states, drug-induced or conversion-induced. Because his society is full of noise and intensity, he seeks, to realize any emotional impact, even higher itensity and greater noise. Because he believes that secularism has failed him,

353

he seeks "spirituality"; and because he thinks rationality has failed him, he seeks refuge in the irrational. As signs of the impending apocalypse abound, he has nothing to gain by the delayed gratification demanded by the Protestant Ethic. He seeks his gratfication now, whether in an ethic of *carpe diem*—an eat, drink and be merry ideology—or in the immediate gratification supplied by ecstatic states, confirming in him the belief in his own worth. Yet, curiously, at this point, the "counterculture" neatly coincides with the morality of the Establishment, the urgings of "fly now, pay later" consumerism.

Perhaps in this coincidence, then, lies the harbinger of the future: the death of the Protestant Ethic and the growth of an Ethic appropriate to a society needing, on the one hand, to reconstruct a sense of community and, on the other, to abandon an inappropriate ideology of scarcity.

1. With apologies to E. R. Dodds and his masterly study of the darker side of classical Greece: *The Greeks and the Irrational* (1951).

2. W. Goldschmidt (1951) following Max Weber identified twelve characteristics of the socio-economic structure of "emergent capitalistic Europe" and of a group of Indian societies of Northwest California. Seven of these twelve characteristics were shared by the cultural types being compared. Also, he identified eight features of the associated ethico-religious system, and six of these were shared. Pressel (1964), following Goldschmidt's example, found an even larger agreement between the socioeconomic structure and the ethico-religious system of emergent capitalist Europe and the Manus of 1928, as described by Margaret Mead. Interestingly enough, both the Californian Indians and the Manus had female mediums, who were consulted to discover causes of illness, which they identified as transgressions, usually the breaking of taboos concerning sex or money.

3. Tylor (1958 vol. 2, p. 210) speaks of "the savage theory of daemonical possession and obsession, which has been for ages and still remains, the dominant theory of disease and inspiration among the lower races. It is obviously based on an animistic interpretation, most genuine and rational *in its proper place in man's intellectual history*, of the actual symptoms of the cases" (my italics).

4. Zaretsky (n.d.) lists the following as some of the groups falling into this category: "Spiritualism, Mormonism, Jehovah Witnesses, Pentecostals Catholic Puerto Ricans (New York), Pentecostals, International Society for

Krishna Consciousness, Subud Movement, Spiritualist-Metaphysical healers, Divine Precept movement, Spiritists, Satanic movement, marginal Fundamentalism, Scientology, Occult churches of Witchcraft and Astrology... (Also) Christian Science, Theosophy (Arcane School, The Astara Foundation), New Thought Churches, Divine Science church, Unity School of Christianity, Seventh Day Adventists, etc." He notes that "a conservative figure of fifteen million adherents and a more liberal figure of twenty-five to thirty million people have been offered." Petersen (1967) has shown the great divergence between various sources of figures on religious adherence in this country. There appears to be no way of identifying marginal groups in these statistics. Thus for 1956-57, claimed church membership gives "other religion" 2.7% of the reported total, the Census Bureau Sample gives 1.3%, and the Gallup Poll finds 11.2% of those who said they attended church at least once a month so list themselves.

5. Among the best know literary accounts perhaps are: Henry James, *The Turn of the Screw* (novel, play, film, television drama, and opera); S. Ansky, *The Dybbuk;* Romain Gary, *The Dance of Genghis Cohn;* Thomas Pynchon, *V;* W. P. Blatty, *The Exorcist*; Aldous Huxley, *The Devils of Loudun* (and the opera and the film based on it); Alfred Hitchcock's film, *Vertigo*; and so on.

6. Not to be confused with the Shakers, founded by Mother Anne Lee.

7. The Children of God (COG) were the subject of two NBC broadcasts, "First Tuesday," December 1970, and "Chronolog," 23 June 1972. In the meantime, they have become the subject of a heated controversy and of a libel suit. They have been severely attacked, in particular by a group of members' parents, called FREECOG. As a result, according to the *New York Times* (13 August 1972) COG is closing its communes in the United States and moving abroad. At present, the group is estimated to have 2,000–3,000 members and some 100 communes.

REFERENCES

Adler, Nathan. n.d. "Ritual, release and orientation: The maintenance of the self in the antinomian personality," in *Pragmatic religions: Contemporary religious movements in America* (editors I. I. Zaretsky and M. Leone). Princeton, N.J.: Princeton University Press, in press.

Bell, Danial. n.d. Comments on E. Bourguignon, 1970, forthcoming.

Bersani, Leo. 1971. Review of *André Breton, the Magus of Surrealism* by Anna Balakian. *New York Times Book Review* (May 30), pp. 15–16.

Bourguignon, Erika. n.d. "The relevance of anthropology: Some reflections on hallucinogenic drugs," in *Ohio State University College of Social and Behavioral Sciences Centennial Symposium: The Relevance of the Social Sciences,* forthcoming.

Bourguignon, Paul-Henri. 1946. *Propos sur le surréalisme: Samuel Hecht.* Brussels: Le Phare Dimanche.

Dodds, E. R. 1951. *The Greeks and the irrational*. Berkeley, Calif.: University of California Press.

Goldschmidt, Walter. 1951. Ethics and the structure of society: An ethnological contribution to the sociology of knowledge. *American Anthropologist* 53: 506–24.

La Barre, Weston. 1962. *They shall take up serpents: The psychology of the southern snake-handling cult*. Minneapolis, Minn.: University of Minnesota Press.

———. 1970. *The ghost dance: The origins of religion*. Garden City, N.Y.: Doubleday.

———. 1971. Materials for a history of studies of crisis cults: A bibliographic essay. *Current Anthropology* 12:3–44.

Moore, W. E. 1963. *Social change*. Englewood Cliffs, N. J.: Prentice-Hall.

Nobile, Philip. 1971. *The con III controversy*. New York: Pocket Books.

Oesterreich, T. K. 1966. (Orig. 1922.) *Possession: Demonical and other among primitive races, in antiquity, the Middle Ages, and in modern times*. New York: University Books:

Peterson, William. 1967. "Religious statistics in the United States," in *The sociology of religion* (editor R. D. Knuten). New York: Appleton-Century-Crofts.

Pressel, Esther. 1964. "Manus socio-economic structure and ethico-religious system: A study of requisite functional relationships." Masters thesis, the Ohio State University.

Reich, Charles A. 1970. *The greening of America*. New York: Random House.

Scholem, Gersom. G. 1961. *Major trends in Jewish mysticism*. New York: Schocken Books.

Tylor, E. B. 1958. (Orig. 1871.) *Religion in primitive culture*, vol. 2. New York: Harper Torchbooks.

Whitehead Harriet. n.d. "Reasonable fantastic: Some perspectives on scientology, science fiction, and occultism," in *Pragmatic religions: Contemporary religious movements in America* (editors I. I. Zaretsky and M. Leone). Princeton N.J.:Princeton University Press, in press.

Zablocki, B. D. n.d. "The social structure of drug-based communes," in *Drug use and drug subcultures*. Washington: U.S. Government Printing Office, forthcoming.

Zaretsky, Irving I. 1970. Personal communication.

Zaretsky, I. I. and M. Leone, eds. n.d. *Pragmatic religions: Contemporary religious movements in America*. Princeton, N.J.: Princeton University Press, in press.

Appendix

Appendix

CODES USED BELOW

1. T-O-O   A society in which ritualized trance behavior is known to occur, but where there is no belief in possession.

2. O-P-O   A society in which a belief in possession exists.

3. O-O-PT   A society in which ritualized trance behavior is known to occur, which is given the native explanation of possession. There is no possession belief referring to other experiences, and there are no trance states with other explanations.

4. T-P-PT   A society in which two kinds of trance states are known to occur, one of which is explained as due to possession and one of which is given another type of explanation. In addition to explaining trance, possession belief also refers to one or more other phenomena.

5. T-P-O   A society in which there is both a ritualized trance state and a belief in possession, but where this belief refers to phenomena other than those of trance,

which, in turn, is explained by other categories.

6. O-P-PT   A society in which a ritual trance state, explained as due to possession, is known to occur. There are no other ritualized trance states. There are beliefs in possession that refer to phenomena other than ritualized trance.

7. T-O-PT   A society in which trance states of two kinds are known to occur, some which are explained by possession beliefs and some of which are explained by other categories. No other phenomena are explained by beliefs in possession.

8. O-O-O   A society in which no ritualized trance states of either kind are known to occur, nor are there any reports of beliefs in possession.

LIST OF 488 SAMPLE SOCIETIES

IDENTIFICATION NUMBER[1]	NAME OF SOCIETY[2]	CODE	MARSH INDEX OF DIFFERENTIATION

1. Sub-Saharan Africa[3]

TYPE I SOCIETIES—POSSESSION TRANCE

| 191067 | Alur | 6 | |
| 110411 | Ambo | 6 | |

1. The identification number is provided as a guide to the listing of societal characteristics in Bourguignon and Greenbaum (1968).

2. The full bibliography on which the coding is based can be found in Bourguignon 1968, pp. 213–86.

3. Societies of Sub-Saharan Africa are grouped according to the classification presented by Greenbaum in chapter 1. Listings for other areas follow the sequence presented in Bourguignon and Greenbaum (1968).

IDENTIFICATION NUMBER	NAME OF SOCIETY	CODE	MARSH INDEX OF DIFFERENTIATION
150111	Ashanti	7	7
180117	Azande	4	5
160012	Bambara	3	
120105	Bemba	6	6
120698	Chokwe	6	5
150924	Edo	3	
150932	Egba	7	
150936	Ewe	6	
150010	Fon	7	
130306	Ganda	6	6
150672	Igbira	3	5
170115	Jukun	6	5
120728	Kongo	6	6
110103	Lozi	6	7
140210	Luba	3	5
110203	Mbundu	6	5
150211	Mende	4	5
130758	Ngonde	4	
120351	Ngoni	7	5
130762	Nyamwesi	4	
110302	Nyaneka	3	
130007	Nyoro	4	6
140641	Ruanda	3	
180218	Shilluk	6	7
130788	Soga	6	
130764	Sukuma	3	4
120750	Tumbuka	6	
110204	Venda	6	
150212	Yoruba	7	7

TYPE I SOCIETIES—NO POSSESSION TRANCE

140209	Bamileke	2	
150942	Fanti	1	
130307	Hehe	5	5

Identification Number	Name of Society	Code	Marsh Index of Differentiation
150922	Itsekiri	5	
120106	Kuba	2	5
150311	Nupe	8	
120005	Pende	2	
140309	Rundi	2	
TYPE II SOCIETIES—POSSESSION TRANCE			
180015	Banda	4	1
150642	Baule	6	
180316	Baya	6	1
130669	Chiga	6	
180317	Dilling	3	4
190677	Dinka	4	
160113	Dogon	4	1
130352	Gisu	3	
110002	Herero	3	2
150643	Ibo	4	
120004	Ila	6	2
150011	Kissi	7	2
120703	Lake Tonga	3	
120205	Lamba	6	4
190219	Lango	6	2
181047	Lugbara	7	1
120668	Luvale	6	
181055	Moro	3	
140807	Ngala	6	
130208	Nyakyusa	6	2
181058	Nyima	3	
120744	Plateau Tonga	6	
120739	Songo	3	
120304	Yao	3	2
TYPE II SOCIETIES—NO POSSESSION TRANCE			
140308	Babwa	1	2

IDENTIFICATION NUMBER	NAME OF SOCIETY	CODE	MARSH INDEX OF DIFFERENTIATION
181038	Bwaka	1	
140699	Duala	2	
150954	Gbande	5	
130774	Giriama	2	
140009	Kpe	1	2
140801	Kutshu	2	
120752	Nyanja	2	
150949	Sapo	2	
160114	Tallensi	8	1
170116	Tiv	8	2
150644	Toma	5	

TYPE III SOCIETIES–POSSESSION TRANCE

110406	Lovedu	6	6
110303	Sotho	4	6
110003	Swazi	6	
110104	Thonga	6	
110405	Tswana	3	6
110404	Zulu	4	7

TYPE III SOCIETIES–NO POSSESSION TRANCE

130107	Chagga	2	4
110401	Ndebele	1	

TYPE IV SOCIETIES–POSSESSION TRANCE

181050	Bongo	3	1
190318	Luo	6	1
190120	Nuer	6	

TYPE IV SOCIETIES–NO POSSESSION TRANCE

140008	Amba	1	
190354	Bari	1	3
100101	Dorobo	8	1
140109	Fang	5	
100726	Hatsa	8	

IDENTIFICATION NUMBER	NAME OF SOCIETY	CODE	MARSH INDEX OF DIFFERENTIATION
130108	Kikuyu	5	2
190648	Kipsigis	5	
100001	Kung	1	1
190678	Lotuko	1	
190119	Masai	1	
170315	Matakam	8	1
100202	Mbuti	8	1
190319	Nandi	1	
100102	Nama	8	3
110402	Pondo	1	5
100301	Sandawe	8	1
190220	Turkana	8	0

NO INFORMATION ON SLAVERY AND STRATIFICATION

181059	Anuak	1	
130772	Digo	4	
150943	Ga	4	
150928	Gbari	3	4
110408	Lenge	6	
120742	Luimbe	3	
120206	Ndembu	6	
171002	Reshe	6	
110410	Shona	6	5
150957	Temne	4	
130783	Vugusu	4	

2. Circum-Mediterranean

210021	Wolof	6	
200019	Somali	4	
200841	Arusi	3	
200846	Sidamo	3	
200707	Gurage	2	
200847	Tsamai	8	
200849	Banna	8	

Identification Number	Name of Society	Code	Marsh Index of Differentiation
200858	Basketo	3	
200860	Kafa	3	
200861	Falasha	3	
200679	Amhara	6	
200862	Barea	3	
200863	Kunama	3	
200320	Bisharin	2	
211084	Zazzagawa	6	
210682	Kanawa	6	
210681	Bororo Fulani	6	
210122	Songhai	6	
220650	Antessar	3	
220880	Ahaggaren	6	
220023	Teda	2	
220123	Siwians	4	
220223	Mzab	6	
290132	Rwala	7	
230125	Riffians	5	
230224	Kabyle	6	
230124	Egypt	4	
230898	Algerians	4	
230892	Ancient Egyptians	2	
240708	Greeks	5	
240025	Gheg	2	
260128	Irish	8	
260029	Icelanders	1	
260129	Lapps	1	
270323	Cheremis	5	
270130	Hutsul	8	
270030	Serbs	1	
270357	Bulgarians	1	

Identification Number	Name of Society	Code	Marsh Index of Differentiation
280908	Ossett	1	
280913	Kurd	5	
280653	Turks	5	
290230	Hebrews	4	
291091	Madan	6	
290413	Babylonians	6	

3. East Eurasia

301135	Iranians	4	
340327	Dard	1	
300324	Nuri	7	
310035	Kazak	6	
310036	Monguor	3	
320136	Yurak	4	
321109	Obostyak	1	
320360	Ket	5	
320038	Yakut	4	
320236	Yukaghir	5	
320135	Chukchee	1	
320235	Koryak	4	
320037	Gilyak	5	
320325	Ainu	6	
321108	Goldi	6	
330137	Manchu	4	
330039	Koreans	4	
330237	Japanese	6	
330326	Okinawans	4	
331110	Shantung	2	
330238	Min Chinese	3	
330138	Miao	1	
330040	Lolo	6	
330361	Minchine	2	
340239	Tibetans	4	

Identification Number	Name of Society	Code	Marsh Index of Differentiation
340140	Lepcha	4	
340630	Sherpa	3	
351092	Kashmiri	1	
350612	Pahari	6	
350328	Bhil	3	
350042	Santal	3	
360654	Baiga	6	
360142	Maria Gond	4	
350362	Oraon	4	
360043	Chenchu	8	
360688	Telugu	6	
360242	Coorg	3	
360044	Tamil	6	
360143	Toda	3	
360243	Kerala	6	
370245	Sinhalese	4	
370145	Vedda	3	
370144	Tanala	6	
370614	Sakalava	6	
370244	Nicobarese	5	
380711	Chin	1	
380147	Lakher	6	
380365	Khasi	2	
380048	Lhota	1	
380421	Angami	4	
380246	Kacki	4	
380426	Palaung	4	
380146	Burmese	4	
380364	Karen	1	
390367	Siamese	4	
390330	Akha	3	
390049	Lamet	5	
390149	Annamese	4	

IDENTIFICATION NUMBER	NAME OF SOCIETY	CODE	MARSH INDEX OF DIFFERENTIATION
390050	Mnong Gar	1	
390712	Cham	3	
390248	Cambodians	3	
390148	Semang	4	
391138	Senoi-Semai	4	
390366	Malay	4	
390249	Selung	3	
4. *Insular Pacific*			
400051	Atayal	1	
401095	Ami	1	
401097	Puyuma	3	
401100	Yami	5	
400331	Paiwan	5	
401139	Kalinga	4	
400150	Ifuagao	6	
401098	Sugbuhanon	5	
400151	Subanun	7	
410251	Dusun	4	
510053	Iban	5	
410153	Batak	4	
410252	Minangkabau	7	
410369	Mentawai	1	
411114	Kubu	6	
410054	Javanese	4	
410152	Balinese	4	
420055	Macassarese	1	
420254	Torada	4	
421115	Ili-Mandiri	3	
420154	Alorese	6	
420155	Belu	5	
421140	Ambonese	6	
421118	Tobelorese	1	
430156	Murngin	5	

Identification Number	Name of Society	Code	Marsh Index of Differentiation
430157	Tiwi	5	
430255	Dieri	1	
431177	Walbiri	2	
430056	Aranda	5	
431141	Tasmanians	6	
440631	Motu	2	
441143	Koita	7	
441144	Mailu	7	
440371	Purari	2	
440656	Kiwai	5	
441119	Marindanim	7	
440057	Kapauku	4	
441101	Kiman	1	
440691	Kutubu	5	
440334	Enga	5	
440713	Siane	6	
440457	Orokaiva	6	
440158	Arapesh	3	
440690	Abelam	3	
440655	Kwoma	6	
441152	Manam	5	
450059	Palauans	4	
450260	Yapese	3	
450427	Chamorro	1	
450161	Ifaluk	4	
450692	Carolinians	4	
450060	Trukese	4	
450428	Ulithians	6	
450259	Ponape	6	
450160	Majuro	5	
460373	Manus	7	
460615	Usiai	7	
460062	Trobrianders	1	

Identification Number	Name of Society	Code	Marsh Index of Differentiation
460261	Dobuans	5	
460162	Kurtachi	3	
460061	Siuai	2	
460262	Ulawans	4	
470063	Mota	6	
470064	Seniang	1	
470263	Ajie	5	
470165	Lau	4	
470694	Vanua Levu	3	
470337	Rotumans	4	
481103	Kapinga-marangi	3	
480265	Ontong Java	3	
480066	Tikopia	6	
480264	Ellice Islanders	2	
480375	Tokelau	3	
481120	Futunans	3	
480166	Pukapuka	4	
481121	Niueans	4	
481125	Uveans	4	
480065	Samoans	6	
481124	Tongans	6	
490167	Maori	4	
490067	Mangarevans	3	
490168	Marquesans	4	
490659	Tahitians	4	
491126	Easter Islanders	6	
490658	Mangaians	6	
490376	Hawaiians	6	

5. *North America*

500068	Nabesna	5	

Identification Number	Name of Society	Code	Marsh Index of Differentiation
500069	Tareumiut	1	
500169	Copper Eskimo	4	
500170	Kaska	5	
500269	Nunivak	5	
500377	Ingal	5	
500458	Aleut	5	
500461	Nunamiut	1	
500463	Polar Eskimo	5	
500468	Carrier	6	
500469	Kutchin	1	
500484	Caribou Eskimo	4	
500486	Labrador Eskimo	4	
500487	Angmagsalik	7	
500489	Tanaina	5	
500490	Tahltan	5	
500494	Eastern Cree	7	
500495	Montagnais	3	
500496	Northern Saulteaux	5	
500497	Pekangikum	5	
500499	Chippewa	7	
500501	Katikitegon	1	
500502	Eastern Ojibwa	1	
500504	Micmac	5	
510070	Haida	4	
510171	Kwakiutl	7	
510172	Yurok	5	
510270	Eyak	1	
510378	Tsimshian	6	

IDENTIFICATION NUMBER	NAME OF SOCIETY	CODE	MARSH INDEX OF DIFFERENTIATION
510470	Haisla	4	
510471	Bellabella	4	
510477	Lummi	5	
510478	Klallam	5	
510481	Chinook	4	
510505	Tlingit	4	
510506	Bellacoola	4	
510507	Makah	2	
510508	Quinault	4	
510511	Alsea	1	
510515	Shasta	7	
510517	Karok	1	
520072	Nomlaki	1	
520174	Yokuts	1	
520272	Atsugewi	4	
520273	Miwok	1	
520339	Diegueno	1	
520379	Yuki	1	
520523	Klamath	7	
520524	Modoc	1	
520525	Achomawi	1	
520527	Maidu	1	
520530	Coast Yuki	1	
520532	Northern Pomo	1	
520535	Wappo	1	
520537	Patwin	1	
520538	Monacho	5	
520546	Cahuilla	1	
520548	Luiseno	1	
530073	Tenino	5	
530074	Southern Ute	2	

IDENTIFICATION NUMBER	NAME OF SOCIETY	CODE	MARSH INDEX OF DIFFERENTIATION
530175	Havasupi	6	
530176	Sanpoil	5	
530340	Washo	5	
530554	Flathead	1	
530557	Sinkaietk	4	
530560	Wishram	4	
530562	Nez Perce	1	
530569	Kuyuidokado	1	
530585	White Knife	1	
530606	Wind River	5	
530607	Walapai	1	
530608	Yavapai	1	
540075	Gros Ventre	1	
540076	Kiowa-Apache	5	
540177	Comanche	5	
540178	Crow	5	
540275	Cheyenne	1	
540341	Mandan	1	
540382	Teton	4	
540616	Arapaho	5	
540618	Assiniboine	5	
540622	Hidatsa	5	
540624	Kiowa	1	
540625	Piegan	1	
540626	Plains Cree	1	
540627	Santee	1	
550078	Winnebago	1	
550179	Omaha	1	
550342	Pawnee	5	
550383	Fox	1	
550384	Hasanai	1	
550695	Iowa	1	

IDENTIFICATION NUMBER	NAME OF SOCIETY	CODE	MARSH INDEX OF DIFFERENTIATION
551104	Ponca	5	
560079	Huron	4	
560180	Creek	1	
560278	Cherokee	2	
560279	Delaware	5	
560385	Natchez	1	
560663	Iroquois	4	
570081	Chiricahua	1	
570182	Navaho	4	
570183	Zuni	5	
570281	Taos	1	
570435	Tewa	1	
570434	Isleta	1	
570439	Mescalero	5	
570440	Jicarilla	1	
570442	Hopi	5	
570445	Mohave	6	
570446	Yuma	7	
570697	Lipan	1	
580083	Tarahumara	1	
580184	Papago	1	
580282	Huichol	1	
580717	Chichimec	1	
581160	Pima	8	
581161	Yaqui	8	
590084	Chinantec	1	
590185	Aztec	1	
591163	Tarascans	1	
591165	Zapotec	1	

6. *South America*

600085	Cuna	2	
600286	Choco	5	
600345	Maya	1	

Identification Number	Name of Society	Code	Marsh Index of Differentiation
600388	Black Carib	6	
600390	Miskito	5	
601166	Quiche	3	
610391	Goajiro	3	
611130	Taino	1	
620088	Warrau	1	
620089	Yaruro	4	
620189	Barama River Carib	4	
620291	Wapishana	2	
620392	Saramacca	3	
620393	Yabarana	1	
620449	Locono	5	
620450	Camaracoto	5	
620451	Macusi	2	
620454	Taulipang	4	
620455	Makitare	7	
630090	Mundurucu	1	
630190	Tapirape	1	
630292	Palikur	7	
630722	Waiwai	5	
640091	Siriono	2	
640092	Tucuna	7	
640191	Jivaro	4	
640293	Cubeo	1	
640347	Witoto	5	
640634	Amahuaca	1	
640666	Conibo	1	
641131	Cocama	5	
650093	Inca	5	
650193	Aymara	2	
650294	Tunebo	1	
650348	Paez	2	

Identification Number	Name of Society	Code	Marsh Index of Differentiation
650395	Chibcha	1	
660094	Yahgan	1	
660195	Mapuche	4	
660295	Ona	7	
660349	Tehuelche	4	
670095	Mataco	4	
670096	Terena	1	
670196	Abipon	1	
670296	Caduveo	1	
670397	Chamacoco	2	
670724	Toba	4	
680097	Bororo	4	
680098	Trumai	1	
680197	Bacairi	1	
680198	Nambicuara	5	
680298	Camayura	1	
681169	Umotina	2	
690099	Caraja	1	
690100	Sherente	1	
690199	Aweikoma	1	
690300	Tenetehara	6	
690399	Apinaye	5	
690400	Tupinamba	5	

REFERENCES

Bourguignon, Erika. 1968. *A Cross-cultural study of dissociational states: Final report*. Columbus: The Ohio State University Research Foundation.

Bourguignon, Erika and Lenora Greenbaum. 1968. *Diversity and homogeneity: A comparative analysis of societal characteristics based on data from the Ethnographic Atlas*. Occasional Papers in Anthropology, no. 1. Columbus: The Ohio State University, Department of Anthropology.

Notes on the Contributors

All of the authors contributing to this volume were associated with the Cross-Cultural Study of Dissociational States at the Ohio State University.

ERIKA BOURGUIGNON is chairman of the Department of Anthropology at the Ohio State University. From 1963 to 1968 she directed the Cross-Cultural Study of Dissociational States under a grant from the National Institute of Mental Health. With Lenora Greenbaum, she is the coauthor of *Homogeneity and Diversity*.

FELICITAS D. GOODMAN is assistant professor of anthropology at Denison University, Granville, Ohio, and the author of *Speaking in Tongues: A Cross-Cultural Study of Glossolalia*.

LENORA GREENBAUM has taught sociology at the Ohio State University and the University of Massachusetts Boston. She is currently visiting professor in the Boston University Overseas Graduate Program of International Studies in Europe.

JUDITH DANFORD GUSSLER spent a year as visiting instructor of sociology and anthropology at Ohio Wesleyan University, Delaware, Ohio. She is currently engaged in field research on the effects of cultural change on food habits in the Caribbean under a grant from the National Institute of Mental Health.

JEANNETTE HILLMAN HENNEY is assistant professor of sociology at Capital University, Columbus, Ohio.

With Felicitas Goodman and Esther Pressel, she is co-author of a forthcoming volume in the series, *Contemporary Religious Movements*.

ANNE P. LEONARD was trained in linguistics and has lived for several years in Micronesia and in Malaysia. At present, she resides in Silver Spring, Maryland.

ESTHER PRESSEL is assistant professor in the Department of Sociology and Anthropology at Colorado State University.

Index

Acculturation, Nguni, 94; Palauan, 337
Acculturative pressures, 22
Adolescent boys, segregation of, 20
Adultery, 24
Africa
  East, 30, 39
  North, 11
  South, 30, 39, 88
  Southeast, 88, 90
  Sub-Saharan, 10 (table 1), 16 (table 2), 18 (table 3), 19, 21, 39, 41,43, 45, 321
  West, 39
African societies, universe of, 44–47
Agriculture: dependence on, and PT, 49 (table 2)
Alertness, 6
Altered state of consciousness, 3–6, 9, 13–15, 28, 29, 33, 187, 337, 343. *See also* Dissociation; Possession; Possession trance; Trance
  and alcohol, 330–31
  behavior in, 291
  learned, 14
  capacity for, 12
  and central nervous system, 7
  cultural meaning of, 3
  culturally patterned, 8, 11, 337
  definition of, 4
  distribution of, 10 (table 1), 18(table 3)
  driving, 199
  drug induced, 34 n. 3, 330, 346, 353
  incidence of, 11, 19
  induction of, 6, 7, 193, 330, 346
  institutional patterning of, 8
  institutionalized, 8, 10, 11, 12, 29

interpretation of, 28
loss of control in, 342
and neurophysiology, 6, 7
private, 8
as possession trance, 28, 337
as psychobiological capacity, 11
as psychopathology, 3
revelatory, 8
sacred, 341
secular, 9
and social change, 29–33, 349–50
as soul absence, 3
as spirit journey, 219
types of, 17, 18 (table 3), 19, 28
unpatterned, 8
utilization of, 345
Amba, 74
America. *See* United States
America, North, 10 (table 1), 16 (table 2), 17, 18 (table 3), 19, 21
America, South, 10 (table 1), 16 (table 2), 18 (table 3), 19, 21
American Indians, 346–47
Anabaptists, 341
Anglican Church, 224
Anxiety, 171, 172, 188, 189, 202, 203, 205
Apostolic Church, 341
Arousal, 6, 7
  of central nervous system, 5, 6
  reduced, 7
  residual, 188, 210, 215, 216
Art Styles, 41
Ashanti, 39, 60, 64

Bantu, 88

Bantu *(continued)*
   traditional, society, 95. *See also* Nguni
Baptism, Shaker ritual of, 240
   call for, 240
   ceremony of, 242
   preparation for, 240
Baptism, by Holy Spirit. *See* Holy Spirit, baptism of
Baptists, 183, 192
Barnett, H. G., 140, 141, 144, 149, 160, 161, 176 n. 2
Beattie, John, 60, 68–69
Belief system, 41
Bersani, Leo, 348, 349
Betel, 153, 156, 169, 170, 177 n. 5, 330
Biocybernetic model, 5, 6
Black Muslims, 343
Blair, W., 187
Body image, change in, 7
Bon Dieu, 27
Bonsam, 39
Bourguignon, Erika, 30, 34 n. 2, 41, 105, 143, 308, 312
Bourguignon, Paul-Henri, 347
Brainwashing, 8
Brazil, 22, 31, 264–75, 326
Bride price, 20
Bushmen, 25

Callaway, Rev. Canon, 97, 98, 101, 102, 329
Camargo, C. P. F. de, 276, 287
Candomble, 284, 285, 313
Catalepsy, 4
Catholic Church, 183, 295
   and Pentecostalism, 344
Catholicism, 27, 284
Catholics, 142, 192
Cavalo. See Umbanda: spirit medium
Change
   adjustment to, 259
   cultural, 4, 175, 195, 215, 216, 274
      and spirits, type of, 314
   economic, 4
   institutionalization of, 33

political, 4
   and possession trance, 336
   and Shakerism, 259
   social, 4, 29, 33, 88
   social, and spirit possession, 88
   and ecology, 88
Chiga, 70
Children of God, 349, 355 n. 7
Chile, 183
Christian Church, enthusiastic, 14, 327, 331
Christian Scientists, 341
Christianity, 27, 313, 322
Church of England (Anglican), 224
Circum-Mediterranean, 10 (table 1), 11, 16 (table 2), 18 (table 3), 19, 21
Class structure, 45 (table 1)
Cognitive dissonance, 311, 312
Cole, Ernest, 101
Community organization and PT, 49 (table 2)
Complexity, cultural, 25
Compensation
   objective instrumental, 328
   subjective expressive, 328
Control
   conscious, 26
   social, 24
Conversion, religious, 8
   story of, 201–2, 203, 205
Counter culture, 345, 347, 348, 349, 354
   and Umbanda, 350, 352, 353
Cousin marriage, duolateral, 20
Crisis, social, 33
Cult, definition of, 124 n. 2
Culture shock, 202

Dawson, John, 67
Deprivation, 216, 328
   socioeconomic, 219
Devil, 206, 207
Dinka, 24
Dissociation, 4, 5, 25, 26, 143, 186, 187, 329. *See also* Trance
   bodily, 24, 25, 27

definition of, 308
physiological features of, 309
as possession trance, 329
as spirit possession, 97, 279, 293
and Umbanda, 279
Dissociative behavior, 105, 185
Divination, 9, 101
Diviner, 39, 42, 60, 324
cult of, 88, 101
female, 101, 102, 108, 120
initiation as, 99–100
as link, 100
male, 102
Palaun, 141
role of, 123
training for, 99
Dodds, E. R., 354 n. 1
Douglas, Mary, 24, 25, 26, 27, 28
Dreaming, 6
Dream, 14, 15, 34 n. 6, 228
as communication, 140
as symptom of possession-illness, 98
Drug states, 7
Durkheim, E., 28

East Indian, 23
East, Near, 11
Economy, 40
Brazilian, 270, 274
Palaun, 134–36
subsistence, 42, 45 (table 1)
of Yucatán, 180–82
Ecstasy, 189
Ecstatic experience, 342, 343
Ecstatic state, 5, 325, 354
Edel, M. M., 70
Ego defense mechanism, 311
Epilepsy, 4, 168
Episcopal Church and glossolalia, 344
Ergotropic excitation, 5
Erikson, Erik H., 121
Euphoria, 188
Eurasia, East, 10 (table 1), 16 (table 3), 19, 21
Europe, eastern, 11

Europe, western, 11
Evans-Pritchard, E. E., 73
Evil eye, 291, 292
Evolution, cultural, 41
Excitation, central nervous system, 7

Faith healing, 343, 346, 350
Family, form of, and possession trance, 43, 49 (table 2)
Favela, 268, 272
Festinger, Leon, 311
Field, M. J., 60, 64–65, 330
Firth, Raymond, 29–30, 60
Fischer, Roland, 5, 6, 7, 12
Fogelson, R., 254, 255
Food taboo, 4, 91, 93, 119, 221
Fugue state, 4, 98

Ganda, 65
Glossolalia: 185, 199, 200, 201, 205, 215, 217 n.5, 331. See also Speaking in tongues
attenuation of, 188–90, 332–34
behavior, evolution of, 187, 202, 203
behavior, learning of, 185, 217 n. 3, 331
emotional reaction to, 188, 189
occurrence of, 331
pattern of, 185, 186, 187
physiological study of, 331
in reverse, 348
role of, 332
Gluckman, M., 30, 109, 257, 258
Goldschmidt, W., 354 n. 2
Goodenough, W., 296
Goodman, Felicitas, D., 185, 217 n. 3, 217 n. 4, 217, n. 5
Great Awakening, 342

Hadley, C. V. D., 222–23
Hallucination, 4–6, 12, 190, 217 n. 8, 247
attitude toward, 250–53
control of content, 247, 252, 253
definition of, 249

Index

Hallucination(*continued*)
and mourning, 243, 335
sensory deprivation, 247–49, 250–53, 335, 346
Hallucinogenic drugs and religious systems, 344
Harris, Marvin, 270
Healing, 8
Hebb, D. O., 247
Hehe, 69
Henry, Pierre, 348
Herskovits, M. J., 260, 284, 294
Herskovits, F. S., 260
High god, 41
Hinduism, 343, 347
Hockett, Charles, 187
Hofstra, Sjoerd, 67
Holiness religions, 344
Holy Spirit, 206
baptism of, 187, 188, 193, 194, 332
possession by. *See* Possession: by Holy Spirit
prayer for, 214
receiver of, 254
receptacle for, 219
Homicide, 24
Huxley, Aldous, 347, 355 n. 3
Hyperarousal, 5, 185, 190, 208
platform phase of, 186, 212
Hyperglycemia, 7
Hypersuggestibility, 7
Hyperventitation, 349. *See also* Over-breathing
Hypnosis, 4, 8
Hypoarousal, 5
Hysteria, 4
of Zulu, 97

Identity, change of
and image, 254–56, 260, 296
and PT, 59, 60, 81
renewal of, 257
Illness, 4, 30, 39, 329. *See also* Sickness
caused by spirit entry, 167–68
diagnosis of, by spirit, 279
mental, 168

spiritual, 287–93
treatment of, by spirit, 279
Industrialization, 264, 271, 272, 312
Innovation, religious, 23, 33, 259, 264, 337, 341. *See also* Shakerism and innovation; Umbanda: as religious innovation
Insanity, 168. *See also* Sickness
caused by magician, 168
by medium, 168.
Insular Pacific, 10 (table 1), 16 (table 2), 17, 18 (table 3), 19

Jehovah's Witnesses, 183, 341
Jesus Freaks, 344, 339 n. 1, 350
Jukun, 39
Jurisdictional hierarchy and PT, 48 (table 2), 50

Kardec, Allen, 294
Kardecism, 276, 281, 295, 316 n. 2, 251
Kentucky Revival, 342
Kikuyu, 75
Kin groups and possession trance, 49 (table 2)
Kinship, 40, 41, 43, 185, 192
Krige, E. J., 96, 113
Krige, J. D., 113
Krishna Consciousness Movement, 343, 345, 350, 353
Kung, 76
Kuper, Hilda, 102

La Barre, Weston, 344, 353
Lalive d'Epinay, C., 183, 184
Landes, R. 294
Latter Day Saints, 183
Leary, T., 347
Lee, S. G., 97, 101, 103, 108, 109
Levy, M. S., 276, 316 n. 3
Lewis, I. M., 26, 28, 31, 33, 258, 328–29
Liverpool Mass, 348
Lopez, J. R. B., 271, 272–73
Lovedu, 112, 113, 114
Lowenthal, D., 223, 254
Lower class, 253, 255, 268, 336

382

LSD, 7
Ludwig, A., 6, 7, 8, 338
Lutheran, German, 142

Macrochange, 29–31, 312, 315
Magic, black, 285
  as cause of death, 166
  practitioner of, 153
Magician, 141, 168
Main (major) morality cults, 26, 27, 31
Mandari, 24
Marital residence, 47, 48 (table 2)
Marriage
  form and PT, 40, 43, 48 (table 2)
  mode of, 49 (table 2)
  polygynous, 20
Marsh, R. M., 44, 52, 53, 56 n. 2
Maya Apostolics, 192, 214, 322, 334, 336, 338, 342, 346
  beliefs of, 187
  case history of, 197–214
  congregation of, members, 192, 194, 195
  church, 184, 195–96, 201
    sections of, 194
    service, structure of, 196–97
Maya Indians of Yucatán, 32, 178, 191, 325
Mayan language, 187, 216
Mazeway resynthesis, 32
Meditation, 6
Medium, 31, 32, 39, 42, 59, 60, 62, 170, 324. See also Spirit medium
  as diviner, 100
  as innovator, 32
  as link, between living and dead, 100
  temporary, 150 (table 2), 165
  as wife of god, 149
Medium, traditional, in Palau, 141, 174, 175, 324
  age of, 150 (table 2)
  divination by, 155
  distribution of, 164, 165
  forbidden to practice, 160
  function of, 158
    and diagnosis of illness, 175

  and link to supernatural, 158, 176
  political, 158, 175
  religious, 175
  and Germans, 160
  opposition to, 159
  Palaun terms for, 143–44
  possession trance in, 154, 170, 176
  removal of, 141, 159
  selection of, 146, 149
    by council of elders, 150 (table 2), 152
    by god, 150 (table 2), 151
    by inheritance, 150 (table 2)
  sex of, 146, 147, 148 (table 1), 149
  sexual deviate as, 176 n. 4
  title of, 146, 147–48 (table 1)
  trance techniques of, 153
  of village god, 146
Mende, 66
Mental illness, spiritual, 293
Mescaline intoxication, 252
Methodism 224, 258, 341
Methodist Order for Morning Prayer, 231
Mexico, 178, 322
Michaux, Henri, 347
Microchange, 29–32, 312, 316, 350
Middle class, 253, 267, 268, 269, 272, 336
Millenial movement, 342
Mischel, F. O., 158, 260 n. 7
Mischel, W., 260 n. 7
Missionizing by Apostolics, 183
Mobility, 180, 267, 268, 269, 324, 325
Modekngei, 32, 142, 159, 174, 176
  and Americans, 163
  and Christianity, 161, 163
  and curing,
  history of, 160
  and Japanese, 162, 163
  and making predictions, 162
  medium of, 144, 163, 164
  as nativistic movement, 161
  opposition to, 161, 162
Momsen, R. R., 266
Moore, W. E., 353
Moravians, 224

Mormons, 341, 345
Motor activity, 6
Mourning, Shaker ritual of, 228, 240,
    252, 332, 334
  and anxiety, 251
  attenuated, 241
  fitness for, 245
  as going to school, 245
  map for, 244
  secret room for, 243
  sign for, 243
  for sins, 242
  spiritual gifts from, 229, 246, 247
  as spiritual journey, 242, 245, 251,
    259
  time limit for, 246
  trance in, 244
Mystical rapture, 5

Nadel, S. F., 24, 31, 60
Native Reserves, 95
Nativistic movement, 161
Neo-Pentecostals, 245, 353
Nguni, 14, 30, 88, 89–109, 123, 124
    n. 1, 321
  acculturation of, 89
  and Christianity, 96, 124
  industrialization of, 94
  modern, 89
  and spirit possession, 90, 96, 326
  traditional, 89, 121
Nuclear family, 20
Nuer, 24, 73
Nyima, 71
Nyoro, 68

Ongesii, 160–62
Orixá, See Umbanda: African deities
Orne, M. T., 248

Palau, 22, 130
  colonial history of, 131
  culture of, traditional, 133
  economic organization of, 134
  gods of,
    clan (female), 140
    village (male), 140

Palauan society, 31, 321
  clans of, 134, 172, 173, 176 n. 2
  nobles and commoners of, 134, 137
  family and marriage in, 136
  men's clubs of, 137, 173
  political organization of, 138, 139
Palauans, 14
  and Americans, 174, 175
  and Germans, 174, 175
  and Japanese, 173, 175
Pathology. *See Psychopathology*
Peasant, 180, 181, 184, 193, 267, 268,
    322, 335, 336
  and race, 269
Pellagra, 115, 116, 117, 118, 120
  and cognitive function, 117
  and mental disorders, 117
Pentecostal movement, 194, 295
Pentecostalism, 27, 183
Pentecostals, 183, 339 n. 1, 341
Perception, 5
  distortion of, 7, 12
Personal identity, discontinuity of, 13
Petersen, W., 355 n. 4
Political organization, 40
  structure of, 43, 45 (table 1)
Population size, 20, 43
  and PT, 40, 47, 48 (table 2)
Portugal, 266
Possession, 25, 27. *See also* Altered
    state of consciousness; Dis-
    sociation; Possession trance;
    Trance
  behavior
    and children, 301
    explanations of, 89
    function of, 89
    religious, 278
    symptoms of, 89
  belief, 15, 16 (table 2), 17, 29
    Nguni, parameter of, 105, 106
    types of, 28–29
  as cause of illness, 143
  cult
    Amandawu, 102, 103, 110, 111
    cure by, 103
    Amandiki, 102, 103, 110, 111

amoral peripheral, 26
dancing in, 114
Izizwe, 102
   cure by, 102
main (major) morality, 26, 27, 31
demonic, 345, 354 n. 3
diagnosis of, 98
by Holy Spirit, 14, 27, 32, 198, 233
illness, 30, 336
   Ukuthwasa, 97, 107–12, 114
   biocultural parameters of, 122
      (figure 1)
   and dreams, 98, 125 n. 9
   and pellagra, 118, 120, 121–23
   and rebirth, 114, 124 n. 6
induced, 24
by male spirit, 167
among Nguni, 90, 96, 110
by sea goddess, 167
spontaneous, 24
Possession trance, 12–15, 17, 19–25,
   27–33, 39, 41, 323, 338. *See also*
   Altered state of consciousness:
   Dissociation; Trance
and amnesia, following, 12, 143, 239
behavior in, 15, 144, 154, 156, 233–
   35, 380, 281
   learned, 14, 329
   rules for, 13–14
breathing in, 236, 237
caused by spirit possession, 145
cult, 26
cultural variation of, 14
as cure, 329
cure of, 39
dancing in, 234
definition of, 42, 81
developing, 235
as experience, 176
experience of, 233, 234, 239, 329,
   330
function of, 327
and impersonation of spirits, 12, 14,
   42
and identity image, 255, 257
as innovation, 338
induction of, 15, 42, 156, 311, 312

institutions of, 23
levels of, 234, 235, 236, 237
motion pattern in, 237
occurrence of, 144, 157, 233
overbreathing in, 239
parameter of
   biological (nutritional), 89
   ecological, 115
performance of, 234, 235
period of, 237, 238
personal identity in, 113
phenomenon
   group, 42, 234
   individual, 43, 234
   private, 327
   public, 15, 327
as rebirth, 114
rhythm in, 234, 236, 237
and Shakers, 258
shaking in, 239
and Shangoists, 260 n. 11
and slavery, 47, 48 (table 2), 50, 51,
   54, 58
societal
   concomitants of, 19
   variables of, 19
as supernatural device, 176
utilization of, 258
words in, 236, 237
Possession trancer, 143
Presbyterians, 183, 192, 214
Pressel, Esther, 354 n. 2
Priest, 42
Prince, R., 60
Proletariat, 267, 268, 335, 336
Protestantism, 192
Protestants, 192
Psychobiological state, 5
Psychopathology, 3, 5, 329

Quakers, 224, 341
Quimbanda, 283, 284

Rage states, 8
Reader, D. H., 91, 95
Recruitment, 184

Redfield, R., 185, 190, 267
Reich, Charles, 344
Rejuvenation, feelings of, 7
Religion, 4, 41, 353
    old Palauan, 175
    realm of, 4
    ritual of, as identity renewal, 254
    role of, 4
    spiritualist, 265
Religious belief
    institutionalized, 41
    and conversion. *See* Conversion,
        religious
Rengul, 160, 161, 162
Residence pattern, 41, 182
    and possession trance, 50
Revitalization movement, 32, 33, 342
Revival meeting, 8, 344
Ribeiró, René, 294, 330
Rigidity, societal
    and flexibility, 80, 81
    and group membership, 63 (table 2)
    and political system, 63 (table 2)
    and possession trance, 23, 59, 60,
        79 (table 5), 80, 81, 84, 323, 337
    and religion, 63 (table 2)
    and residence, 63 (table 2)
    and status, 63 (table 2)
    and stratification, 79 (table 6), 81
Ritual
    curative, 30
    of rebellion, 31, 109, 257
Role, 22, 23, 30, 264, 293, 300, 312
Rorschach test, 172
Routledge, K., 75
Routledge, W. S., 75
Rural way of life, 191

Sacrifices, 24
St. Vincent, 14, 27, 219, 321
    economy of, 221, 222
    history of, 220
    political affairs of, 222
    slavery of, 221
Salman, D. H., 278
Salvation, 256, 335, 350
Samādhi, 5

Samburu, 34 n. 1
Santos, J. F., 297
Satan, 211–14, 216
Schaefer, J. M., 56 n. 2
Scheibe, K. F., 248
Schizophrenia, 5
Schultes, R. E., 177 n. 5
Scientologists, 346
Scrying, 9
Second Coming, 32, 193, 199, 206,
    207, 216, 336, 349
Sensory deprivation, 8, 247, 248, 346
    and anxiety, 251
    and cultural factors, 253
    and mourning, 248, 249, 335
    and psychological factors, 253
    and suggestion, 252
Separatist church, 32, 346
Settlement pattern, 20, 21, 34 n. 7
    and possession trance, 40, 43, 48
        (table 2), 50
Seventh Day Adventists, 142, 341
Sex division of labor, 45 (table 1), 49
    (table 2)
Shaka. 94
Shakerism and innovation, 259
Shakers in United States, 341
Shakers of St. Vincent, 31, 33, 219–
    63, 322, 338, 346
    church
        elder of, 228
        improvised, 227, 228
        nurse of, 228
        obedience in, 228
        structure of, 228
    church service, 230, 231
        dissociation in, 231, 233
        memorial, 232
        possession trance in, 233. *See
            Also* Possession trance
        of thanksgiving, 232
    congregation, 226, 227
        leader of, 229
        men in, 229
        pointer of, 225, 228, 229, 259
        pointer's control over, 229–30,
            232

women in, 229
interference with, 225
legalizing of, 225
originators of, 230
praise house. *See* prayer house
prayer house, 227
center role of, 226
Shangoists of Trinidad, 258, 260 n. 7, 260 n. 11
Sickness, 24. *See also* Illness
causes of, 287
diagnosing of, in trance, 143
and evil eye, 291
magical etiology of, 289
and reincarnation, 231
and religious negligence, 237
and unhappy spirit, 290
Simpson, G. E., 258
Sin, 24, 25, 325
Slavery, 20, 22, 47, 48–49 (table 2), 50–51, 221, 222, 253, 265, 266, 270, 396
Sleep, REM (rapid eye movement), 6, 14, 15
Smith, G. E., 258
Smith, T. L., 265
Smythies, J. D., 250
Social. *See also* Rigidity, societal
action, 28
differentiation and possession trance, 52, 54, 53 (table 5), 53 (table 6)
order, 28
structure, 23, 29, 31, 32
Brazilian, 265, 267
flexible, 81–83
rigid, 85 n. 2, 172
Society
complex, 19–21, 23, 80, 323, 324, 326
egalitarian, 64
elite, 253, 266
flexible, 326
"the others" in, 179
rigid, 23, 31, 326. *See also* Rigidity, societal
rural, 180
simple, 23

stratified, 34 n. 6, 175
structure of, 30, 253. *See also* social: structure
tribal, 321, 336
urban, 180
the very rich in, 179
West Indian, 253
Somali, 26
Sommambulism, 4
Sorcery, 41
Soul, 3, 4, 12
Sovereignty, administrative, 41
Speaking in tongues, 103, 185, 190, 193, 194, 332, 344, 346. *See also* Glossolalia
definition of, 185
interpreting of, 207
Spies, T. D., 117, 118
Spirit, 4, 26, 30
of ancestors, 22, 39, 100
of animals, 22
cult, 60
of dead, 99, 140, 145, 167, 279
of East Indians, 22, 103
female, 30
of foreigners, 22
of humans, 22
imitating actions of, during trance, 12
impersonation of, 22
journey of, 12
medium, 60, 81. *See also* Medium
official, office of, 135, 176
personality of, 301
training of, 302
Umbanda *(cavalo)*, 276, 279, 280
messages of, 12
never embodied, 32
possession, 5, 8, 26, 39, 42, 279
belief, distribution of, 16 (table 2), 88
cultural structuring of, 301, 303
as microchange, 312
sickness, caused by, 167–68
signal of, 302
as witchcraft, 194
role, 311
of Swazi, 22

Spirit *(continued)*
of Thonga, 22
tribal, 8
type of, 29, 281, 313, 314
of Umbanda medium, 281
Spiritism, 194
Spiritual Baptists, 260 n. 4, 260 n. 6. *See also* Shakers of St. Vincent
Spiritual fluid, 281, 287
Spiritual operation, 292
Spiritualism, 341
State, comalike, 42
State of consciousness, 5
biocybernetic model of, 5
Statistical analysis, 11
findings, 44
methods, 44
Status, 179, 325
and rigidity, of social structures, 80
and role, 40, 42, 52, 54, 59, 60, 173
Stimulation, exteroceptive, 6
Stratification, social, 20, 22, 222
and PT, 40, 47, 48 (table 2), 50, 51, 58, 77 (table 3), 78 (table 4)
Stress, 327
Sudan, 39
Sundkler, B., 96, 104
Supernatural
being, 42
contact with, 165, 166
entity, 3
power, 34 n. 6
premise, 216
sanction, 32, 328
Surrealism, 347
Swazi, 39, 102, 103

Tallensi, 71
TAT test, 172
Tarantism, 34 n. 1
Temple sleep, 8
Temudad, 160, 161, 162
spirit of, 161
Thonga, 103
Time sense, 7
Trance, 4, 5, 9, 12–15, 17, 19, 20, 22,

24, 25, 27–29, 34 n. 6, 190 *See also* Altered state of consciousness; Dissociation; Possession trance
acquisition of, 215
behavior in, 215
body image, change of, 310
culturally patterned, 9
dance in, 145
and emotional states, 309, 311
feelings after, 309, 311
at funeral rite, 145
healing in, 8
as hyperarousal, 187
as induced by spirit, 43
induction of, 156, 165, 169, 302, 309, 310
memory of, 12
as microchange, 312
preparation for, 309, 310
private, 15
as private enterprise, 12
release produced by, 189
residual, 210
rules for behavior in, 14
societal concomitant of, 19
variables of, 19
sustaining of, 305, 310
as soul absence, 12
as soul, adventures of, 12
as soul, journey of, 12, 245
symptoms of, 144
techniques of, 153
termination of, 309, 310
types of, 19 (table 3), 21, 23, 29, 309
vision in, 15
visionary, 14, 15, 32, 334, 336, 338, 346
Tranquilization, 6, 7
Transvestite medium, 149
Turkana, 76
Tylor, E. B., 354 n. 3

Ukuthwasa. See Possession illness
Umbanda, 22, 31, 264, 265, 275–315, 335, 336, 350–52

and African deities *(orixá),* 284, 285, 286, 287, 313
and Catholic saints, 284, 285
center, 276, 277, 279, 316 n. 3
and health services, 295
medium
 biological aspects of dissociation in, 309–2
 structures and functions of personality in, 301–8
membership of, 276, 322
prestige of, 277
possession states
 in novice, 303, 306, 311
 and rewards, 307, 308
 as social behavior, 297
as religious innovation, 265, 312
spirit and client, 298
and interpersonal relations, 299–300
spirits
 personality of, 283
 type of, 281, 282, 283, 284
and spiritual self, 296, 297
and urbanization, 294
United States of America, 27, 265, 339 n. 1, 340
Upper class, 255, 256, 269
Urban way of life, 191
Urbanization, 272, 312
Useem, J., 139, 176 n. 2

Variable, societal, 29

Venda, 112, 113, 114
Vermont-Salas, R., 187
Vidich, A. J., 141, 160
Vilakazi, A., 96, 106, 107
Voodoo (vodû), Haitian, 26, 27, 30
Vision, 12, 205, 206, 208, 209, 211, 213, 215, 228, 246. *See also* Hallucination

Wagley, Charles, 267, 268, 314
Wallace, A. F. C., 30, 249, 252, 329
Weber, Max, 28, 354, n. 2
Weber's Protestant Ethic, 342, 354
West Indians, 25
Whitehead, H., 346
Witch, smelling out of, 100
Witchcraft, 60, 194
 belief, 24, 31
Wolf, E., 184

Xangô cult of Recife, 330

Yorubaland, 284
Yucatán, 14, 27, 33, 178–84

Zaretsky, I. I., 354 n. 4
Zionism, Zulu, 104, 108, 124
Zionest church, Zulu, 104
Zubeck, J. P., 249
Zuckerman, M., 249
Zulu, 22, 23, 32, 72, 90, 94, 323. *See also* Nguni